TELEWARS

IN THE STATES

Telecommunications Issues in a New Era of Competition

Thomas W. Bonnett

Library of Congress Cataloging-in-Publications Data

Bonnett, Thomas W., 1952-
    Telewars in the states: telecommunications issues in a new era of competition/Thomas W. Bonnett
      p. cm.
    Includes bibliographical references (p. 157)
    ISBN 0-934842-16-7 (pbk.: alk. paper)
    1. Telecommunication policy – United States – States.
    2. Competition – United States – States. I. Title.
    HE7781.866 1996
    384'.066 – dc20

HE 7781 B66 1996

The Council of Governors' Policy Advisors began the Telecommunications Project in the fall of 1995 to prepare information about state telecommunications for its membership. Early in the following year, when the Telecommunications Act of 1996 was enacted, CGPA produced a series of "issue alerts" to inform members about emerging issues in a new era of competition.

The issue series, this book, and other activities were made possible by generous support from AT&T, the Alliance for Competitive Communications, MCI Telecommunications Corporation, GTE Telephone Operations, and others. In addition, CGPA corporate supporters have included: Ameritech Foundation, AT&T Foundation, Bell Atlantic Corporation, BellSouth, Dun & Bradstreet, General Electric Company, IBM, Northern Telecom, NYNEX Corporation, Pacific Telesis, Southwestern Bell Foundation, and U S West.

This is the fourth CGPA publication on state telecommunications in the past decade, reflecting both the significance of these issues to the states and the strong interest of our members. The first was published as a working paper in 1986 and was entitled: *The Challenge of Telecommunications: State Regulatory and Tax Policies for a New Industry*. Two additional reports came out in 1992 and were well received by members as well as leaders in the telecommunications industry: *New Alliances in Innovation: A Guide to Encouraging Innovative Applications of New Communication Technologies to Address State Problems* by Nancy Ginn Helme; and *State and Local Tax Policy and the Telecommunications Industry* by Karl E. Case.

The Council of Governors' Policy Advisors (CGPA) is a nonprofit, nonpartisan membership organization whose members are the top four advisors to each of the nation's Governors. Through its office in Washington, D.C., the council provides assistance to states on a broad spectrum of policy matters. CGPA also conducts policy and technical research on both state and national issues. CGPA has been affiliated with the National Governors' Association since 1975.

Council of Governors' Policy Advisors
400 North Capitol Street
Hall of the States–Suite 390
Washington, D.C. 20001
Tel: 202.624.5386
Fax: 202.624.7846
Internet cgpa.sso.org

Cover design by Hasten Design Studio, Inc.

Printed in the United States of America.

CONTENTS

LIST OF FIGURES AND BOXES

February 8, 1996 was a historic day. It marks President Clinton's signing of the *Telecommunications Act of 1996*, the first major rewrite of telecommunications legislation in sixty-two years. The purpose of the legislation was to promote competition in telephone and cable services and partially deregulate much of the industry. As expected, its enactment unleashed a flurry of activity, including two Baby Bell mergers (SBC & Pacific Telesis and Bell Atlantic & NYNEX).

The new law poses tough policy choices for states and territories. This book was written to provide information on state telecommunications issues to CGPA members and others who advise state Governors.

Rapid advances in computing and related information technologies have expanded the nature and scope of telecommunications. Plain old telephone service, or POTS, no longer describes what is now an expanding array of services in most areas of the country. In addition to voice, the information transmitted now includes data and images in the form of digitized bits. Other innovations such as fiber optics, satellites, and wireless technologies are an integral part of many newly built telecommunications networks.

As directed by the Telecommunications Act, the Federal Communications Commission (FCC) is establishing new ground rules to guide the industry: universal service; a 14-point competitive checklist that regional Bell operating companies (RBOCs) must meet before they sell long-distance services in their own territories; interconnection agreements between incumbent local exchange carriers and prospective competitors; and a host of other issues affecting the price and quality of telephone service in every state and territory.

Soon, perhaps even before the FCC issues its rulings, Governors' offices, state legislatures, and state public utility commissions (PUCs) will be drawn into state debates on how to ensure a "level playing field for competition" among those firms seeking to provide local and intrastate telephone services. Policymakers will need to decide whether to create universal-service programs, and how to achieve equity in state and local taxation. State PUCs also will approve interconnection agreements and will render an opinion to the FCC to determine whether an RBOC is meeting the competitive checklist defined in the act.

The outcome of these policy debates will have an enormous impact on business revenues. Given the financial magnitude of public decisions on private telecommunications companies, Governors should expect major battles in the approaching state "telewars":

- Heated controversy will arise over the 14-point competitive checklist. The RBOC will contend that it meets checklist conditions, while prospective competitors will make counterclaims. The typical state PUC may not have an easy time resolving this conflict. To be sure, the terms and price of interconnection agreements will be at issue.

- Virtually every major firm in this industry will be eager to share its persuasive information with the Governor's office, state legislators, and the PUC. The term "venue shopping" may characterize the aggressive lobbying style of telecommunications firms that hope to find a sympathetic ear.
- The public interest will be difficult to define in a chorus of discordant voices. "Competition will benefit consumers." "Maintain the integrity of the network to provide reliable services." "Keep residential rates low to preserve universal service." And so on.

In the course of these debates, the most common question will be: *"Why are we messing with the best telephone system in the world?"* Congress enacted the Telecommunications Act of 1996 in the belief that creating competition in regulated industry—the trucking industry in 1978, the airlines in the early 1980s, and now also the electrical utilities—stimulates innovation, increases efficiency, and speeds the development of new and better technologies, products, and services. Competition is now the touchstone for the future evolution of telephone and cable services. Although consumers have benefited from competition in long-distance service for the past two decades, the federal act now provides a framework for competition in local telephony and cable-TV.

The transition from monopolistic to competitive local telephony will be rocky and uncertain. Adding to the confusion is the emergence of new wireless and satellite systems, which may soon rival the wireline networks. Technological innovation was a significant factor in influencing how national policymakers think about telecommunications. Why should governments regulate monopolistic providers of telephone and cable services if new technologies will enable new companies to enter the competitive arena? Why not let telephone companies offer video programming? Why not let cable-TV systems provide telephone service? Why not let any qualified provider of a viable technology compete to provide any telecommunications service? The role of government in answering these questions is to set reasonable terms and conditions for fair competition and ensure that social objectives are met.

Many countries provide telephone, telegraph, and postal services through national, publicly owned systems. Others have a national regulatory system to monitor privately owned telephone companies. The United States is the only Western nation with a dual regulatory structure for telephone service. For most of the twentieth century, the FCC has regulated interstate telephony, while states have regulated local and intrastate services. This system has been both attacked and applauded. The new Telecommunications Act and ensuing state telewars will constitute the latest chapter in the evolution of our dual regulatory structure and possibly renew the debate over appropriate roles.

This book is limited to a discussion of states' roles in telecommunications. There are principally three: states regulate local and intrastate telephone service; states and their localities tax telecommunications firms and services; and state leaders understand that quality telecommunications are critical to promoting economic development.

The first chapter begins with an overview of the social significance of telecommunications in an era of convergence and competition. Convergence refers to mergers and alliances among firms in the computing, electronics, media, and communications industries. Convergence also refers to communications technologies that have come about from the microelectronic and digital revolutions, culminating in the telecommunications revolution. Understanding both corporate and technological convergence provides additional context for state debates on telecommunications policy. This chapter also presents a brief overview of existing telecommunications networks.

The second chapter explains why telecommunications issues are so important to states. It summarizes recent state actions to improve economic competitiveness by promoting infrastructure investment and improving the quality of telecommunications services. It also presents a summary of various telecommunications applications to provide public services and manage state resources and operations.

A short history of the development of the telephone industry appears in chapter three. Why did government begin to regulate the industry? How did our dual regulatory system evolve? A central theme is the significance of universal service as a national objective, an issue that will likely remain one of the top priorities for most states in the new era of competition.

The fourth chapter summarizes recent trends in state telecommunications regulation. The twelve years between the 1984 AT&T divestiture and the Telecommunications Act of 1996 included three regulatory phases at the state level: reaction, retrenchment, and restructuring. The chapter gives special attention to the bold innovations of several states in promoting competition and establishing ground rules for effective competition. Indeed, some observers claim that the states provided important precedents in deregulation, pricing, and competition policies, which served as models to Congress as it debated federal telecommunications policy.

Chapter five is the core of this book. It is a summary of the new federal telecommunications legislation and an analysis of policy choices that states face. What are the issues before the FCC and how will they affect states? What are interconnection agreements? How will they promote competition in the local loop? How will universal service be defined at the federal level? Should states establish their own universal-service funds? Will urban consumers benefit from competition at the expense of rural customers? Is rate rebalancing inevitable? The policy choices will vary across the states, but these central questions are common to all.

The sixth chapter presents a summary of the current status of local competition in telephony, a discussion of the potential competitors in these local markets, and an overview of promising technologies that could affect the industry in the near future. This chapter presents two pressing issues for Governors and other state policymakers: achieving tax equity for telecommunications providers, and establishing privacy protections for citizens and consumers. The chapter concludes by summarizing the major state policy choices in a new age of competition.

Whence the Title *TELEWARS in the States?*

In anticipation that Congress would enact federal legislation to deregulate much of the telecommunications industry, CGPA began a telecommunications project in the fall of 1995 to prepare information about state telecommunications issues. A series of "issue alerts" was prepared in the spring of 1996, following the enactment of the Telecommunications Act of 1996, to help states and CGPA members prepare for new responsibilities and challenges under the federal act. CGPA received many requests for additional information from members and others in state government. One call was vividly memorable. It was a conversation with a Governor's legal counsel who described an army of lobbyists from telecommunications firms besieging the state legislature. During the call, he used the phrase *state telewars* to describe the ensuing battle in the state capitol. The phrase was transposed to form the title of this book.

Appendices include a summary of major themes ("for those who never have time to read anything for more than ten minutes"), a list of state responsibilities under the Telecommunications Act of 1996 prepared by the National Association of Regulatory Utilities Commissions (NARUC), and an extensive glossary of telecommunications terms.

For those of us not trained as engineers, the terminology in this field can be bewildering. Basic concepts are explained in the narrative, but most technical terms and industry jargon have been kept out of the text. The glossary includes definitions of technical terms to help CGPA members and other state decisionmakers better understand the complexity of the issues.

Encroaching state telewars may follow the rough contours of congressional debates of the past four years. Major battles between the incumbent local exchange carriers and prospective competitors will capture newspaper headlines, frustrate the patience of state regulators, and even find their way into state legislative chambers. There also will be important battles between public advocates who want to include advanced telecommunications services in the state definition of universal service, and consumer advocates who want to protect consumers. The outcome will vary from state to state, but the central themes—how to establish fair rules while promoting competition and preserving universal service—are likely to dominate the state policy agenda for many years to come.

The next few years will be important and turbulent times. Telewars in the states will be bitterly fought. Yet the policies formed in these debates may well signal another period of innovation. Moreover, it is likely that states will continue to serve the nation as important policy laboratories. As always, CGPA would be pleased to hear from members and others about the issues being debated in state capitols and whether this publication has been helpful.

ACKNOWLEDGMENTS

I really like thanking people who have helped me do my work. Telecommunications is a fascinating topic, but I have found much of it rather complicated. Without doubt, I could not have written this book had I not been exceptionally fortunate to have had the assistance of so many kind and generous people.

When I started the CGPA Telecommunications Project in the fall of 1995, I had only general knowledge of this issue. Fortunately, the organization had published exceptional work on telecommunications. I got started by reading those publications. My good fortune continued when I assembled an advisory group for the telecommunications project. I am not a technical person,[1] but the individuals in this group were patient and generous with their time. They helped me learn a difficult subject. Individually and collectively, they also provided excellent advice on how CGPA could best serve its members. It was the group's idea to push ahead with the three "issue alerts" that were distributed to our members in the spring of 1996, following the enactment of the Telecommunications Act in that same year. I also received good comments—although sharply divergent views—on my draft manuscript from members of the advisory group.

I am grateful to these individuals for their personal support, advice, and friendship, and I am grateful to their organizations for providing financial support to this project. The group includes: Cindy Cox and Jim McCollum, BellSouth; Patrick Gaston, NYNEX; David Mack, Pete Kirchhof, and Edie Ortega, U S West; Patrick Nugent, MCI; Ron Scheberle, GTE; Marc Rosen, AT&T; Frank Thompson, Bell Atlantic; and Robert Lloyd and Kathryn Falk, NECA. The last two—Bob and Kathryn—deserve special thanks for their gracious assistance, providing mountains of information.

The next group of people I want to thank are my colleagues at CGPA. They were very supportive while I was researching telecommunications issues and laboring at writing this book. They were always cooperative and helpful. They also provided many good suggestions. With gratitude, I thank: Eric Brenner, Leslie Fain, Nadine Frazier, Richard Gross, Jeanette Hercik, and Gabriela Nosari. My special appreciation goes to Gabriela Nosari for more than I could possibly mention here, but it includes managing the production process of this book with good cheer and enthusiasm. It was a pleasure to work with Sandie Macdonald and Laura Miller, who did a wonderful job editing my work, and Kim Hasten, who always does an outstanding job designing my books. I thank them all.

---

[1] I once made the mistake of trying to pass for a technical person at a telecommunications conference. It was a mistake I shall never repeat. Seconds after the conversation began, a blast of acronyms, technical terms, and industry jargon whizzed past my ears: "T-1, ISDN, SONET, ATM, interoperability, ethernet, encryption…" It became so intense I felt like the target dummy at an NRA firing range. I finally broke away from the hypnotic rhythm of acronyms in search of the comfort of another non-technical person.

I want to thank a special friend, Matthew Bonaiuto, who was a mentor to me on technology issues during his time at CGPA. If there is a social division between the information-haves and have-nots, it may be greater between generations than across various family income levels. The young folks seem to get it. This reminds me of the story about the six-year-old running ahead of his father and stopping at the corner to ask: "Which way, Dad?" After shouting, "Right, right," the father adds, "It's the hand you use the mouse with!" I did know how to use my mouse before Matt joined CGPA, but I certainly learned a great deal from him. He was a good teacher and I thank him.

My dear friend, Cindy Cox, suggested at the beginning of this project that I keep the material simple. Keeping it short was another objective. (I think it was T.S. Eliot who said, "I did not have time to keep it short.") As I wrote this book, I tried to keep the profile of the most likely reader in mind. The typical Governor's policy advisor is intelligent, quick, and heavily burdened with the responsibilities of keeping the Governor informed on twenty to thirty different matters. He or she has little free time to read policy books on emerging state issues. I was constantly asking myself: What do Governors' policy advisors need to know? Furthermore: What do they want to know about these issues? Readers are welcome to judge for themselves how well this book meets these standards.

I wanted this book to present the best possible information on state telecommunications issues to members, so I cast a wide net for potential reviewers of the draft manuscript. I sent copies to members of the CGPA executive board, those who had called me asking for additional information after our issue alerts were distributed, a handful of experts whose work I greatly respected, some old friends who I knew would give me an honest assessment, and others with expertise in the field. They are busy folks and I asked for comments within a ridiculously short time. I was delighted to have received so many responses.

These comments were very helpful. Several people made excellent suggestions, forcing me to think hard about the material and how it was presented. I added a section summarizing the major themes of the book because a CGPA member conceded, "I don't have time to read anything for more than ten minutes." I worked hard to incorporate all but a few of these suggestions, and I think the book has been improved by peer review.

My debt to the reviewers is large. I gratefully thank: Stephen Adams, Massachusetts Taxpayers Foundation; Brent Anderson, Kansas; Rod Armstrong, Nebraska; Scott Barkan, CLASP; Jennifer Bosworth, NADO; Robert Bradley, Florida; Cindy Brinkley, SBC; Will Carter, West Virginia; Dan Ebersole, Georgia; Mary Power Foerster, MCI; Francis Dummer Fisher, University of Texas; David Gabel, Queens College; Jack Gallt, NASTD; Lawrence Gasman, CATO; Rick Gowdy, ALEC; Bob Greeves; Tim Johnson, Colorado; Robert Kelley, Guam; Kathy Kelly, Washington; Carolyn Lane, Louisiana; Patricia Lewis, University of Florida; Ted Lightle, South Carolina; Shirley Marshall, IBM; Phil McClelland, Office of Consumer Advocates, Pennsylvania; Richard McHugh, Georgia State University; Milton Mueller, Rutgers

University; James Bradford Ramsay, NARUC; Louise Spieler, NASHIRE; Paul Teske, SUNY at Stony Brook; and Tim Totman, GTE. (Unless otherwise identified, these individuals work in the Governor's office or in an executive branch agency in state government.)

Incorporating good suggestions and reconciling different views was a challenge. Notwithstanding the assistance of so many, the author alone is responsible for any error of fact or interpretation contained in this book.

I want to express my appreciation to my wife, Karen Kahn, and my son, Stephen Kahn Bonnett, for their love and support as I blundered through the difficulties of writing this book. Finally, I want to remember my father, Robert W. Bonnett, who died in March of this year. He was a storyteller, not a writer. I think he would have been pleased and proud to have been remembered in this way.

Tom Bonnett
[twbparkslo@aol.com]

CHAPTER ONE

CONVERGENCE AND COMPETITION IN TELECOMMUNICATIONS

Many have argued persuasively that in the second half of the twentieth century, our society has experienced an information revolution comparable in scope to the Industrial Revolution.[1] Telecommunications means the transmission of information over distance. Rapid advances in computer and information technologies have expanded the nature and scope of telecommunications services. Plain old telephone service, or POTS, no longer describes the array of services available in most areas of the country. In addition to voice, the information transmitted now includes data and images in the form of digitized bits. The networks built to transmit this information use fiber optics, satellites, and various wireless technologies.

Our ability to transmit data in innovative forms has barely matched the explosive demand for information. The convergence of computing and telecommunications has, in short, changed the way we communicate, the nature of our work, and the quality of our lives. It may be premature to categorize these changes as a *telecommunications revolution*, although certainly they have transformed our social patterns and have great potential to reshape our future.[2]

This chapter describes two major trends in the telecommunications industry: convergence and competition. These trends are important for state policymakers to

---

[1] Here is an assessment by an eminent historian, J.M. Roberts, The Penguin History of the World, third ed., (New York: Penguin Books, 1992), 971:

> The single greatest technological change since 1945 in the major industrial economies has come in Information Technology, the complex science of handling, managing, and devising electronically-powered machines to process information. Few innovatory waves have moved so fast. Applications of work...were diffused in a couple of decades over a huge range of services and industrial processes. Rapid increases in power and speed, reduction in the size, and improvement in the visual display capacity of computers only meant, in essence, that much more information could be ordered and processed than hitherto. *But this was an example of a quantitative change bringing a qualitative transformation.* Calculations which until recently would have required the lifetime of many mathematicians to complete can now be run through in a few minutes. Technical operations which would have had to wait decades for such calculations, or for the sorting and classifying of great masses of data, have now become feasible. Intellectual advance has never been so suddenly accelerated. At the same time as there was revolutionary growth in the capacity and power of computers, their technology made it easier and easier to pack their potential into smaller and smaller machines. Within thirty years, a "microchip" the size of a credit card was doing the job which had first required a machine the size of an average British living-room. *The transforming effects have been felt in every service—and, indeed, almost every human activity, from money-making to war-making.* [Author's emphasis]

[2] One astute observer of the telecommunications industry has written that the word *revolution* along with the phrase *information superhighway* are among the most overused terms in telecommunications. He called the information revolution oversold, lamented the perpetual "hype" of the industry, and dismissed the word *revolution* as a marketing buzzword. He argued, in contrast, that long-term change occurs slowly and unpredictably. (See Edmund L. Andrews, "Changing the Wiring Takes Time," *New York Times* [October 30, 1994]). Evidence of this assessment comes from Massachusetts Congressman Edward Markey, who said, "The good news from Washington is that every single person in Congress supports the concept of an information superhighway. The bad news is that no one has any idea what that means." Markey's quote as cited in William J. Drake, ed., "Introduction," *The New Information Infrastructure: Strategies for U.S. Policy* (New York: Twentieth Century Fund Press, 1995), 1.

understand as they make strategic decisions to improve telecommunications infrastructure in their states.

CONVERGENCE

From a business perspective, corporate convergence refers to the anticipated merger or consolidation of diverse communications firms to form "a single, ubiquitous digital network that can be called an *information superhighway.*"[3] In recent years, the range of alliances among firms in the telecommunications, computing, and media industries has been broad and the rate of convergence, explosive. Seldom does a day pass without yet another announcement of an alliance between a media giant, a large telecommunications provider, a computer or software company, and an entertainment producer. Richard Adler, vice president for development for SeniorNet, notes:

> **AT&T** and **Intel** have formed an alliance to develop a computer-based "video telephone"....**MCI** and **CNN** have jointly created an interactive television program called "TalkBackLive"....**Intel** and **CNN** are developing a system that will deliver video news programming directly to desktop PCs....Book publisher **Random House** and software publisher **Brøderbund** have set up a joint venture to create "interactive books" for children....**Microsoft** and **Southwestern Bell** are collaborating on a project to provide interactive services to Southwestern Bell customers....The **Walt Disney Company** has formed a joint venture with **Ameritech, BellSouth Corporation**, and **Southwestern Bell Corporation** to provide such services as movies-on-demand, interactive games, and home shopping. **U S West** is working with seven movie studios and **Visa** to offer a new service called GO-TV.[4]

These alliances reflect the convergence of media to provide communications, information, and entertainment. Not so long ago, we used telephone wires to transmit voice communications and airwaves to broadcast radio and television signals. Now many different delivery systems can transmit many forms of information.[5] (See Box I-1.)

Technological convergence has been achieved because of the capacity to convert voice, data, and image into digital bits (a series of ones and zeros) and also because of

---

[3] Robert W. Crandall, "The Economic Impetus for Convergence in Telecommunications," *Crossroads on the Information Highway* (Annual Review, Institute for Information Studies/The Aspen Institute, Queenstown, Maryland, 1994), 1. Crandall warns against assuming that industrial convergence will result in "one large, interactive terrestrial network with a variety of interconnected wireless adjuncts." He concludes: "Communications technology is changing so rapidly and is opening up so many new potential applications for which we have little or no information on consumer demand that all forecasts must be taken as something between speculation and an informed guess."

[4] Richard P. Adler, "Introduction," *Crossroads on the Information Highway* (Annual Review, Institute for Information Studies, The Aspen Institute, Queenstown, Maryland, 1994), xiii-xiv.

[5] The rate of technological advances has been so rapid that it is difficult at times to appreciate the evolution of various technologies. For example, the General Instrument Corporation in 1990 made one of the breakthroughs that accelerated digital convergence. According to "Telecommunications Timeline" *Congressional Quarterly* (February 3, 1996): 293, the company developed a "way to compress and transmit high-quality television pictures in digital form—the same binary language of ones and zeros used to ship computer data—rather than the traditional analog method that uses sound waves to ship video and audio signals. The breakthrough allows data flowing over television, telephones and computers to be interchangeable." For more about digital compression and future social implications of digital media, see Nicholas Negroponte, *Being Digital* (New York: Alfred A. Knopf, 1995).

advances in telephony and computing that rely on wireline, satellite, or wireless networks. (See Box I-2.) Investments in fiber optics, modern digital switches, and other improvements have increased the capacity of conventional telephone networks to transmit voice, data, and images. Similar advances in technology and switching equipment have enabled cable-TV systems to provide telephone service and a range of interactive information services. The development of wireless technologies represents an opportunity to provide independent delivery systems for telephone, television, and other services. With these technological advances comes accelerated demand for telecommunications services and increased competition to provide them.

In 1983, Ithiel de Sola Pool, a distinguished political scientist at MIT, anticipated the "convergence of modes that is blurring the lines between media." Pool predicted that "different services that had previously been carried by different physical media might be carried by a single medium, and a service that had previously been carried by a single medium might be distributed through several different physical media."[6]

Supply and demand functions also help explain the current era of telephony. On the supply side, the capacity to provide services has grown tremendously as a result of technological improvements and wireless systems, industry investments in infrastructure (i.e., fiber optics, digital switches, ISDN) and new networks built by new competitors. The demand for expanded telecommunications services is equally significant. Growing corporate and consumer interest has enticed large corporate users to develop their own networks and new firms to build new networks in selected urban markets.[7]

Until recently, it appeared that the supply of capacity was keeping pace with growing demand.[8] The investment challenge for the industry is to increase supply to satisfy the future demand for advanced services. Expanding supply requires capital and time to build the infrastructure. Demand for new services, such as broadband access to the Internet, may be explosive. Although most analysts expect both supply and demand to continue to grow, the demand for new services is particularly difficult to forecast.

COMPETITION

Competition in long-distance telephone services began in the 1970s and has since accelerated. In the 1980s, companies began to vie for in-state toll calls, while competition in local telephone services only emerged in recent years and in selected markets. Competition comes from new firms that build new networks or purchase capacity from existing providers. Ian Craig, President of Broadband Networks, Northern Telecom Inc., predicts that "fortunes will be made with the building of networks for voice, data, and image to carry all sorts of information in the form of digitized bits."[9]

New technologies have also spurred competition. For example, the Federal Communications Commission (FCC) recently auctioned radio spectrum for personal communications services (PCS), which may enable new firms to compete with providers of cellular service and local telephone companies. Also, the popularity of direct broadcast satellite (DBS) and the emergence of wireless cable technologies could lure customers from cable-TV systems at the same time that cable companies are installing switching equipment to compete in providing telephone service.

---

[6] As quoted by Adler, "Introduction," xiii.

[7] Technical clarification: the word *network* gives the impression that corporations are building hardware networks for internal use; rather, corporations form virtual networks by leasing dedicated lines and capacity from common carriers for their own communications traffic. The author thanks Patrick Nugent of MCI for making this distinction.

[8] Does the supply of telecommunications services create the demand, or did the demand for new and better services stimulate investment to expand capacity? In 1926, H.B. Thayer, president of AT&T said, "Telephone service was not created to fill a demand....The service creates the demand. That is the business of our system, to try to discover and determine what it is that will be helpful to the people of the United States in the way of service and then to provide it. The demand follows the creation of the service instead of being impelled by it." As quoted in David Gabel, "Federalism: An Historical Perspective," in *American Regulatory Federalism & Telecommunications Infrastructure* (Lawrence Erlbaum Associates, Hillsdale, New Jersey, 1995), 28.

[9] Ian Craig, "Foreword," *Crossroads on the Information Highway* (Annual Review, Institute for Information Studies, The Aspen Institute, Queenstown, Maryland, 1994), v-vi.

Increased levels of competition are well on the way. Since 1934, most forms of telecommunication—television, radio, cable TV, various radio frequencies, and interstate long-distance telephone service—have been regulated by the FCC. Historically, states have had the authority to regulate local and intrastate telephone service. Over the past two decades, the FCC has supported increased competition among telecommunications firms, and in recent years several states have allowed new firms to provide local telephone service.[10]

Since the Modified Final Judgment (MFJ) in 1982 and the consequent dismantling of the AT&T Bell system in 1984, many industry leaders have argued that telecommunications firms should be allowed to compete in government-restricted markets. Local telephone companies want to provide long-distance services and cable TV; in a few cases, cable-TV firms are providing phone service; and long-distance companies are entering local telephone markets and forming alliances with cable-TV companies. The convergence of the media in providing communications, information, and entertainment services has only strengthened the argument for increased competition.

Since the Telecommunications Act of 1996, the rate of convergence has accelerated. U S West spent $5.3 billion to acquire Continental Cablevision, the nation's third largest cable company. AT&T purchased a large share of a direct broadcast satellite company. MCI and Robert Murdoch's News Corporation agreed to pay $682 million "for the last unclaimed orbital slot for a satellite that can beam television straight to individual homes across the United States."[11] SBC Communications (formerly Southwestern Bell) announced its $17 billion acquisition of Pacific Telesis on April 1, 1996.[12] On April 22, 1996, the long-awaited merger of Bell Atlantic and NYNEX was announced.[13] Some market analysts expect other telecommunications companies to form alliances, perhaps resulting in joint ventures, mergers, or consolidations.

This activity represents more than a game of musical chairs; it is the beginning of an era of robust competition and convergence among different providers of telecommunications services. It promises to be an exciting and, quite possibly, confusing time for

---

[10] As discussed in chapters four and five, allowing new firms to provide local telephone service does not mean that competition in the local market exists. What matters is whether the terms and prices for resale established by a state and the nature of the interconnection agreements approved by the state commission constitute a "level playing field for effective local competition."

[11] Edmund L. Andrews, "News Corp. and MCI Win Satellite Slot," *New York Times*, January 26, 1996, D1.

[12] If successful, this $17 billion merger would combine the 15.8 million local-access lines of Pacific Telesis with the 14.1 million local-access lines of SBC Communications and enable it to carry as much as 50 percent of the long-distance traffic to Latin America. The merger must be approved by the California PUC, the FCC and the Department of Justice. See the *Washington Post* or *New York Times*, April 2, 1996.

[13] This merger combines the 17.1 million local access lines of NYNEX with the 19.8 million access lines of Bell Atlantic. According to the reporting of Mark Landler ("NYNEX and Bell Atlantic Reach Accord on Merger; Links 36 Million Customers," *New York Times*, April 22, 1996), the proposed merger "is subject to approval by Federal and state regulators, as well as by the Internal Revenue Service and the Securities and Exchange Commission." Landler quoted an industry analyst who said that "30 percent of the long-distance calls originate in the territories of the two companies. By merging, he said the two companies had a good chance to grab many of those calls." The advocates of this merger stressed the potential benefits of vertical integration, cost efficiencies due to consolidation, and creation of the capacity with which to compete on a "global platform." Landler also quoted Eli M. Noam, director of the Columbia University Institute of Tele-Information, "This is another step in the inexorable march of telecommunications to a world of four or five giant players." If Noam is correct, the word that leaps from *Webster's Ninth New Collegiate Dictionary* (1983) is *oligopoly*, "a market situation in which each of a few producers affects but does not control the market." For a dissent against mergers, see Monroe E. Price, "Making Antitrust Work," *The Nation*, June 3, 1996, 28.

most of us, especially as consumers. It surely will be an important time for Governors and other state policymakers who will be making state telecommunications policy choices.

The state role in telecommunications policy is limited in scope, but not significance. Historically, states have regulated local and intrastate telephone services, and state regulators have sought to juggle several conflicting goals:

- Keeping telephone rates as low as possible while allowing regulated companies a reasonable rate of return on their investment.
- Ensuring that everyone has access to basic telephone service and, in some circumstances, trying to provide special services to handicapped populations.
- Encouraging company infrastructure investment and innovation in enhanced services.
- Resolving a variety of other complex issues.

In recent years, as Governors have pressed for increased investment in telecommunications infrastructure to promote state economic development, state regulators have added yet another objective to their collective responsibilities. These topics are better understood in the context of existing telecommunications networks.

EXISTING TELECOMMUNICATIONS NETWORKS

Most of the discussion in this book focuses on the existing wireline telephone network. Although this system is likely to remain the foundation of the information superhighway, an overview of cable-television and wireless networks is appropriate.[14] Neither system poses an immediate competitive threat to the wireline network in providing basic telephone services; however, future advances could enable both to compete aggressively with the wireline network and potentially drain essential revenues from it.

On the other hand, these systems may ultimately complement the wireline network and create an integrated and expanded capacity for telecommunications services. Eli M. Noam has argued that "the central institutions of future telecommunications will not be carriers but systems integrators that mix and match transmission segments, services, and equipment, using various carriers....The new issues will be those of integrating the emerging 'network of networks.'"[15]

The Wire-based Voice and Data Telephone Network
The telephone system consists of 145 million access (local) lines, fixed investment of US$200 to 300 billion, and more than 1,200 telephone companies. Most of these

---

[14] Much of the material in this section is drawn from *Information Superhighway: An Overview of Technology Challenges*, GAO/AIMD-95-23 (General Accounting Office, Washington, D.C., January 1995).

[15] Eli M. Noam, "Beyond Telecommunications Liberalization: Past Performance, Present Hype, and Future Direction," *The New Information Infrastructure* (Twentieth Century Fund, New York, 1995), 31.

companies are small and independent. The twenty-two Bell operating companies that were divested from AT&T in 1984 were organized into seven holding companies known as regional Bell operating companies, or RBOCs. Together, RBOCs and GTE (the largest non-Baby-Bell local exchange carrier) control 90 percent of the local telephone lines in this country. According to *Fortune*, the RBOCs' estimated 1994 revenues from local phone services were $74.7 billion. (Total revenues for local exchange carriers were approximately $90 billion.) Estimated 1994 revenues from long-distance services from AT&T, MCI, and Sprint—the three largest interexchange carriers—were $61.7 billion.[16] Most other long-distance companies do not have their own facilities for transmitting services; they are called *resellers* because they purchase capacity from other companies and resell services to the public.

This composite of many parts provides the world's largest distributed network, according to the GAO report, for "point-to-point voice, fax, data, and videoconferencing services to hundreds of millions of subscribers....It is ubiquitous, highly interoperable, and reliable. It is capable of handling millions of simultaneous calls, and it provides accurate usage tracking and billing....Although the industry is rapidly introducing advanced digital communication technologies, the telephone network continues to be dependent on analog transmission."[17] Figure I-1 diagrams a typical local telephone network.

The range of services this network can provide varies considerably. At the highest end, using fiber-optic cable and digital switches, the network provides voice, data, videoconferencing, interactive video, and other bandwidth-intensive applications to business, government, and institutions. State governments have encouraged telephone companies to accelerate high-end infrastructure investment to provide advanced telecommunications services to schools, hospitals, and other public institutions. Similarly, Section 254 of the 1996 Telecommunications Act designated "elementary and secondary schools and classrooms, health care providers, and libraries" to receive discounted rates for advanced telecommunications services. Telephone companies, for their part, will more readily invest in this infrastructure if they are confident of the "effective demand" (willingness and ability to pay) among their consumers. (See chapter two.)

At the lowest service level is the party line, which 1 percent of phone subscribers receive. These subscribers cannot make private calls, send or receive facsimile messages, or use a modem to access information services. As discussed in chapter five, one of the major issues concerning universal service is the definition of basic, essential telephone services that will be made available to all who want them. A related concern is who pays to ensure that the standard is met.

The debate over developing "the last mile" is typical of the many challenges facing the telecommunications industry. Most telephone subscribers are connected to the wire-based telephone network through an analog voice frequency (VF) system. This

---

[16] Andrew Kupfer, "The Future of the Phone Companies," *Fortune*, October 3, 1994, 98.

[17] GAO, *Information Superhighway*, 45.

Figure I-1: A Typical Local Telephone Network

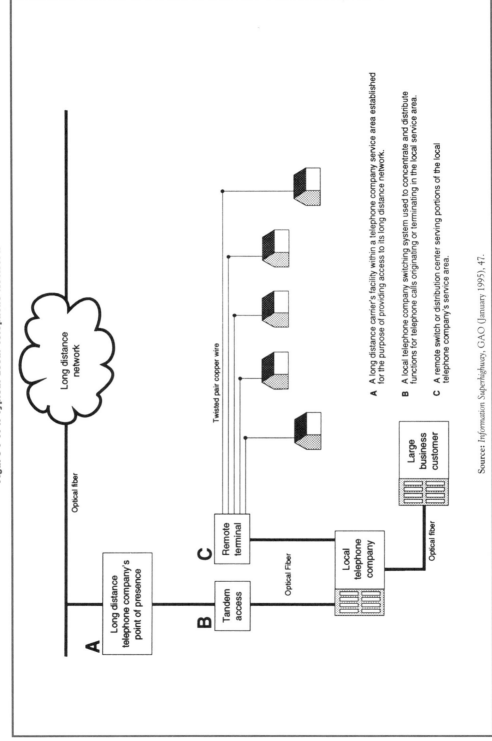

Source: *Information Superhighway*, GAO (January 1995), 47.

system transmits voice over a twisted pair of copper wires—often called the local loop—to the central office where switches then route the call to its destination. Completely converting the network to digital transmission, and especially replacing copper wire with fiber-optic cable, would provide glorious bandwidth[18] to every subscriber. With this kind of connection, one could view any video program, download videos for future viewing, or send a family video to Grandmother on Mother's Day.

As stated, telecommunications providers will make huge private-sector infrastructure investments only if persuaded that their customers are willing to pay for broadband services. Many consumers would delight at having "fiber to the curb" but others would have little interest. Consumer advocates have been critical of aggressive plans to provide new services for which demand has not been demonstrated. The burden of financing an overbuilt infrastructure would fall on ratepayers. On the other hand, underinvesting in technology and infrastructure would delay the development of advanced telecommunications services, which are advantageous for state economic competitiveness and business development.

As with most public policy matters, there is no single answer to this infrastructure dilemma, only policy tradeoffs. The question itself becomes more challenging as technological innovation proceeds.

The Cable Television Network

The cable-television industry has experienced tremendous growth in the past two decades. In 1980, approximately 4,225 cable systems provided video services to 17.7 million subscribers; in 1990, 11,075 cable-television systems provided services to more than 57 million subscribers. Of greater significance, the GAO reports that cable service is available, through "ready access to the service provider's coaxial cable," to more than 96 percent of households in this country.[19] Simply because this network could connect via broadband coaxial cable to so many homes, it could become a competitive threat to the wireline network in providing basic telephony and other services.

The technical challenge to the cable-television industry is how to install modern switches to enable existing coaxial cable to transmit telephone calls both to and from the home. The subscriber network of a typical cable system has been compared to an urban bus route in which the bus only goes in one direction. Most cable systems can deliver communications to the home, but as presently designed, they cannot receive them. (See Figure I-2.) The GAO report explains:

> The telephone system is based on a switched, distributed network architecture, and uses standard switching and transmission protocols capable of supporting global, narrowband, two-way, point-to-point communications. The cable systems, on the

---

[18] See Lawrence Gasman, *Telecompetition: The Free Market Road to the Information Highway* (Cato Institute, Washington, D.C., 1994), especially chapter one. Gasman (11) defines bandwidth as "the measure of the capacity of a communications channel. The bigger the bandwidth, the more information that is, the more bits you can send down the channel....The telegraph did not need very high bandwidth. Telephones need somewhat more bandwidth than telegraph communications. Television required higher bandwidth than either telephone or telegraph."

[19] GAO, *Information Superhighway*, 47.

Figure I-2: A Typical Cable System Architecture

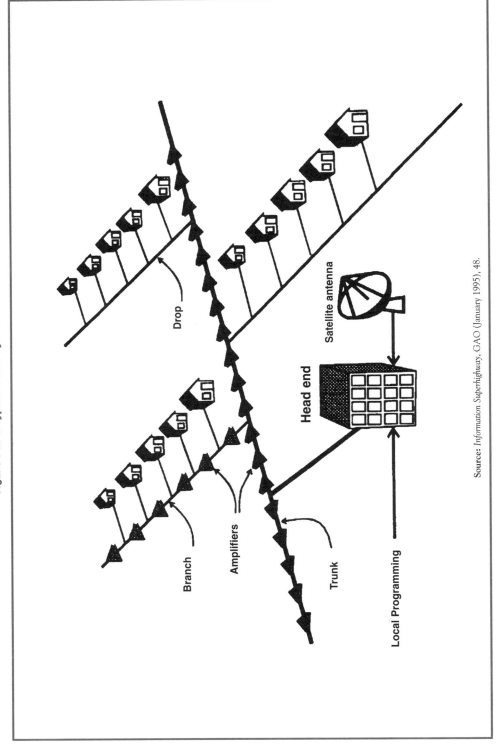

Drop

Branch

Amplifiers

Trunk

Satellite antenna

Head end

Local Programming

Source: *Information Superhighway*, GAO (January 1995), 48.

other hand, are based on a tree-and-branch network architecture and proprietary transmission protocols *designed to support one-way broadband analog transmission with little or no provision for "upstream" communications*. [Author's emphasis][20]

Cable companies in the United Kingdom have enjoyed substantial success in offering telephony service. According to Crandall and Waverman, "By pricing telephony services at 10 to 15 percent less than rates charged by British Telecom and by arranging long-distance interconnection with Mercury, U.K. cable companies have been able to enroll about 20 percent of their cable subscribers in their local telephone service."[21]

The British experience is well understood in this country. Witness the heavy investments made by major cable companies to build fiber optics into their feeder plants and install digital switches to enable them to provide local telephone services. According to industry analysts, one reason that telephone companies—which have expertise in switching technologies—have purchased distant cable companies is to convert them into competitors in other telephone markets. Cable systems have also invested heavily in cable modems to provide high-speed, broadband access to the Internet and other online information services.

Federal rate regulation for all but the basic tier of cable services will end in 1999, according to the new federal legislation. Congress assumed that by that date, cable television would be subject to vigorous competition from both telephone companies (providing video programming) and direct broadcast satellite companies. Federal price regulation would end because competition would prevent cable rates from soaring. The underlying theory is sound, but it rests on critical assumptions about industry behavior over the next few years:

- Direct broadcast satellite currently has only 2 million customers compared to 63 million households served by cable companies in 1996. While most analysts expect DBS to grow rapidly, will growth be sufficient to serve as a competitive check on cable rates?
- In contrast to a short time ago when enthusiasm was high, most of the RBOCs are scaling back plans to break into television. Will telephone companies or others enter the video programming market in such force as to keep cable rates in line?[22]

---

[20] *Ibid.*, 48.

[21] Robert W. Crandall and Leonard Waverman, *Talk is Cheap: The Promise of Regulatory Reform in North American Telecommunications* (Brookings Institution, Washington, D.C., 1995), 259-260. The authors continue: "This share is expected to increase with time. Their success is partly because they have no universal service obligation; nor do they have to pay access charges to British Telecom that include a contribution charge. Cable companies in the United Kingdom have been so successful that British Telecom has reconsidered its pricing policies to slow the pace of customer defections."

[22] Mark Landler and Geraldine Fabrikant, "Even Before Deregulation, Cable Rates Are on the Rise," *New York Times*, April 12, 1996, D4. The authors provide another insight:

> Indeed, some analysts said the industry was pushing its rates now primarily to capitalize on its monopoly position. "They still have a window," said Dennis Leibowitz, a cable analyst at Donaldson, Lufking & Jenrette. "They are doing it now because later competition will make it harder."

Wireless Networks

Two distinct networks provide wireless transmission of information over distance: cellular and satellite. Cellular radio operates within a grid of low-powered radio sender-receivers. As a user travels to different locations on the grid, the signal is passed along from cell to cell to different receiver-transmitters that automatically support the message traffic. Analog cellular systems are based on the "advanced mobile phone services" standard, which "provides 416 voice channels and employs a seven-cell frequency reuse pattern." The FCC requires that new digital cellular systems "be fully compatible with the current analog system."[23] (See Figure I-3)

Cellular telephony provides mobile services as a complement to the wireline network. Its recent growth has been spectacular. From December 1991 to December 1994, the number of subscribers increased from 7.6 million to 24.1 million. In 1994 cellular companies gained 8.1 million subscribers while investing $5 billion in plant and equipment. Some applications of this technology have replaced or supplemented existing wireline services. Crandall and Waverman report on variations of this technology in different geographic locations:

- Basic Exchange Telecommunications Radio Service is a radio-based technology used by rural telephone companies to provide extended services or replace existing copper wiring. BETRS was first used in Glendo, Wyoming and Allen, Kansas in 1986. Since then, other rural telephone companies have used digital wireless technologies; Bell Atlantic is using a similar technology to provide telephone services in rural Mexico. Some experts claim that digital wireless will become the dominant network in many less-developed nations that currently lack wireline networks.
- Urban Wireless Systems were designed by NYNEX to reduce the use of copper wires and other costs in high-cost, urban areas. A system that used "a fiber-optics backbone to connect a series of radio ports mounted on telephone poles" to communicate to nearby subscribers was successfully operated in Brooklyn, N.Y.[24]

Of potentially greater significance, some experts expect that cellular systems—in the form of digital cellular service or personal communications service—could substitute for regular wireline telephone services. A close cousin to cellular, PCS is a radio-based technology that transmits voice and low-speed data applications directly to subscribers, rather than to a specific location. The FCC recently held several spectrum auctions for PCS licenses, generating billions of dollars from the winning bidders.[25] Crandall and Waverman make the assessment that PCS "is not likely to compete with

[23] GAO, *Information Superhighway*, 49.

[24] Crandall and Waverman, *Talk is Cheap*, 223-38. Also see George I. Zysman, "Wireless Networks," *Scientific American* (September 1995).

[25] In October 1994, three large cable companies (Tele-Communications, Inc., Comcast, and Cox Communications) formed an alliance with Sprint to offer telephone services. This Sprint-led group spent $2 billion on FCC licenses to offer personal communications services in selected metropolitan markets. AT&T, already the largest cellular carrier, won PCS licenses in nineteen of the fifty-one Metropolitan Trading Areas.

Figure I-3: A Typical Cellular System Architecture

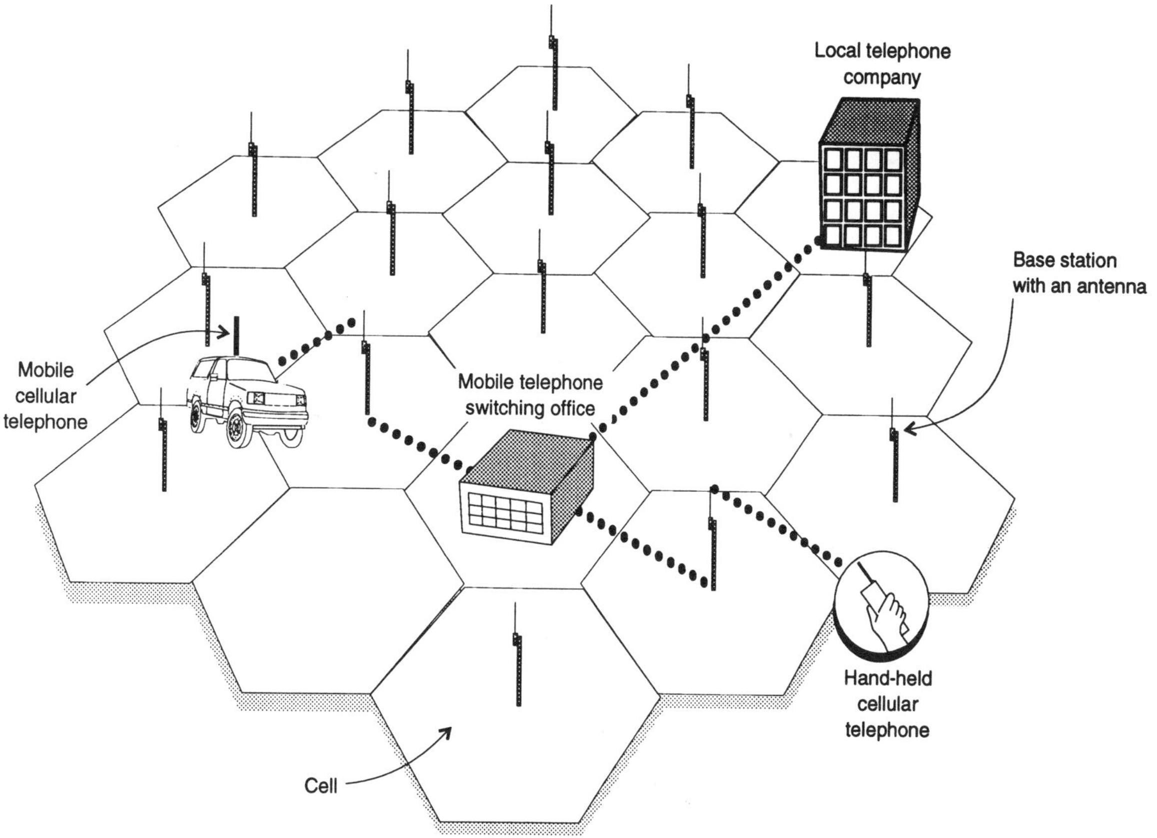

Base station
with an antenna

Local telephone
company

Hand-held
cellular
telephone

Mobile telephone
switching office

Cell

Mobile
cellular
telephone

Source: *Information Superhighway*, GAO (January 1995), 50.

the integrated fiber/coaxial broadband network being built by cable and telephone companies, but it could discipline the telephone companies that attempt to raise residential access rates for voice services." Nevertheless, they boldly conclude:

> The rapid development of wireless technologies and their declining costs provide opportunities for developing a truly contestable local telephone industry. Forecasts of the growth of the wireless technology have proven far too conservative. By the end of the century, there will likely be one wireless telephone for every three Americans and Canadians.[26]

Satellite Networks

There are two kinds of communications satellites: GEO and VSAT. The approximately 150 geosynchronous orbit satellites are 22,300 miles above the equator and rotate with the earth. According to the GAO report, these satellites "have advantages over terrestrial networks because they are accessible from any spot on the globe; can provide broadband digital services, including voice, data, and video, to many points without the cost of acquiring right-of-way and cable installation; and can add receiving and transmitting sites without significant additional costs." The disadvantages of a satellite network include the expense of launching a satellite and the need for large antennas to receive weak signals from space.[27]

Very small aperture terminal (VSAT) satellites transmit energy in a narrow beam to a small geographic area and connect to small ground antennas to provide point-to-point network services. Most of the VSAT satellites launched in the past two decades have been used by large corporations to link multiple branch offices and worksites. This network uses a hub-and-spoke relay system that requires communications to flow through the hub, as illustrated in Figure I-4.

STATE POLICY CHALLENGES IN AN ERA OF COMPETITION

This summary of existing telecommunications networks presents a convincing argument that the convergence of technologies has the potential to foster a competitive environment in the near future. This logic was fundamental in persuading Congress to pass the Telecommunications Act of 1996. (See chapter five.)

In preparing for the policy challenges that lie ahead, Governors need to understand both convergence and the robust forces of competition. For most of the century, states have regulated telephone companies. With the convergence of media based on a digital format, these public policy issues are now appropriately called *telecommunications*. Technological convergence of media now enables the transmission of more than just

---

[26] Crandall and Waverman, *Talk is Cheap*, 240-41.

[27] GAO, *Information Superhighway*, 51.

Figure I-4: Broadcast and VSAT Satellites

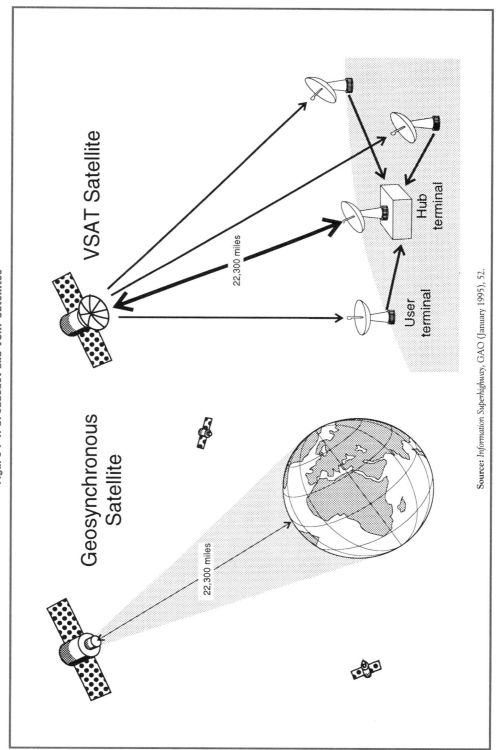

Source: *Information Superhighway*, GAO (January 1995), 52.

voice. George Gilder, a gifted technology seer, has observed that "in 1995, PCs outsold TVs, the number of e-mail messages surpassed snail mail, and RBOC data traffic (driven by an unbelievable increase in Internet usage) exceeded voice traffic for the first time."[28]

Nicholas Negroponte, Director of MIT's Media Lab, explains: "The mixing of audio, video, and data is called 'multimedia'; it sounds complicated but is nothing more than commingled bits."[29]

Negroponte presents this context for understanding telecommunications policy:

> There are five paths for information and entertainment to get into the home: satellite, terrestrial broadcast, cable, telephone, and packaged media (all those atoms, like cassettes, CDs, and print). The Federal Communications Commission, the FCC, serves the general public by regulating some of these paths and some of the information content that flows over them. Its job is a difficult one because the FCC is often at the thorny edges between protection and freedom, between public and private, between competition and broadly mandated monopolies.[30]

To varying degrees, the FCC has regulated the first four paths. All states have regulated telephone services. Only a few have regulated cable-television services, since most cable systems have franchise agreements with municipalities.[31] The Telecommunications Act of 1996 will enable competition in both industries and has established a new set of state responsibilities for promoting local and intrastate telephone competition and preserving and enhancing universal-service objectives for telephone services.

The major point state policymakers need to keep in mind is the immense scale of the various telecommunications industries and the implications for policymakers as competition flourishes and state telewars begin. The business of providing local telephone services, which the states regulate, generates an estimated $90 billion. The

---

[28] As quoted by Anthony B. Perkins, "Bandwidth or Bust," *Wired*, March 1996, 80. See George Gilder's recent work at http://homepage.seas.upenn.edu~gaj1/ggindex.html. Note also this observation by Bill Gates, Microsoft CEO (as quoted in "All about E-mail," *Microsoft Magazine*, April/May 1996, 18):

> Electronic messaging is the beginning of this information highway. In fact, all of the issues being addressed here are the fundamental issues: security, administration, and interoperability of all these different systems. Certainly this broad connectivity will be available on business desktops long before it is available to everyone in their homes. In fact, I think we'll see a dramatic rise in the kinds of networks that connect businesses, whether they're private networks or the Internet backbone, whether it's employees being able to work at home with an ISDN line, or whether it's companies putting information about their products on bulletin-board servers. That kind of bottom-up, business-driven use of communication is where the information highway starts.

[29] Nicholas Negroponte, *Being Digital* (New York: Alfred A. Knopf, 1995), 18. Negroponte continues:

> These two phenomena, commingled bits and bits-about-bits, change the media landscape so thoroughly that concepts like video-on-demand and shipping electronic games down your local cable are just trivial applications—the tip of a much more profound iceberg. Think about the consequences of a broadcast television show as data which includes a computer-readable description of itself. You could record based on content, not time of day or channel....And if moving these bits around is so effortless, what advantage would the large media companies have over you and me?

[30] Ibid., 51.

[31] Because few states regulate cable-television services, the focus of this book is on telephone services. For more about cable regulation, see Robert W. Crandall and Harold Furchtgott-Roth, *Cable TV: Regulation or Competition?* (Brookings Institution, Washington, D.C., 1996). See also Anthony Crowell, "Local Government and the Telecommunications Act of 1996," *Public Management*, Vol. 78, No. 6 (ICMA, Washington, D.C., June 1996): 6-12.

long-distance telephone business, which the FCC regulates, generates an estimated $70 billion. In addition, revenues from providing home video services are estimated conservatively at $74 billion.[32]

Revenues of this magnitude attract robust competition. As the FCC completes its rule-making procedures to implement the new Telecommunications Act, states will become the venue for difficult decisions about how to promote local competition and enhance universal-service objectives. Firms that are competing for billions of dollars in revenue may not be reticent in expressing their corporate views on pressing public policy issues.[33]

State telecommunications policy has long been confounded by difficult tradeoffs, but the movement toward deregulation and competition will yield new challenges: What do deregulation and convergence in telecommunications mean for the states? What are the important issues during the transition from heavy regulation to competition? Competition in local telephone services may herald a new era of enhanced services and lower prices, but for whom? Who will benefit? Will competition in selected markets shift costs to other ratepayers and threaten the goal of universal service? These questions will be addressed in subsequent chapters.

Governors, state regulators, and state legislators will soon find themselves thrust into state telewars. Convergence and competition will define the new era of state telecommunications policy, but there also are immediate and practical reasons for understanding these issues. The next chapter explains the significance of telecommunications in promoting state economic development and improving state services and management.

---

[32] *Ibid.*, 22.

[33] That a firm in a regulated industry should seek to influence, in a rational and strategic way, its own regulatory environment hardly needs documentation. For a good case study of an RBOC active in the states, see Paul E. Teske, "Rent-seeking in the deregulatory environment: State telecommunications," *Public Choice* (1991): 68:235-243. Teske's abstract states: "U S West executives correctly perceived that the political environment in which they operated differed greatly from that in the rest of the country and that a different deregulatory strategy was appropriate. The firm exploited institutional differences by bypassing state regulators and going directly to state legislators to get favorable policies." See also Ken Auletta, "Pay Per Views," *New Yorker*, June 5, 1995.

CHAPTER TWO

THE IMPORTANCE OF STATE TELECOMMUNICATIONS ISSUES

Governors and other state policymakers understand that advanced telecommunications services are essential for the economic development of their states. The ability to provide these services reliably and quickly has become paramount to state efforts to attract and retain industry. States also are using advanced information technologies to improve service delivery and government operations, but they lag behind the private sector in exploiting new technologies to improve in these areas. This chapter presents three compelling reasons why telecommunications issues are important to the states:

- Telecommunications infrastructure and quality services are essential for state economic development.
- Emerging telecommunications applications can give citizens access to public information and services, often in ways that are more effective and efficient than traditional ones.
- Advanced telecommunications services and related information technologies have tremendous potential to improve state management of people, programs, and data.

STATE ECONOMIC DEVELOPMENT

In the early 1990s, Wisconsin's Tommy G. Thompson was among several Governors who understood the importance of telecommunications issues to their states and led efforts to promote competition and investment in this vital sector. In a report on his Blue Ribbon Telecommunications Infrastructure Task Force, he writes:

Nearly every aspect of our lives is being revolutionized by telecommunications. And the only way to maintain Wisconsin's competitiveness for the 21st Century is to make sure that we have a first-rate telecommunications network in place. This electronic network will serve as an infrastructure, just as important as our highways, bridges, and railroads. Telecommunications will be a crucial link between Wisconsin and the rest of the world.[1]

---

[1] As quoted in "Convergence, Competition, Cooperation: The Report of the Governor's Blue Ribbon Telecommunications Infrastructure Task Force" (Department of Administration, Madison, Wisconsin, November 8, 1993).

Box II-1 Telecommunications and Rural Development

Telecommunications is as important to the economic development of rural areas as the interstate highway system that links outlying communities and major consumer markets. Already the emergence of advanced communications has reversed outmigration and declining job opportunities in many nonmetropolitan areas. In 1989 Premium Standard Farms (PSF), a pork-production facility, chose to locate near Princeton, Missouri, a community of 3,600 residents 90 miles northwest of Kansas City. PSF selected Princeton for its facility in part because the local, independent phone company could offer electronic, fully digital communications. Initially employing only three people, the PSF workforce grew to 700 employees within five years. The company's need for high-technology telecommunications continues to grow. This year the local telephone company will install a direct fiber-optic link between its facilities and PSF.

Source: *Telecommunications: The Next American Revolution* (National Governors' Association, 1994).

Quality telecommunications services have become an important asset for states in the competition for firms and employment. Growing sectors of our economy require modern telecommunications infrastructure to transmit voice, data, and video quickly and reliably throughout the world. Many firms in information-intensive sectors make locational decisions based, in part, on the quality of a state's telecommunications infrastructure. According to Russ Kesler of GTE, "Eighty-two percent of relocation businesses list telecommunications capacity as a key factor in selecting a new site."[2]

Several studies also conclude that the location decisions of the largest users of telecommunications (e.g., the financial industry, business services, printing and publishing, computers, airlines, and corporate headquarters of large firms) are "partly driven by the cost and quality of available telecommunications services." William Shapiro, senior vice president of a site selection company, argues that "telecommunications is absolutely critical in any facilities decision....The more telecommunications intensive a business is, the more telecommunications plays a role in site selection."[3] L.C. Mitchell is a telecommunications consultant at Deloitte & Touche who has consulted with New Jersey and Pennsylvania state governments. As he observes, "Advanced telecommunications are increasingly being recognized by states as a competitive weapon in economic development and business retention and attraction."[4]

---

[2] Kesler continues: "In North Carolina, we helped build a 100 percent digital fiber-optic system that has the route diversity firms require. This gives the state the competitive edge it needs to lure new business into the next century." As quoted by Whitney Chamberlin, *Telecommunications and Community Economic Development in North Carolina* (Center for Policy Alternatives, Washington, D.C., 1995), 1.

[3] Paul E. Teske, "State Telecommunications Policy in the 1980s," *Policy Studies Review* (spring 1992): 11:1, 121.

[4] Steven Prokesch, "Wiring into the Future: The High Stakes of Telecommunications," *New York Times*, January 12, 1993, B1.

Over the past decade, many state-commissioned studies of telecommunications argued forcefully that investing in telecommunications infrastructure would foster state economic development.[5] One scholar noted, "Telecommunications is often cited as the infrastructure for the 21st Century information economy with analogies to railroads and the manufacturing economy of the 19th Century."[6] Dr. Edwin Parker, a telecommunications consultant, cited empirical data that demonstrates the linkage between telecommunications investment and the creation of wealth over time: "The richer you get, the more you spend on telecommunications; and the more you spend on telecommunications, the richer you get." Telecommunications is not an isolated "cause" of economic development, but it is surely a vital catalyst. From every indication, the importance of telecommunications to economic development will only grow in the future.[7]

In Walter Wriston's book, *The Twilight of Sovereignty*, he uses the term "global conversation" to capture how telephone and computer networks are shrinking the world. He notes that every hour, over 100 million telephone calls are made throughout the world, using 300 million access lines. The estimated volume of phone transactions will triple by the year 2000. In reviewing Wriston's book in the *Harvard Business Review*, Alan W. Webber concludes:

> Those who are most plugged into this global conversation stand to gain the most from it. Those outside the conversation—by virtue of political ideology, personal choice, poverty, or misfortune—risk total economic failure, a fact that is as true for countries as it is for companies.[8]

Using Governor Thompson's analogy, it would appear to be as important to states' economic development to have advanced telecommunications infrastructure as it was in past decades to have physical infrastructure such as highways, bridges, and railways. For this reason, most Governors and state economic development agencies have worked closely with industry leaders in recent years to ensure that infrastructure investment is sufficient to improve the capacity of existing systems and enhance service levels.[9]

Governors' policy advisors need to be concerned with two issues: the political nature of the debate on infrastructure investment, which is addressed in chapter four; and whether rural businesses are competitively disadvantaged to the extent that they

---

[5] It should be noted, parenthetically, that some of these studies focused too narrowly on telemarketing as a growth industry. Improving telecommunications in a particular state, it was thought, would lure telemarketing and certain back office operations to locate in that state—following the Nebraska example. State economic development officials are far more sophisticated now because they understand that every business in their state that is competitive in regional, national and international markets has a severe disadvantage if it lacks quality telecommunications services.

[6] Teske, "State Telecommunications Policy in the 1980s," 121.

[7] As quoted in "Convergence, Competition, Cooperation," 12. Although these data are persuasive, one must not confuse correlation with causality. Wealthy states have the resources to invest in their infrastructures. Prudent infrastructure investment does promote and facilitate economic development. Poor investments, of any kind, are never wise.

[8] Alan M. Webber, "What's So New About the New Economy?" *Harvard Business Review* (January-February 1993): 25.

[9] See especially, Gail Garfield Schwartz, "Telecommunications and Economic Development Policy," *Economic Development Quarterly*, Vol. 4, No. 2 (May 1990): 83-91.

have limited service areas for local calling and lack access to enhanced telecommunications services.[10]

IMPROVING STATE SERVICES

State governments have been exploring the landscape of telecommunications to find innovative ways to improve operations and provide services. According to a memorandum of the National Association of State Telecommunications Directors, the range of telecommunications applications being planned or implemented by state governments includes:

> Statewide voice/data backbone networks; digital data networks; integrated e-mail/voice mail systems; videoconferencing capacity; local area networks (LANs) and wide area networks (WANs); online information systems; imaging; 800MHz trunked radio systems for public safety; enhanced 911 systems; inmate telephone systems; call processing/voice response units/automated attendants; disaster preparedness/recovery plans; dual party relay systems (for the hearing impaired); and ISDN (Integrated Services Digital Network) open systems standards.

The annual report of the National Association of State Telecommunications Directors also constitutes an important source of information about state telecommunications activities.[11] It would appear, judging from this list, that the potential benefits of advanced telecommunications services in state government operations are extraordinary.

---

[10] For more on this last point, see especially Edwin B. Parker and Heather E. Hudson, with Don A. Dillman, Sharon Strover, and Frederick Williams, *Electronic Byways: State Policies for Rural Development Through Telecommunications* (Boulder, Colorado: Westview Press and The Aspen Institute, 1992). See *Telecommunications and its Impact on Rural America* (NADO Research Foundation, Washington, D.C., April 1994); and Thomas W. Bonnett, *Strategies for Rural Competitiveness: Policy Options for State Governments* (CGPA, Washington, D.C., 1993). Citing the work of Parker et al., this author provided the following assessment (93):

> Telecommunications represent a tremendous potential to assist rural development, to overcome the economic development disadvantages of isolation and the distance penalty, and to create vital linkages with the robust economic sectors in the urban, national, and global economies. The policy challenge is complicated by numerous factors:
>
> • State legislators and regulators often do not fully comprehend the potential of telecommunications as an economic development tool, especially for rural communities;
>
> • The regulatory transition has changed from pricing subsidies toward pricing at actual costs;
>
> • A broad range of competitors is seeking to meet new and growing telecommunications demands of urban markets, but often fails to do so in rural communities—effectively outdistancing the technology curve; and
>
> • Many rural communities are already poorly served by the existing services, such as the lack of single-party, touchtone service, which is required to transmit data through computer, modem, and facsimile.

[11] Jack Gallt, NASTD staff director, "State Telecommunications Activities" (Memorandum, April 6, 1993). For current information about state telecommunications activities, also see "1995 State Reports" (National Association of State Telecommunications Directors/Council of State Governments, Lexington, Kentucky, 1995). Also see *State Technology Inventory: A Compendium of Innovative Technology Projects Designed to Improve Government and Reduce Costs* (State Management Task Force, National Governors' Association, Washington, D.C., July 1994).

Health
Electronic Verification
Telemedicine
Mobile Communication
Health-care Education Networks

Education
Distance Learning
Home-to-School Messaging
Learning and Evaluation Tools

Public Assistance
Electronic Fund Benefits Transfer (EBT)
Information Systems and Program Integration
Video Touchscreen Prescreening

Criminal Justice and Emergency Services
Remote Video Arraignment
Apprehension and Conviction Systems
Emergency Services

Environment
Telecommuting
Remote Emissions Monitoring
Geographic Information Systems (GIS)

Citizen Access
Kiosks
Electronic Democracy
Home Access

Source: *New Alliances In Innovation* (CGPA, 1992), 10.

Applications that are receiving the most public attention include the following: distance learning programs for rural schools;[12] "telemedicine" programs that link medical experts to remote patients with special needs; electronic bulletin boards that

---

[12] Unfortunately, much of the recent literature about the role of technology and distance learning has been influenced by those so enamored by the "whiz-bang, rah-rah" of the applications that they seem to have forgotten underlying educational goals. The market for educational goods and services is so large that it has attracted the impressive advertising and marketing skills of gifted entrepreneurs. As quoted by Peter Applebome, "Computer Idea Gets Mixed Response," *New York Times*, January 25, 1996, Edward Miller, editor of *The Harvard Education Letter*, offered this opinion: "The evidence from research on the usefulness of technology is not very encouraging. The idea that you put computers in classrooms and kids learn better is just not the case." For an excellent discussion of telecommunications technologies in the schools, see Arthur Sheekey and Richard T. Hezel, "Telecommunications Development for Schools: Implications for Governance, Finance, Policy-Making and Management of Schools" (Paper commissioned by the Institute for Educational Finance, Governance, Policy-Making and Management, Washington, D.C., 1996). For a contrary view, see chapter nine in Clifford Stoll, *Silicon Snake Oil: Second Thoughts on the Information Highway* (New York: Doubleday, 1995).

provide information about state bidding and contracting procedures; and kiosks placed in shopping centers to provide information about state services and employment and enable citizens to renew licenses and obtain state permits. The range of innovations pursued by state governments in cooperation with telecommunications firms is extensive. The potential benefits—in terms of improving services, providing greater citizen access to information, and reducing public expense—are extraordinary.[13]

Important lessons for state policymakers about implementation strategies are summarized in a recent GAO report: *Telecommunications: Initiatives Taken by Three States to Promote Increased Access and Investment*. This report reviews "the experiences of three states that experts in the field consider to be leaders in the development of statewide advanced telecommunications: Iowa, whose network provides two-way video communications; Nebraska, which uses less advanced technology to provide high-speed data connections and video conferencing; and North Carolina, which provides two-way video communications to several sites simultaneously using the most advanced technology available." [14] The term *advanced telecommunications services* refers to any service, such as two-way video or high-speed data connections, not currently available over a standard telephone line.

This report acknowledges that telephone companies are investing billions of dollars to improve infrastructure (replacing copper wires with fiber-optic cables and installing advanced computerized switches) "mainly in business districts and high-density residential areas where there are opportunities to make a profit" (and to recover the cost of these investments). But the report notes, "In rural areas, where there are fewer businesses and the cost of delivering service is usually higher, the current profit incentives are generally not high enough for companies to invest in providing such services."[15]

---

[13] Nancy Ginn Helme, *New Alliances in Innovation: A Guide to Encouraging Innovative Applications of New Communication Technologies to Address State Problems* (CGPA, Washington, D.C., 1992). This work is an excellent introduction to how states began to harness the power of telecommunications in the early 1990s to improve the quality of public services. For current information about state and local applications, see *State and Local Strategies for Connecting Communities: A Snapshot of the Fifty States* (Benton Foundation and Center for Policy Alternatives, Washington, D.C., 1996), and recent issues of *Governing* and *Government Technology* magazines.

[14] General Accounting Office, *Telecommunications: Initiatives Taken by Three States to Promote Increased Access and Investment*, GAO/RCED-96-68 (Washington, D.C., March 1996), 2-3.

[15] *Ibid*, 2. Although the conventional view is that rural telephone companies have failed to make sufficient infrastructure investments, contrary evidence is presented in the "1995-96 NECA Access Market Study" (National Exchange Carrier Association, Washington, D.C., 1996). Eighty percent of the companies that are part of NECA's traffic sensitive pool participated in this survey. Here are the survey highlights from a NECA summary:

- **SS7** The deployment of Signaling System 7 technology has continued at an accelerated pace. More than 32 percent of the central offices representing 50 percent of the customer access lines now have access to this capability. Before the end of 1998, 255 central offices with more than 250,000 access lines plan SS7 deployment.

- **Digital** Ninety additional companies have converted to digital central offices since the 1993 survey. In the last survey, member companies had 91 percent of their central offices converted to digital.

- **ISDN** Integrated Services Digital Network is gaining support from end users, and member companies are installing ISDN equipment to meet this demand. Five percent of the switches already have ISDN. Companies plan on doubling that number in 1996 and adding another 5 percent in 1997. This represents a total of 16 percent of central offices and 38 percent of customer access lines having access in ISDN by 1997.

- **Internet** More than 200 companies are now involved in some way in providing Internet service to their customers. These companies are located in 38 states and serve more than 1.5 million or 25 percent of the total access lines provided by the small member companies.

Box II-3 State Experiences Offer Lessons

Successful project implementation depends on reaching consensus among interested parties about how to provide and use advanced telecommunications services. Participants said that telecommunications companies are willing to provide advanced services to public organizations if the proposal makes "business sense." Long-term customer agreements with states, prior experience working with public agencies, and the ability to sell advanced services to commercial customers can encourage companies' acceptance of this kind of proposal.

State and private-sector officials indicated that reaching agreement with potential users on how to use an advanced telecommunications system can help ensure that the system provides the services they want at a price they are willing to pay. Identifying a source of financial support to help pay the costs of connection is also important so that future users will receive some assistance.

Legislative support for project financing can help prevent delays that can result from reductions in funding. And while officials of a state's executive branch can serve as advocates to keep a project on track, administrative responsibilities for implementing that project also must be clearly defined.

Source: *Telecommunications: Initiatives Taken by Three States to Promote Increased Access and Investment* (GAO, March 1996).

Therefore, the role of public leadership—as demonstrated in Iowa, Nebraska, and North Carolina—is paramount in making strategic public investments, encouraging private investment, and coordinating with potential users to expand advanced telecommunications services throughout their states. Three basic strategies are profiled in these case studies:

- **Make Public Investment.** Each state made a major commitment to fund infrastructure investments in telecommunications to improve public services. Iowa was an exception because it financed and built its own network.
- **Encourage Private Investment.** Both Nebraska and North Carolina encouraged local telephone companies "to make improvements faster than they would have on their own."
- **Coordinate with Potential Users.** Each state sought funding from a variety of federal and state agencies to leverage strategic investments. A specific strategy called "aggregating demand" involved three steps: first, identify potential users and potential applications for advanced services; second, pull together the buying power of disparate public agencies and potential users in the community; and third, use the pooled demand for advanced services as leverage to persuade the private sector to make substantial infrastructure investment. Efforts to aggregate

demand and integrate programs have proved to be important strategies to convince the private sector to make major telecommunications investments in underserved areas.[16]

These state initiatives have not taken place without controversy and consternation. Iowa, for example, "faced early difficulties in attracting private-sector involvement" and is now attempting to share future costs of its public network with the private sector. Nevertheless, each state already has made advanced services available to between 100 and 400 sites in public buildings, even though networks are at an early stage of development. According to this report, state officials believe these networks will "provide education, health care, and other public services more effectively and more equitably. They also believe these services will make their states more attractive to new and expanding businesses and allow their rural residents to participate more fully in state government."[17]

Other states have experimented with various approaches to encourage private-sector investment in advanced telecommunications services for schools, hospitals and other public institutions. Florida, Texas and Tennessee have enacted legislation that requires service providers to assist these organizations. Service providers in Texas must contribute to a fund that supports distance-learning applications and provides toll-free access to the Internet and discounted services to public institutions. In Tennessee, service providers must contribute to an economic development fund that supports small business development.[18]

The potential to improve service delivery using advanced telecommunications applications is unheralded; yet extensive experimentation has been performed by state governments in recent years. Multiple approaches are being tested to make information readily available to the public. Many federal and state agencies have created electronic bulletin boards that are accessible to citizens who have computers with modems.[19]

States have not been left behind in the telecommunications revolution. State governments are often the largest single consumer of telecommunications services in their states. Also, some state agencies operate their own special systems and networks. In recent years, several Governors have appointed chief technology officers to coordinate

---

[16] Ibid.

[17] Ibid., 16.

[18] Patricia F. Lewis, "Universal Service: How States are Planning for the Future" (Unpublished paper, University of Florida, December 17, 1995).

[19] With a modem, computer, and telephone line, one can connect electronically with a menu of choices on a full range of topics and issues. Check the National Technical Information Service's "Fed-World" electronic bulletin board, which lists more than 3000 files and provides gateway access to more than 100 individual federal agency databases, with this dial-up computer number (703.321.8020) [8N1]. Browse the Library of Congress electronic card catalog with 25 million entries at Internet address: locis.loc.gov. Or send electronic mail to the White House: president@whitehouse.gov. See Office of Technology Assessment, U.S. Congress, *Making Government Work: Electronic Delivery of Federal Services*, OTA-TCT-578 (U.S. Government Printing Office, Washington, D.C., September 1993), 27. See also Bruce Maxwell, "Washington Online 1995" *Congressional Quarterly* (Washington, D.C., 1995).

telecommunications investment and management. Some states have chief information officers to coordinate and plan investments in information technologies.[20]

California, Colorado and Texas were among the first states to experiment with interactive kiosks in public settings to improve citizen access to information and public services. Oregon was the first state to allow contractors to bid on state contracts

---

Box II-4 Center for Technology in Government

CTG is a partnership of government, business, and the university community. Through small-scale testing, the center saves agencies the cost and risk of buying expensive computer systems and software without knowing if the equipment will work. CTG's six objectives are to: 1. examine how technology can help reduce government spending and the cost of doing business with government; 2. allow government to reduce the risks inherent in adopting new technologies; 3. support innovations that improve productivity, streamline operations, and enhance public services; 4. encourage standards to support effective sharing of information; 5. leverage the benefits of single projects through a technology transfer program; and 6. serve as the focal point for other government technology initiatives. CTG is funded by the state legislature and SUNY Albany. In 1995, it received a $100,000 Innovations in American Government Award from the Ford Foundation and Harvard University's Kennedy School of Government.

Source: *State and Local Strategies for Connecting Communities: A Snapshot of the Fifty States* (Benton Foundation and Center for Policy Alternatives, Washington, D.C., 1996), 79.

---

through its electronic "vendor information program." Texas claims to have been the first state to create a Web page (in 1993), but now many have their own World Wide Web sites to provide information via the Internet. For example, Europeans planning a trip to this country frequently visit Maine's Web site. The Web has attracted such interest that *Government Technology* began a "Best of the Web" award for state and local governments.

Several articles in the May 1996 issue of *Government Technology* illustrate the range of advanced applications used by the states:

- Illinois Governor Jim Edgar unveiled a Web site that enables firms to locate sources of assistance that can help them become more competitive by modernizing technical and business operations. The site was designed by the National

---

[20] A good source of information about chief information officers is the National Association of State Information Resource Executives (NASHIRE), 167 W. Main St., Suite 600, Lexington, Kentucky 40507, (606) 231-1884 or lspieler@ ukcc.uky.edu. Also of interest is a forthcoming report by Harvard's Kennedy School of Government, entitled "Information Technology and Government Procurement: Priorities for Reform," as part of an initiative between NASHIRE and the National Association of State Purchasing Officials to focus on improving the procurement of information technology and telecommunications products and services in state government.

Box II-5 What Is a Kiosk?

Info/Texas is a statewide network of multimedia kiosks that resemble automatic teller machines. At a kiosk, a customer can access information about government services in either English or Spanish. Soon, customers will be able to use kiosks to do business interactively with the state. Kiosks are located in shopping malls, grocery stores, convenience stores, and similar locations. They are not located in state offices. The idea is to move the service point out of state offices and into the community, where people can use them in the normal course of their day. As the network expands, kiosks may be placed in public libraries, colleges and universities, military facilities, community centers, or other sites where people need access to state government services.

Source: *State Technology Inventory* (National Governors' Association, July 1994).

Center for Supercomputing Applications at the University of Illinois at Urbana-Champaign and is the first of its type in the country to be electronically connected to a major on-line manufacturing publisher. (The URL address for the site is http://www.ncsa.uiuc.edu/illcoalition.)

- Under the leadership of Utah Governor Michael O. Leavitt, the Western Governors' Association is attempting to develop a "virtual learning system" that will offer courses "taught in traditional classrooms, via two-way interactive video over fiber-optic cable and satellite, using CD-ROMs and floppy disks, electronic bulletin boards and the Internet."[21]

As experimentation continues, some states may be entering the rocky terrain of implementation and the inevitable growing pains of expanding to scale. Ironically, state funds for InfoCal, one of the most innovative prototypes of a state kiosk system, were cut in the fall of 1995. State funding for FYI Hawaii, the prototype for an interactive state information system accessible through any computer/modem, was also eliminated in late 1995. These cutbacks represent ominous warning signs, for they suggest that advocates of advanced telecommunications have not made their case convincingly to state decisionmakers. The cuts may also reflect the frustrations of state budgeters who are still looking for measurable returns on past investments in communications technologies and are growing more skeptical about future investments.

In 1992, CGPA published an excellent monograph by Nancy Ginn Helme about state government innovation in communications technologies. A prominent theme of Helme's study is the difficulty of overcoming organizational barriers to new

---

[21] Governor Michael Leavitt, "The Century of the States," *Government Technology* (May 1996), 48.

technologies. Program turf and coordination problems are serious institutional obstacles to innovation within a bureaucracy. Budgets and costs also constitute obstacles, but opponents sometimes use the phrase "too expensive" when, in fact, other interests are being threatened. Indeed, Helme notes that fear—of both change and technology—is an important sociological obstacle to innovation.

Regulatory and legal obstacles also block innovation, but Helme's report cites numerous examples of how states have used flexibility in regulating telephone companies to encourage modernization, direct private investment, and promote the expansion of services. The Helme report also identifies technical obstacles to innovation that state governments must be prepared to address.

Jerry Mechling, director of the Program on Strategic Computing and Telecommunications in the Public Sector at Harvard University's Kennedy School of Government offers astute advice about the process of implementing information technologies. Mechling asks whether the benefits of cross-organizational reforms are worth the effort, and answers by providing these guidelines:

Box II-6 IBM's Government of the Future Studio

IBM's electronic global village is located at 1301 K St., N.W. in Washington, D.C. and presents technologies in true-to-life settings. Demonstrations will include:

- Public access kiosks for government information and services such as registering vehicles, filing tax forms, or obtaining information about a water bill.
- Emergency 911 dispatch and mobile police communications, digitized fingerprinting, and mugshots.
- Environmental applications such as air quality monitoring.
- Transportation planning using remote sensors and geographic information systems.
- Electronic town meetings.
- A digital library and interactive school classroom.

"Technology is changing the lives of police officers and judges, teachers and school children, public servants and citizens," said Janet Caldow, director of the Institute for Electronic Government at IBM. "The Government of the Future Studio is designed to show public officials how they can take advantage of technology to reduce costs and improve service."

Source: IBM (May 16, 1996).

- Reduce the confusion of cross-organizational initiatives through explicit analysis.
- Manage the conflicts of cross-organizational initiatives through leadership.
- Avoid initiatives that are just too risky.[22]

Perhaps at this point, one could argue that the promise of telecommunications to improve service delivery has been tarnished, not because technology, hardware, or software is lacking, but because land mines scattered along the path of implementation thwart progress. According to Mechling, public leadership is necessary to avoid these land mines and transcend organizational boundaries to implement new systems.

Telemedicine serves as a good example of why so little has been carried out despite the glow of potential social benefits. In 1991, the Congressional Office of Technology Assessment offered this summary:

Telecommunications and information technologies can also improve health-care delivery in rural areas. From online databases that provide physicians with indexed scientific periodicals, to remote defibrillation and monitoring of heart patients, to inventory control systems that link suppliers and hospital administrators, to diagnostic services that connect general practitioners with specialists at research hospitals, communications technologies can provide rural communities with levels of health care now available only in urban centers. These technologies can also help cut costs so that rural hospitals could remain open when they otherwise could not.[23]

To be sure, many telemedicine projects have begun in the past five years. Indeed, virtually every state has initiated a demonstration project. Individually, each is

---

Box II-7 Pennsylvania's HealthNet

The Rural Health Telecommunications Network "uses video conferencing to link patients at 12 remote, rural sites with specialists at four major teaching hospitals." HealthNet, which received an award from the National Association of State Information Resource Executives for its innovative use of technology, allows consulting specialists to do "almost everything but touch the patient." The system "creates a video link for long-distance examinations...using advanced telecommunications equipment, high-speed graphic processors and state-of-the-art medical tools such as electronic stethoscopes."

Source: Marilyn J. Cohodas, "A Guide to Award-Winning Technology," Governing.

---

[22] Jerry Mechling, "Reaching Across Organizational Lines, Governing, June 1995, 106. See also Thomas M. Fletcher and Jerry Mechling, "Information Technology and Government: The Need for New Leadership" (Summary Report, Kennedy School of Government, Cambridge, Massachusetts, 1996).

[23] Office of Technology Assessment, U.S. Congress, Rural America at the Crossroads: Networking for the Future (U.S. Government Printing Office, Washington, D.C., April 1991), 105-6.

impressive, yet on the whole one must consider the general lack of progress in implementing telemedicine programs a disappointment. One might also ask: Who will provide the public leadership to plan and coordinate a telemedicine program? Who pays to install the T-1 line that links the rural hospital or clinic with the urban hospital? When will public policy issues be addressed, such as state licensing restrictions, third-party reimbursements for telemedicine consultations, standards for data transmission, and establishment of medical protocols for various services?

In this context, it is significant that innovators—in the land of bureaucratic mazes—have enjoyed as much success as they have. State policymakers who seek to implement program innovations using telecommunications applications need a great deal more attention and assistance. Strategies from the private sector may be helpful to those who are struggling with this challenge in state government.

IMPROVING STATE MANAGEMENT

Following the November 1994 elections, Congress and many Governors sought to give states greater autonomy for social welfare programs such as AFDC, Medicaid, and work force training and development. Part of the argument for devolving domestic

---

Box II-8 Reengineering and Information Technologies

"Organizations have been using reengineering to dramatically speed up work processes. Using a private sector example, an insurance company recently found that each new policy application had to be seen by fifteen specialist workers and required twenty-two days for processing. While the customer waited more than three weeks for an answer, the application was actually being worked on for less than forty-five minutes; the remaining time was consumed by hand-offs. In this case, *information technology* enabled the company to redesign the process completely. They began by creating an expert system to aid in applying the many rules involved in reviewing an application. The system allowed the company to create a new category of worker—the case worker—to handle all the processing steps for a typical application; in cases requiring specialists, hand-offs were made via an electronic image on the computer network, thereby allowing the involved specialists to work on it simultaneously. The results have been dramatic: the redesigned process requires 50 percent less labor and 90 percent less time. Customers who previously waited twenty-two days now get answers normally within two hours and, in the worst case, within two days."

Source: Jerry Mechling, "Reengineering Government: Is There a 'There, There'?" *Public Productivity and Management Review.*

---

responsibility to the states was the Governors' claim that states could manage these programs better and would not have to comply with endless federal requirements. Advocates for greater autonomy assert that states will reform and consolidate programs; states also will develop and integrate information systems, which will improve service delivery and reduce redundancy.

The primary vehicles for managing additional social welfare responsibilities will be advanced telecommunications and related information technologies.[24] Many experts suggest that advanced information technologies can radically restructure large bureaucracies.[25] Pointing to the corporate downsizing that began in the 1980s, reengineering advocates contend that the skillful employment of information technologies can profoundly reshape state governments. This contention has received considerable attention as state governments gradually assume additional responsibilities for domestic programs and the federal government reduces its financial support.

STATE POLICY CHALLENGES

Following the Nebraska and North Carolina examples, can states use their purchasing power to encourage local telephone companies to shift private investment toward infrastructure improvements that provide social objectives such as telemedicine or distance learning? Integrate and coordinate telephone networks to streamline operations and cut costs? Minimize the number of dedicated networks? Work to maximize the capacity of existing networks? Maintain interoperability among networks? Work with local communities to aggregate demand for telecommunications services to justify new investment and modernization? Engage public leadership to develop information infrastructure across organizational boundaries?

Lessons from the past can help us prepare for the future. The next chapter describes why government became involved in regulating the telephone industry in this country and how regulation has evolved throughout the century.

---

[24] See *The States Forge Ahead Despite the Federal Impasse: CGPA's January 1996 Survey of the States on the "Devolution Revolution"* (Council of Governors' Policy Advisors, Washington, D.C., February 1996).

[25] See Michael Hammer and James Champy, *Reengineering the Corporation: A Manifesto for Business Revolution* (New York: HarperBusiness, 1993); and Sharon L. Caudle, *Reengineering for Results: Keys to Success from Government Experience* (National Academy of Public Administration, Washington, D.C., 1994).

CHAPTER THREE

A SHORT HISTORY OF TELEPHONY[1]

There is often a lag between invention and widespread acceptance of the refined product. The public was slow to understand the potential of the telephone, long after Alexander Graham Bell spoke the first message to his assistant: "Watson, come here, I need you." John Brooks, a historian and journalist, writes:

> In 1877 when Bell and Thomas Watson were giving public demonstrations of the telephone in New England and New York, the newspaper reports were full of forebodings of witchcraft. "It is difficult," said the *Providence Press*, "to really resist the notion that the powers of darkness are in league with it." The Boston *Advertiser* spoke of a "weirdness" never before felt in that city; and the New York *Herald* found the telephone "almost supernatural."[2]

Just two years later, Sir William Preece, the chief engineer of the British Post Office, predicted that the telephone had a limited future in Britain:

> I fancy the descriptions we get of its use in America are a little exaggerated, though there are conditions in America which necessitate the use of such instruments more than here. Here we have a superabundance of messengers, errand boys and things of that kind....The absence of servants has compelled Americans to adopt communication systems for domestic purposes. Few have worked at the telephone much more than I have. I have one in my office, but more for show. If I want to send a message—I use a sounder or employ a boy to take it.[3]

---

[1] Before the telephone came the telegraph. According to Eli M. Noam, "Telecommunications in the United States began in 1836 with Samuel Morse and his electromagnetic telegraph." Also of interest, the first telegraph message, which was sent from Baltimore to Washington in 1844, was "What hath God wrought?" (See Eli M. Noam, "Beyond Telecommunications Liberalization: Past Performance, Present Hype, and Future Direction," in *The New Information Infrastructure: Strategies for U.S. Policy*, William J. Drake, ed. [Twentieth Century Fund, New York, 1995]), 34, 31. And a final point, Congress appropriated $30,000, not an insignificant sum, to subsidize Morse's experimental line from Washington, D.C. to Baltimore. See Gerald W. Brock, *The Telecommunications Industry* (Boston: Harvard University Press, 1981), 56.

[2] John Brooks, "The First and Only Century of Telephone Literature," *The Social Impact of the Telephone*, Ithiel de Sola Pool, ed. (Cambridge, Massachusetts: MIT Press, 1977), 209-10.

[3] As quoted by de Sola Pool, Craig Decker, Stephen Dizard, Kay Israel, Pamela Rubin, and Barry Weinstein, "Foresight and Hindsight: The Case of the Telephone," *The Social Impact of the Telephone*, 128.

Around the same time, the mayor of a midwestern city in the United States had a broader appreciation of its social utility: "I can envision a time in which every city might have a telephone."[4] As is often the case, the inventor himself had a compelling vision. This is what Alexander Graham Bell wrote to a group of British investors just two years after he invented the telephone:

At the present time we have a perfect network of gas pipes and water pipes throughout our large cities. We have main pipes laid under streets communicating by side pipes with various dwellings, enabling the members to draw their supplies of gas and water from a common source.

In a similar manner it is conceivable that cables of telephone wires would be laid under ground, or suspended overhead, communicating by branch wires with private dwellings, counting houses, shops, manufactories, etc., uniting them through the main cable with a central office where the wire could be connected as desired, establishing direct communication between any two places in the city....I believe in the future wires will unite the head offices of telephone companies in different cities, and a man in one part of the country may communicate by word of mouth with another in a distant place.[5]

A few historical anecdotes enrich our understanding of how the modern telephone network evolved. One historian claims that the first switchboard was unintended. The licensee in New Haven in 1878 had run "all wires through his office for ease of servicing," but when Bell learned of this approach, he said that he "had always anticipated this development, which was central to his idea of the role of the telephone in society."[6] As another curious event, the first automated switchboard was invented by an undertaker who thought he was losing business because the switchboard operator was married to the other funeral director in town.

In the early years of this century—soon after the Bell patents expired—there was vigorous competition among telephone companies in many urban markets. In cities with populations above 5,000, more than half the Bell exchanges had local competitors. Sometimes the competition was short-lived, because there were inherent advantages in a single system with uniform standards for the telephone network and

---

[4] Personal communication with Michael Kirk Stauffer, NYNEX. Note this assessment by S.H. Aronson, "Bell's Electrical Toy: What's the Use? The Sociology of Early Telephone Usage," In de Sola Pool, *The Social Impact of the Telephone*, 15: "Even after the telephone had been widely discussed and its principle had begun to be understood, for many the telephone as remarkable as the idea seemed had no obvious use. There is even evidence that some who should have known better did not immediately appreciate the possibilities of the amazing device." Aronson also reports that William Orton, president of Western Union, rejected the opportunity to buy the original Bell telephony patents for $100,000, saying, "What use could this company make of an electric toy?"

[5] de Sola Pool et al, "Foresight and Hindsight," *The Social Impact of the Telephone*, 156-57. The full letter, dated March 20, 1878 and addressed "to the capitalists of the Electric Telephone Company" is reprinted as an appendix.

[6] de Sola Pool, *Forecasting the Telephone: A Retrospective Technology Assessment of the Telephone* (Ablex, Norwood, New Jersey, 1983), 22, 24, as quoted by Susan G. Hadden, "Technologies of Universal Service," *Universal Telephone Service* (Northern Telecom Inc./The Aspen Institute, Queenstown, Maryland, 1991), 62.

equipment. Competition had its critics. Rival networks were seldom connected, and businesses had to install and maintain two or more telephones, one for each network. Thus many argued that rival networks caused duplication and economic waste.[7]

In this environment, AT&T enjoyed a tremendous advantage, because it was able to construct a network that linked many different local exchanges. Robert Crandall, an economist at the Brookings Institution, provides this summary:

> AT&T's early power derived from its patents on the basic technology of transmitting voice signals over copper wires, which allowed AT&T's forerunner company to establish local telephone exchange monopolies through a series of license agreements. When these patents expired in the 1890s, a rush of new entry into local telephone service took place, but the new entrants did not have access to a service that would interconnect their exchanges with distant exchanges in other cities or states. AT&T had pioneered the development of long-distance technology, and it used its patents in this field to control the interexchange (long-distance) business.[8]

AT&T was aggressive in this formative period in acquiring competitive local exchange companies. Associated with this acquisition strategy was Theodore Vail's vision of *universal service*,[9] as articulated in the 1910 AT&T annual report:

> The Bell system was founded on broad lines of "One System," "One Policy," "Universal Service," on the idea that no aggregation of isolated independent

---

[7] Richard H. K. Vietor, *Contrived Competition Regulation and Deregulation in America* (Boston: Belknap/Harvard, 1996), 171. Vietor also quotes the Michigan Public Utilities Commission in 1921: "Competition resulted in duplication of investment, the necessity for the business man maintaining two or more telephones, economic waste to the company, increased burden, and consequent continuous loss to the subscriber. The policy of the state was to eliminate this by eliminating as far as possible, duplication."

[8] Crandall, *After the Breakup*, 17. For an alternative interpretation of this era, see Milton Mueller, *Universal Service: Competition, Interconnection, and Monopoly in the Making of the American Telephone System* (Cambridge, Massachusetts: MIT Press/American Enterprise Institute, 1996).

[9] The phrase *universal service* has an interesting history of its own. One view holds that T. Vail pioneered the concept because it furthered his "drive to achieve political support for the elimination of competition and the establishment of regulated monopoly" (Mueller, 1993), 365. The original concept did not refer to geographic ubiquity or provision of service to the entire population.

Oettinger comments: "AT&T's Theodore Vail spoke about the idea of universal service around 1907. The idea was written into the preamble of the Communications Act of 1934, but there is very little legislative history on why and how it got in there. And even though the words were grand, nothing really happened until around 1945. By then, penetration of telephones...was only about 40-50 percent. So after 40 years of rhetoric, universal service as we now know it came into place somewhere between 1945 and the early 1960s." Both quotations appear in Harmeet Sawhney, "Universal Service: Prosaic Motives and Great Ideals," *Towards a Competitive Telecommunications Industry* (Lawrence Erlbaum Associates, Mahwah, New Jersey, 1995), 214-5.

Indeed, vast rural sections of the country had no telephone service many years after cities and towns were first wired. (See Hadden, "Technologies of Universal Service," 61.) The cost of installing and maintaining telephone wires in rural areas greatly exceeded what residents could pay for service. Direct federal loans and subsidies to rural telephone cooperatives—similar to the program that brought electricity to rural America—proved to be an important strategy to expand access to basic telephone services. Subsidies benefited rural residents, but also added value to other users by linking more people to the network. Even so, it took most of this century to achieve universal service.

Rising affluence may have had more of an effect on expanding telephone access than government regulatory policies. As cited in Hadden (55), it took more than 70 years for the telephone to penetrate half of American households. In 1920, 35 percent had telephones; in 1940, 36.9 percent did; in 1960, 78.3 percent; and in 1980 and again in 1990, 93 percent. Currently, about 94.3 percent of U.S. households have telephones. This discussion continues in chapter five.

systems not under common control, however well built or equipped, could give the country the service that an interdependent, intercommunicating, universal system could give. One system with a common policy, common purpose and common action; comprehensive, universal, interdependent, intercommunicating like the highway system of the country, extending from every door to every other door, affording electrical communication of every kind, from every one and every place to every one at every other place.[10]

Indeed, the first users of telephones were limited to calling a very small number of people who also had phones. These pioneers used their telephones much like an intercom might be used in a modern office. Only when a sufficient number of households and businesses joined the telephone network did it provide convenience and value to the average consumer.[11]

Similarly, the more people connected to this network, the more valuable the network became to all users. AT&T's ability to provide long-distance service in the early years enhanced the value of its local exchange services. The inability of independent companies to provide long-distance access and connections to other networks diminished the value of their local service and left them vulnerable to an aggressive AT&T merger and acquisition campaign.

Foreshadowing subsequent debates over market power, the Interstate Commerce Commission (ICC) began in 1910 to regulate AT&T's interstate telephone business. The ICC received authority that year to regulate telephone and telegraph carriers (defined as common carriers) to ensure that their rates were "just and reasonable." Then in 1913, the Justice Department negotiated a settlement with AT&T in which the company agreed to "cease acquisitions of direct competitors, to interconnect independent local companies with its long-distance network, and to dispose of its Western Union stock."[12]

Heightened concern with monopolies was one of the factors leading to state regulation of telephone service. Municipalities granted the first local telephone franchises; but around 1907, states began to assume some regulatory responsibilities. Some historians claim that the shift from municipal to state regulation came from public distrust of corrupt, urban political bosses in the Progressive era, but the move also stemmed from the changing structure of the telephone industry.

States preempted municipal regulation following AT&T's merger with its Bell operating companies. One historian used New York as an example of organizational consolidation:

---

[10] Hadden, "Technologies of Universal Service," 62-3.

[11] This insight comes from de Sola Pool, *Forecasting the Telephone*, 82, as quoted in Hadden, "Technologies of Universal Service," 89. de Sola Pool observes: "The problem the phone promoters faced in the 1870s was to find potential users of the new device who would get value from it, even when linked to only one or a few other sets. Businesses or professional people who had to maintain regular communication among limited operating points were thus the natural clients. Starting with initial subscribers to such 'intercoms,' the phone system could grow gradually and incrementally."

[12] Crandall, *After the Breakup*, 17.

Prior to 1909, seven BOCs served New York state....But during that year, operations were consolidated into one firm, New York Telephone. At that point, it seemed to make little sense to leave the regulation of Bell to local authorities. Yet another reason is that AT&T advocated regulation to block competition from the Independents in the largest urban markets.[13]

Indeed, in the 1910 Annual Report in which Theodore Vail articulated the AT&T philosophy of universal service, he also wrote, "Effective, aggressive competition and regulation and control are inconsistent with each other, and cannot be had at the same time." Hence, most business historians conclude that AT&T accepted government regulation to avoid competition.[14]

Early state efforts to regulate telephone services were significant but inconsistent. Many state legislatures responded to the problem of rival (nonconnecting) networks by enacting laws that required physical interconnection of local telephone exchanges: twenty-six states enacted such laws between 1907 and 1913.[15] A few states tried to conduct studies of the cost of providing telephone services, a difficult task even when telephone companies chose to cooperate. AT&T, for example, tried to deter states from determining its revenue requirements and argued instead for "value of service" pricing, which requires little or no cost data and gives the regulated firm the greatest pricing freedom. Aside from these efforts, most states did not establish formal regulatory commissions (public utility commissions, or PUCs) until soon after World War I.

The rationale for establishing PUCs included all of the factors mentioned: the concern that telephone companies would use their market power as monopolies to overcharge consumers;[16] the need for rival networks to interconnect to eliminate duplication and increase the value of the networks to users; and the desire to protect AT&T from competition from independents in its largest urban markets. In addition, many progressives argued that state regulation of big business was an enlightened policy for expanding and improving quasi-public goods such as telephone services.

State legislatures created the PUCs to act in the public interest, but such a move was also pragmatic. In regulating telephone companies (as well as investor-owned

---

[13] See David Gabel, "Federalism: An Historical Perspective," in *American Regulatory Federalism & Telecommunications Infrastructure,* (Lawrence Erlbaum Associates, Hillsdale, New Jersey, 1995).

[14] As quoted in Vietor, *Contrived Competition,* 171. Vietor offers this assessment: "This was the only politically acceptable way for AT&T to monopolize telephony and extend the network externalities (benefits to all from greater connectivity) and economies of scale inherent in the technology. It seemed a necessary trade-off for the attainment of universal service, the strategic vision that Vail had adopted for AT&T." See also Mueller, *Universal Service* (1996).

[15] *Ibid.*

[16] According to economists, a monopoly occurs when one company, due to inherent economies of scale, can produce a good or service cheaper than two or more companies providing the same commodity. Without effective competition, however, a monopoly can price its products or services at a level higher than at marginal cost. Hence, the justification for public regulation of natural monopolies is to impose a price structure that protects consumers from being overcharged for essential services. Consumers are not the only ones who seek regulation to protect themselves from monopoly pricing; business leaders also fear that revenues from monopoly pricing may cross-subsidize other business activities, constituting unfair competition. The concern with cross-subsidies has become acute since local exchange companies have entered non-telephone businesses. It was one reason that long-distance companies and cable-television systems long opposed the entry of local exchange carriers into these markets.

electric and gas companies), the state was taking the path of least resistance amidst a swirl of debate about the economic concentration of industrial organizations, free enterprise, and rising expectations for public and quasi-public services. One historian offers this assessment:

> Neither the hearings nor the legislation that authorized the establishment of state public utility commissions (PUCs) provides much insight into the policies that the legislature wanted the PUCs to pursue. Although they were clearly concerned that rates be "fair," there was little guidance as to how these agencies should balance fairness with policies that promoted the state's infrastructure. Instead, as is often the case with the U.S. legislative process, broad authority was granted to the delegated agency.[17]

Congressional action in 1921 to liberalize the antimerger law represented a significant shift away from earlier concerns about monopolies. Speaking on behalf of the 1921 Willis-Graham Act, a Republican congressman said, "It is believed to be a better policy to have one telephone system in a community that serves all the people, even though it may be at an advanced rate, properly regulated by state boards or commissions, than it is to have two competing telephone systems." The Senate Commerce Committee declared that "telephoning is a natural monopoly."[18]

With mergers continuing, AT&T grew to substantial dominance in the domestic telephone industry. By the late 1930s, it had all but a fraction of the long-distance market, provided local service to 80 percent of the telephones in the country, and maintained a huge share of the equipment manufacturing market.

For the next several decades, AT&T continued to dominate the telephone industry, but not without some restraint. The Communications Act of 1934 created the Federal Communications Commission to regulate long-distance telephone service, shifting this responsibility from the Interstate Commerce Commission and the radio-broadcasting industry (replacing the Federal Radio Commission).[19]

Federal regulators also were concerned with AT&T's relationship with Western Electric. In 1949, the Department of Justice filed an antitrust suit against AT&T, which alleged that it monopolized the telephone equipment business "through its exclusive purchases from Western Electric." The case was settled in 1956 with a consent decree that allowed AT&T to keep Western Electric but "prohibited AT&T from entering any markets other than regulated telecommunications."[20]

---

[17] Gabel, "Federalism: An Historical Perspective," 25.

[18] As quoted in Vietor, Contrived Competition, 173.

[19] The preamble to this act includes a phrase many cite as the major universal-service objective of the federal government: "to make available, so far as possible, to all people of the United States a rapid, efficient, nation-wide, and world-wide wire and radio communication service with adequate facilities at reasonable charge." Mueller in Universal Service (1996) argues that the legislative intent of this act did not explicitly make access to basic telephone services a government objective. In chapter thirteen, he concludes, "The subject of universal service, in either its modern or classical sense, did not appear in the deliberations."

[20] Crandall, After the Breakup, 19.

In 1974, the Justice Department again filed an antitrust suit against AT&T, alleging that it violated Section 2 of the Sherman Act by monopolizing the long-distance and telephone-equipment businesses. It also sought the divestiture of Western Electric and Bell Laboratories from AT&T. In 1982, AT&T negotiated a consent decree with the Department of Justice, which shocked many observers. Here is Crandall's summary:

> AT&T would divest itself of all operating companies but retain its Western Electric and Long Lines divisions....The newly independent operating companies would be allowed to provide only "local" services so as to prevent the reassembly of the vertical monopoly that provoked the case in the first place. Finally, AT&T was to be freed of the restrictions on its activities that were built into the 1956 decree, thereby permitting it to enter other electronics businesses, including computers.[21]

In 1984 the Bell operating companies were organized into seven regional Bell operating companies; according to the Modified Final Judgment, RBOCs were required to "move quickly to install switches that would enable equal access" to any long-distance carrier, but were forbidden to enter competitive telecommunications businesses, such as equipment manufacturing, information services, and long-distance service outside designated areas (known as local access and transport areas or LATAs).[22] (See Boxes III-1 and 2.) The prohibition against information services was removed by court action in October 1991.

Box III-1: What Is a LATA?

The 1982 Modified Final Judgment established 164 geographic areas called local access and transport areas. Telephone service within each LATA is provided by local telephone companies, also known as local exchange carriers (LECs). These local and regional telephone services are usually regulated by states; small companies and telephone cooperatives are exempt from some regulation in some states.

  Long-distance companies, also known as interexchange carriers (IXC), generally carry calls that originate in one LATA and terminate in another. The state may regulate service between one LATA and another within the state (Intrastate-InterLATA); but the FCC regulates telephone calls originating in one state and terminating in another (Interstate-InterLATA).

Source: "NARUC Report on the Status of Competition in Intrastate Telecommunications" (National Association of Regulatory Utility Commissioners, October 4, 1995).

---

[21] *Ibid.*, 38-9.
[22] *Ibid.*

Box III-2 National LATA Map

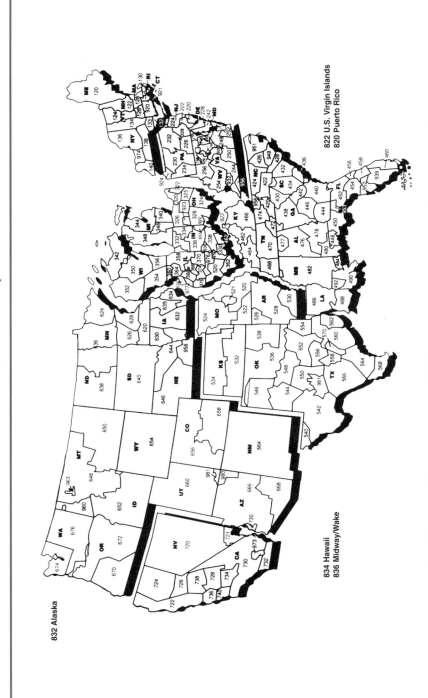

Note: The regional divisions on the national LATA map represent the service areas of the seven regional Bell operating companies as established under the "Modification of Final Judgment."

Source: *State Technology Inventory* (National Governors' Association, July 1994).

Also in 1984, the Cable Communications Policy Act codified long-standing FCC cross-ownership rules that prevented telephone companies from providing video programming in their service areas. Ever since 1984, the RBOCs and other local telephone companies have sought congressional action to allow them to compete in the long-distance market and to enter the cable-TV market in their service areas. In recent years, as competition has increased in the local telephone markets, the RBOCs have expanded their nonregulated businesses by marketing cellular telephones and selling telephone systems and services abroad.

SUMMARY OF HISTORICAL THEMES

Emerging from this historical narrative are three principal themes. The first involves public concern with telephone monopolies. In its first decade of business, AT&T's strategy included: "horizontal integration of local exchanges, backward integration (into equipment manufacturing), forward integration (through the leasing of retail equipment), and the development of the first interexchange (long-distance) transmission."[23] For their part, public policymakers viewed telephone companies as natural monopolies; yet they deemed it necessary to regulate them to protect consumers from unfair pricing. AT&T's divestiture in 1984 reflected similar concerns with anticompetitive practices due to excessive market control in different segments of the industry. In short, for most of this century, policymakers were willing to accept telephone monopolies as long as they were publicly regulated.

The second theme is the effect of competition on the development of the telephone industry after the original Bell patents expired in 1894. Early competition in many cities kept rates low; nevertheless, the Bell operating companies that merged with the long-distance capacity of AT&T enjoyed important competitive advantages. After a half century of slumber, competition in the long-distance business emerged slowly in the 1970s and accelerated in recent years, fostered in large part by the FCC's procompetitive actions. Drawing on past FCC and state experiences, policymakers currently face a new era of competition in all aspects of telecommunications.

The third theme concerns the evolution of public regulation. Twice in our history, regulation of the telephone industry shifted from a lower to a higher level of government. At the beginning of the century, states began to replace municipalities in regulating telephone companies.[24] Then in 1934, Congress passed the Communications Act, creating the FCC and giving it authority to preempt state regulation of interstate telephone services. The Telecommunications Act of 1996 follows this pattern by preempting state regulation in some areas and reframing the context for state regulation of intrastate services.

The recent congressional debate on deregulating the telecommunications industry often reflected these historic themes: how to prevent monopolistic control of local

---

[23] Vietor, *Contrived Competition*, 169.

[24] Although the Mann-Elkins Act of 1910 gave the ICC authority to regulate interstate telephone services, it did not preempt state authority.

Box III-3 Telephone Milestones

1876 Patent for telephone issued to Alexander Graham Bell.

1894 Bell Telephone patents expire, allowing independent companies to develop.

1913 To solve antitrust problems, AT&T sells Western Union and agrees to interconnect with independent telephone companies.

1934 Communications Act of 1934 moves regulatory responsibility for interstate communications from the Interstate Commerce Commission to the newly created Federal Communications Commission.

1949 Department of Justice antitrust suit charges AT&T with monopolizing the telecommunications equipment business.

1956 AT&T settles antitrust case by agreeing to limit its participation in nonregulated telecommunications markets.

1968 FCC Carterphone decision opens terminal equipment market to competition by allowing interconnection of non-telephone company-provided equipment.

1971 Specialized Common Carrier decision allows open entry into the business telecommunications market.

1972 FCC's Open Skies decision permits competitive provision of domestic satellite communications.

1974 Department of Justice files antitrust suit against AT&T for monopolizing the long-distance and telecommunications-equipment businesses.

1982 AT&T and the Department of Justice settle antitrust case and agree to consent decree (MFJ).

1984 Divestiture implemented.

1988 Judge Harold Greene allows divested Bell companies to provide certain information services, including voice mail, electronic mail and gateways.

Source: "Preserving Long Distance Competition and Promoting Local Competition: 21st Century Telecommunications Policy" (MCI Communications Corporation, 1995).

---

networks, structure meaningful, effective, fair competition, and determine appropriate federal and state regulatory roles. Indeed, hard-fought battles centered on these questions: What constitutes fair competition among firms? What is a "level playing field for competitive telecommunications?" How can effective competition be achieved without undermining universal-service objectives? Given the business revenues at stake, these issues were hotly contested, and the debate often included arguments made earlier in this century.

The long-distance companies (AT&T, MCI, and Sprint being the largest) long opposed congressional legislation that would allow the RBOCs, GTE, and other local telephone companies to enter the long-distance market. For most of the twentieth century, the local exchange companies have been monopolies, and there was general concern that they would use their local access "bottleneck" to compete unfairly in the long-distance business. There also was a specific concern that they would use revenues from their monopoly operations to cross-subsidize their entry into the long-distance market. Finally, there were concerns that they would resist local competition, using their formidable political clout in state capitols.[25]

The history of the telephone industry in this country suggests that such concerns about market power and its effect on fair competition are not unwarranted.[26] For example, the local loop—the link that extends from a central telephone office to the telephone instrument—is likely to remain a monopoly at least in the short term. In a few years, perhaps, alternative networks based on coaxial cable, wireless technologies, and satellite transmission will have advanced sufficiently to represent effective competition. Until then, however, how is competition possible when local exchanges own and control the loop? According to federal legislation, what are the states' responsibilities in fostering competition without jeopardizing the social objective of universal access?

These questions are addressed in chapter five in the context of the Telecommunications Act of 1996 and its provisions for creating effective competition. The next chapter presents an overview of state innovation in telecommunications policies in the twelve years between the 1984 divestiture of Ma Bell and passage of the Telecommunications Act of 1996.

---

[25] The interexchange companies were sensitive to the presence of local exchange carriers (LECs) in state capitols. The LECs have had extensive experience with state commissions. They may have lobbyists representing them in the state capitol and may contribute to highly visible charities and campaigns, most of which earns them the goodwill of the political community. From a sociological perspective, local exchange carriers are part of a state's political community. Hence, long-distance companies were concerned that they would be at a political and institutional disadvantage if state commissions were given the authority to rule on issues of local competition in telephony.

The academic literature includes a rich discussion of the appropriate form and control of regulatory agencies, as well as behavioral models that test various theories. A good summary is provided by Paul Teske, "Interests and Institutions in State Regulation," *American Journal of Political Science*, Vol. 35, No. 1 (February 1991): 139-140:

> The original public interest theories of regulating monopolies were challenged first by proponents of capture theory, who doubted the ability of regulators to counterbalance industry power over time. Economists went even further in the "theory of economic regulation," arguing that regulation was established from the start to favor the regulated firms. Political scientists challenged this view, using arguments about political entrepreneurs and the impact of ideas to explain how majoritarian politics could overcome the power of concentrated interests.

See also Heather E. Campbell, "The Politics of Requesting: Strategic Behavior and Public Utility Regulation," *Journal of Policy Analysis and Management* Vol. 15, No. 3, (summer 1996). Campbell specifies a new model that includes "stylized actors representing the firm, the regulator, the intervener, and customers all acting under uncertainty about the future. Also there are important information asymmetries: *the firm knows the most about its costs, the regulator less, interveners little, and customers essentially nothing.*" [Author's emphasis]

[26] For a vigorous rebuttal, see Daniel F. Spulber, "Deregulating Telecommunications," *Yale Journal of Regulation*, Vol. 12, No. 1 (winter 1995): 25-67. Spulber challenges conventional "arguments that the local exchange network was a natural monopoly, that the carriers benefited from barriers to entry, that they could leverage their monopoly power into other markets, and that they would use revenues from local service to subsidize their entry into other lines of business." He contends that these arguments "are no longer valid because of technological and market changes in the telecommunications industry." George Gilder ("From Wires to Waves," *Forbes ASAP*, June 5, 1995) holds a similar view: "Today, in the name of deregulation, politicians are preparing to impose a series of new competitive requirements upon the Bell operating companies, on the assumption that they still wield monopoly power. Pundits still seem to believe that the copper cage protects local telephone companies from outside competition. But in fact, the cage incarcerates them in copper wires, while the world prepares to pass them by."

CHAPTER FOUR

TWELVE YEARS OF POLICY INNOVATION IN STATE TELECOMMUNICATIONS REGULATION

This chapter discusses recent policy innovations in the regulation of state telecommunications. Prior to the 1984 AT&T divestiture, the state regulatory role was undistinguished. Periodically, a major rate case would capture the headlines of state newspapers, but with a few exceptions, there was little policy innovation. For this reason, critics argued that the dual system of regulation (FCC regulation of long-distance services coupled with state regulation of local and intrastate long-distance) was unwise, unnecessary, and redundant. Among the strongest criticisms were that the system resulted in fragmented policies across the fifty states and that state commissions, especially in less populous states, had inadequate resources to protect the public interest. Adding to this quiet controversy were difficult jurisdictional battles between the states and the FCC, many of which involved major court decisions.[1]

Following the AT&T divestiture, the FCC continued to provide policy direction, primarily on interstate issues. The FCC also "expanded its regulatory jurisdiction whenever areas of uncertainty developed."[2] And Congress continued to grant authority to the FCC to preempt the state role periodically.[3] These important qualifications

---

[1] See generally Paul Eric Teske, ed., *American Regulatory Federalism & Telecommunications Infrastructure*. For one of the stronger criticisms of the states, see Teske's "Introduction and Overview" in which Roger Noll, a Stanford economist, is quoted: "In the long run the telecommunications system might better serve society's objectives if, as in broadcasting, state regulation played no role at all; and as a practical matter the jurisdictional boundary between state and federal authorities is now quite blurry, so that debate about where it should be drawn is timely." Note, however, that this statement was made in 1986. For more about preemption and the court decisions on jurisdiction issues, see Henry Geller, "Legal Issues in Preemption," 125-131. Also see Henry Geller, "Reforming the U.S. Telecommunications Policymaking Process, in *The New Information Infrastructure: Strategies for U.S. Policy*, William J. Drake, ed. (New York: Twentieth Century Fund Press, 1995), 115-135.

[2] Teske, *After Divestiture: The Political Economy of State Telecommunications Regulation* (Albany, New York: State University of New York, 1990). Here is Teske's fine summary (40):

The FCC made several important decisions on depreciation issues, interstate revenue pooling arrangements, lifeline programs, and other issues with interstate dimensions....As Kenneth Robinson, of the National Telecommunications and Information Administration, notes: "It has certainly been the case at the federal level for 20 years that state regulators have been viewed as poor relations....Federal agencies have viewed them with suspicion and guarded distrust." Courts generally rejected state efforts to avoid implementation of the spirit of FCC decisions. The 1986 *Louisiana PSC vs. FCC* depreciation case halted this trend and affirmed two-tiered regulation by upholding state regulatory jurisdiction on issues with largely intrastate implications.

[3] Congress limited the state role in regulating mobile services—radio common carriers, private carriers, cellular, and personal communications services—when it adopted the 1993 Budget Act, which granted generous authority to the FCC to preempt state regulation. See Jeffrey Tobias, "Notwithstanding Section 2(B)....Recent Legislative Initiatives Affecting the Federal-State Balance in Telecommunications Regulation," in *American Regulatory Federalism & Telecommunications Infrastructure*, 133-140.

notwithstanding, states emerged as important decisionmakers in the post-divestiture period.

The dismemberment of Ma Bell, the world's largest corporation, pushed a tangled web of public policy issues before the state commissions and forced them to confront difficult problems concerning pricing and competition. One scholar offers this assessment:

> State public utility commission regulators were thrust into the limelight in 1984, after playing minor roles in telecommunication regulation for 75 years. They have faced difficult policy choices, compounded by complex economic issues and the interests of several different groups. While much media attention has focused on Washington policymakers...state regulators have emerged collectively as vital decision-makers in the implementation of telephone deregulation.[4]

The shock of divestiture was widely felt by state regulators. According to one scholar, Bell telephone companies requested $7 billion in rate increases during the eighteen months following the Modified Final Judgment.[5]

Sharon Nelson, a Washington State regulator and former president of the National Association of Regulatory Utility Commissions (NARUC), divided the post-divestiture period into the three Rs. The first was "reaction" to divestiture. The late 1980s was a period of "retrenchment," in part because the 1986 Tax Reform Act reduced the taxes paid by local telephone companies. Nelson predicted that the third R in the 1990s would be a "restructuring" phase that might include innovative regulatory policies and deregulation of competitive services, among other approaches.[6] Our concern, in this chapter, centers on this period of restructuring.

RATE STRUCTURES AND COMPETITION

Economists have generally advocated reforming rate-of-return policies, pricing closer to actual costs (increasing local rates and lowering in-state toll-call charges), and promoting competition in deregulated services to lower prices and spur efficiencies. Paul Teske frames the states' policy choices in the 1980s this way:

---

[4] Teske, *After Divestiture*, xiii. See also Jeffrey E. Cohen, The Politics of *Telecommunications Regulation: The States and the Divestiture of AT&T* (M.E. Sharpe, Armonk, New York, 1992).

[5] Roger G. Noll, "State Regulatory Responses to Competition and Divestiture in the Telecommunications Industry," in *Antitrust and Regulation*, Ronald E. Grieson, ed. (Lexington, Massachusetts: D.C. Heath and Company, 1986), 166. Teske in *After Divestiture* (40) presents this summary:

> State regulators approved $10.5 billion in rate hikes from 1982 to 1986, out of $70 billion in annual BOC (Bell operating companies) revenues. The high-water point of these increases was 1984 in which $3.9 billion in rate hikes were approved, representing 53 percent of telephone company requests. In 1982, $2.9 billion were approved (55 percent of requests), $2.4 billion in 1983 (40 percent), and $1.3 billion in 1985 (45 percent). Thus, the telephone companies sought substantial rate relief in the five years after the Consent Decree and state regulators granted about half of the requests.

[6] Teske, "State Telecommunications Policy in the 1980s," 120.

First, how should local service be priced, given that large business users threatened to leave the regulated network because toll prices were well above marginal costs? Second, given that many of the services provided by the local operating companies, including intraLATA long-distance transmission, may not have been natural monopolies, should free entry be allowed into these markets? States responded differently to these two questions. Some states altered prices to reflect marginal costs while others maintained pricing systems filled with cross-subsidies. Some states encouraged intraLATA competition while others continued to restrict entry totally.[7]

An overview of pricing policy is necessary to appreciate the tradeoffs inherent in state regulatory deliberations.[8] Historically, state public utility commissions (PUCs) have determined the rate structure for different services: local calls (residential and business lines), intrastate toll calls, measured service, pay phones, and directory assistance. Until recent years, most public utility commissions (PUCs) have set an appropriate rate of return for the local companies that provided these services.

To keep residential rates low, PUCs usually set higher rates for businesses. Similarly, both the FCC and most state PUCs charged rates for long-distance service (interstate and intrastate, respectively) higher than at cost, which provided cross-subsidies to keep local residential rates as low as possible. Many regulators believed that subsidizing local residential service was the most effective way to achieve universal service.[9] This strategy proved popular with the public as well.

States introduced two policy innovations in the 1980s, first, to restructure pricing, and second, to allow competition in intraLATA toll calling. Although these two concepts are linked, states varied in their approach to them. During the first wave of policy reform (1984-87), seventeen states adjusted intraLATA toll charges downward (reducing cross-subsidies to stabilize local calling rates) or established an unbundled intrastate

---

[7] Teske, *After Divestiture*, 17.

[8] Pricing policy for telephone services is complex. An accessible source for the noneconomist is Teske, *After Divestiture*, 33-38. As evidence of both points, here are selected paragraphs:

Telephone pricing is so difficult and controversial, in part, because telephone networks provide multiple products using some of the same facilities. Access, local usage, intraLATA toll, intrastate interLATA toll, WATS, private line services, PBX, Centrex, and pay telephones....Telephone pricing is difficult in reality because regulators must deal with two types of costs. *The first are embedded costs, which are historical or book costs. The second are marginal or incremental costs, which are forward looking, economic costs.*....Efficient prices require a flat rate for network access and incremental cost-based prices for all local and toll usage, matching the board-to-board view of pricing. Access to the switched network is a separate service from usage as access allows incoming calls to be received without any outgoing usage, and access lines are related to individual subscribers, while usage equipment is shared....Marginal cost pricing will not recover all of these common costs when marginal costs are below average costs. Telephone firms need to recover the fixed costs of equipment, such as switches. Thus, Ramsey pricing marks up prices above cost for those services with the most inelastic demand.

[9] Many experts think the cross-subsidies in the rate base are too large and distorting because consumers do not experience prices based on actual costs. Writing in 1990, Teske in *After Divestiture* (38) makes this observation: "For the bulk of residential consumers, however, the subsidy to access has been large and perhaps unnecessary to achieve universal service over the past fifteen years." Roger Noll (1986) notes, "It is a transfer of too much from too few to too many in too inefficient a manner." See also the discussion in chapter five.

residential subscriber access charge. Sixteen states approved "facilities-based competitive entry into intraLATA markets. Only seven states made both changes: Illinois, Massachusetts, New York, Oregon, New Mexico, Pennsylvania, and Maryland."[10] (See Box IV-1 for an example of Illinois' leadership on efficient pricing policy.)

Box IV-1 Illinois' Leadership on Pricing

After 1984, regulators in Illinois adopted efficient prices more rapidly and more completely than did any other state....The Illinois Commerce Commission has a tradition of progressive regulation and a concern for efficiency in pricing; the commission implemented local measured service for some telephone customers in the 1930s.

The Illinois commission was the first in the nation to unbundle access from local usage (resulting in local measured service) and then to deaverage access rates across the state. The commission led the way in simplifying local rates by reducing ninety-three previous plans to two, residential and business, both of which reflected economic efficiency by implementing off-peak price reductions and volume discounts. The commission accelerated depreciation to eliminate the reserve deficiency, reduced the business access subsidy to residential consumers, allowed intraLATA competition in 1987 and intraexchange competition in 1989, and deaveraged the toll rates of local operating companies in the state.

Source: Paul Teske, *After Divestiture*, 105.

Most states that granted entry into intraLATA markets later realized that past pricing policy was no longer sustainable in a competitive environment. Many pioneering competitors sought to provide phone services, including intrastate long distance, to large corporate users at rates below those set by state tariffs. The resulting loss of revenue to the dominant local exchange carrier from corporate "bypass" threatened to raise rates for everyone else. The clear winners would be businesses that would receive cheaper service; but regulators feared that everyone else would have to pay higher rates as a result. One expert in state regulatory policy provided this summary:

> Put most bluntly, the policy problem for states is how to balance a seeming economic need to reduce intrastate long-distance prices closer to their marginal costs

---

[10] Teske, *After Divestiture*, 65, attempted to explain this puzzle (85):

> Why are pricing and competition choices not more closely linked? One possibility is that regulators use competitive entry more as a symbolic policy choice to respond to external pressure, but do not expect it to materialize in the near future to threaten existing cross-subsidies. Price changes, on the other hand, are more substantial policy changes that more accurately reflect regulatory climates and attitudes. Price changes immediately harm large numbers of consumers, who can easily trace the change to regulators.

so that large corporate users will not leave the public network of the local operating company, or "bypass," versus the widespread desire by residential consumers for affordable local service.[11]

For most of this century, local phone companies have been monopolies. The rates for local and intrastate calls were established after review by the state PUC, but only one company provided services. Indeed, almost all local phone companies still are monopolies. Yet after divestiture, local exchange carriers in some urban markets began to experience varying degrees of competition. Their competitors included private companies with their own private branch exchanges (PBXs); local area networks (LANs); wide area networks (WANs); other private networks that bypass the public switched telecommunications network (PSTN)[12]; competitors that build fiber-optic networks for large users; and developers of new wireless technologies such as cellular telephones and personal communication services. In a few cases, cable companies began to provide telephone service over their networks. Some industry analysts expect that other regulated utilities such as electric or gas companies will start to use their distribution networks to enter local telephone markets as well.

ALTERNATIVES TO RATE-OF-RETURN REGULATION

In the mid-1980s, partly in response to these developments, some state PUCs began to experiment with different ways to set rates for local telephone services, including deregulation of competitive services, incentive regulation, social contracts, and alternatives to regulating the rate of return.[13] (See Box IV-2.) A few examples of state experimentation in rate formulation are presented below.

Deregulation of Rates. In 1986, the Nebraska legislature deregulated all telecommunication service rates. Now, local exchange rate increases of up to 10 percent are permitted without prior PSC (public service commission) approval, although a certain percentage of customers may petition the PSC to review rate increases for basic services. This action was part of a larger economic strategy to encourage the development of a telemarketing industry in the state. Former Governor Robert Kerrey explained, "If you live in a rural, isolated state like Nebraska you absolutely need to be connected to the

---

[11] Teske, "State Telecommunications Policy in the 1980s," 119. Stripped of the controversy, *bypass* simply means that a direct connection from a telephone customer is made to the interexchange carrier, eliminating the local loop of the LEC.

[12] According to Wilson and Teske, "Many companies with multiple locations have found it advantageous, for reasons of cost, reliability, or security, to develop their own telecommunications systems. Some of the private systems are enormous. General Motors' private network links 250,000 telephone sets and computer terminals located throughout the world." Robert H. Wilson and Paul E. Teske, "Telecommunications and Economic Development: The State and Local Role," *Economic Development Quarterly*, Vol. 4, No. 2 (May 1990): 160. As noted above, most corporate networks are virtual networks, composed of leased lines from common carriers.

[13] Rate-of-return regulation provides a fair return on investment to regulated monopolies; it has been described as a cost-plus approach. Some of the contemporary criticism of rate of return derives from the seminal article by Harvey Averch and Leland Johnson, "Behavior of the Firm under Regulatory Constraint," *American Economic Review*, Vol. 52, No. 3 (June 1962): 1053-69. Averch and Johnson argue that rate of return provided an incentive for firms to substitute capital for labor, which increased the base of fixed investment. See also Clifford Winston, "Economic Deregulation: Days of Reckoning for Microeconomics," *Journal of Economic Literature*, Vol. 31 (September 1993): 1263-89.

rest of the country. But to get it, we have to move away from arguing, 'What should the price of the product be?' and into 'What should the product be?'"[14]

Box IV-2 What is Rate-of-return Regulation?

In simplified terms, a local exchange carrier would submit its expenses and capital investment records to the state PUC. The PUC decides which costs are allowable, and adds them to determine the total cost of providing services. After public hearings, the PUC determines the company's revenue requirement, which includes expenses and a reasonable rate of return on the rate base. The PUC must then set rates on all regulated services so that the revenue requirement will be met. Typically, basic phone rates are set below cost; other rates, such as interLATA long distance, are priced above cost to make up the difference.

Source: "Everything you always wanted to know about telecommunications—but didn't know who to ask" (GTE Telephone Operations, 1995).

Social Contract Regulation. Sometimes a PUC would offer rate flexibility if the local exchange carrier made or accelerated socially desired investments. Vermont pioneered this approach in 1987 when its PUC "offered greater pricing flexibility to local exchange carriers, in exchange for the telephone companies' commitment to upgrade their systems and provide a basic level of service to every community." Southwestern Bell agreed to invest $160 million to accelerate the upgrade of its network in Kansas "in exchange for a more flexible pricing structure from Kansas' utility commission."[15]

Incentive Regulation. This approach allowed telephone companies to keep part of the profit when they earned more than the allowable rate of return. In 1987 the New York PSC extended a moratorium on rate increases with an incentive to encourage New York Telephone to cut costs and increase productivity. (New York Telephone was allowed to "keep one-half of the profits earned above the 14 percent target rate of return.")[16] Some PUCs experimented with various profit-sharing incentives in which ratepayers got to share some of the additional profits through rebates. The intent of this approach was to encourage telephone companies to increase their operational efficiency.

Alternative Regulation. According to a NARUC report, by January 1994, forty-two states had some form of alternative regulation plan, including: thirty-three plans that allowed flexible pricing for some services; twenty-seven plans that classified

---

[14] T. Reid, "Phone Deregulation, Phase 2" *Washington Post*, May 27, 1986, as quoted in Teske, "State Telecommunications Policy in the 1980s," 122. As several experts have emphasized, deregulating rates is not the same as allowing competitive entry into regulated markets. The initial Nebraska legislation did not allow competition.

[15] Helme, *New Alliances in Innovation*, 33.

[16] Teske, *After Divestiture*, 93.

services by level of competition for regulatory purposes; nineteen plans that were tied to infrastructure improvements; nineteen plans that were permanent; and twenty-three that were temporary.[17]

Price Caps. By October 1995, about half of the states were using price caps as part of an alternative to traditional rate-of-return regulation for local exchange telephone companies.[18] Setting maximum price schedules for various telephone services supposedly creates incentives for companies to become more efficient, reduce costs, and improve general operations. Companies can price their services up to specified, maximum price caps, but must manage their resources and reduce expenses to obtain profits for stockholders. Some suggest that price caps are superior to rate-of-return regulation, in part because they remove the financial incentive to make capital investments, but this issue remains controversial.[19]

Capital Depreciation Rate Regulation. PUCs in most states set depreciation rates for capital investments made by local exchange carriers. The ability to depreciate capital investment quickly enables companies to recover costs over a relatively short period of time. The disadvantage of this approach is that rapid depreciation imposes a higher immediate cost on ratepayers. As mentioned, many states have revised their depreciation schedules based on a growing appreciation for the economic benefits of investing in telecommunications infrastructure.

From this review, it is clear that state PUCs have been active policy innovators since the MFJ forced the divestiture of the old Bell system in 1984. Many states adopted alternative rate structures prior to 1989, when the FCC established price caps for long-distance services. Many have embraced and encouraged increased competition in intrastate toll calling and have begun to allow competition in local phone service.

In brief, the legislative actions and policy innovations of several state PUCs have been in the forefront of progressive telecommunications policy. They have influenced Congressional and FCC efforts to deregulate the industry and have delineated clear policy options for the future. Box IV-3 presents a summary of state regulatory reform as of 1994.

PROMOTING INVESTMENT IN TELECOMMUNICATIONS INFRASTRUCTURE

As discussed above, states have been active in pursuing strategies to improve their telecommunications infrastructure: accelerating depreciation schedules, experimenting with incentive and social-contract regulation, and forming public-private partnerships to plan network upgrades. States such as Iowa, North Carolina, and Nebraska have developed specific strategies to encourage private-sector investment so that advanced

---

[17] "NARUC Report on the Status of Competition in Intrastate Telecommunications" (National Association of Regulatory Utility Commissioners, Washington, D.C., August 1995), 180-81.

[18] *Ibid.*

[19] For a different, strongly argued view on this issue, see William Page Montgomery, "Promises Versus Reality: Telecommunications Infrastructure, LEC Investment and Regulatory Reforms" (Paper supported by MCI Communications Corporation, Montgomery Consulting, Chestnut, Massachusetts, August 1994).

telecommunications services reach rural areas, which lack aggregate demand. The discussion below addresses, in a general way, the broader issue of telecommunications investment and poses important questions for state policymakers about who benefits from investments and who pays for them.

In the late 1980s through the early 1990s, Governors began to focus on telecommunications as a crucial element of state economic development strategy. The economic benefits of investing in telecommunications infrastructure made such investments more politically desirable, and also increased the responsibilities of state regulators. During the same period, some local exchange carriers were developing ambitious plans to install fiber optics and digital switches and were seeking approval from state commissions for major infrastructure investments.

Local telephone companies often make what can be called a supply-side argument: state actions such as rate reform and liberal depreciation schedules will benefit the public by enhancing and improving telecommunications infrastructure. Build capacity, says the industry, and it will be used. Not only will it be used, but it will be well used, because it will promote business development and location, as well as state prosperity.[20]

Consumer advocates are often more skeptical. They make the demand-side argument that the need for new services must be demonstrated before a state PUC approves a major investment in infrastructure. Ratepayers (who also are voters) are not eager to pay any more than necessary for the telephone services they require. Unfortunately, few ratepayers can accurately anticipate their own future demand for services, especially when these services are rapidly evolving. As in the past, perhaps demand will indeed grow with capacity.

One way to understand the continental divide on this issue is to consider the two most extreme positions: an overbuilt or an underbuilt infrastructure. This summary comes from the Wisconsin study:

> An "overbuilt" infrastructure might serve some interests (large business customers, hospitals, government, and schools, for example), but it would increase rates for local residential and small business telephone service beyond acceptable limits. An "underbuilt" infrastructure would drive large customers away and hinder the state's economic and social development goals.[21]

A similar analysis of the infrastructure dilemma was presented by the International Communications Association, which represents more than 700 companies and institutions that are very large telecommunications consumers. This is how an ICA-commissioned white paper defines the public policy challenge:

> Underinvestment in new technology by the LECs could delay or entirely foreclose the development of new telecommunications applications and markets, risk harm to the LECs' financial strength, and possibly reduce the competitiveness of U.S. companies for whom LEC services are an important input to production. On the other hand, LECs that overinvest relative to new services demand could saddle themselves and basic ratepayers with underperforming investments, driving up basic telephone rates and imposing a drag on the national economy.[22]

---

[20] In 1926, H.B. Thayer, president of AT&T said, "Telephone service was not created to fill a demand...the service creates the demand. That is the business of our system, to try to discover and determine what it is that will be helpful to the people of the United States in the way of service and then to provide it. The demand follows the creation of the service instead of being impelled by it." As quoted in Gabel, "An Historical Perspective," 28.

[21] "Convergence, Competition, Cooperation," 25.

[22] ICA Telecommunications Public Policy Committee and Economics and Technology, Inc., *The Infrastructure Dilemma: Matching Market Realities and Policy Goals* (International Communications Association, Washington, D.C., January 1993), 2.

A related challenge concerns the choice of technologies. Which technology will provide the best social return? For example, will wireless systems become a better investment at some future point than increased capacity in existing wire networks? Who has the wisdom to make these choices? Should states promote investment and guide these decisions? Some state PUCs are cautious about major investment decisions for this very reason: ratepayers will suffer if the local exchange carrier makes investment decisions that turn out badly.

CREATING A LEVEL PLAYING FIELD FOR FAIR LOCAL COMPETITION

One of the most contentious issues in telecommunications policy is defining the terms for competition in local (e.g., non-toll) telephone markets. According to the FCC, in the spring of 1996 the following states had competing firms offering switched local service: "Massachusetts, Michigan, California, Illinois, Maryland, New York, and Washington. At least some local competition rules are in place in Virginia, North Carolina, Colorado, Louisiana, Arizona, Connecticut, Florida, Georgia, Iowa, Ohio, Oregon, and Tennessee....Generally, new competitors are small and are still experimenting in the market."[23]

Those who write about state telecommunications policy sometimes fail to emphasize the tremendous chasm between having a state law that allows local competition in telephony and actually having robust competition. For example, according to a recent report by the National Conference of State Legislatures, fifteen states enacted legislation during 1994 and 1995 that related to local competition and rates.[24] Also, a January 1996 New York Times article stated that, "At least twenty-nine states, including New York, have approved measures to end telephone monopolies."[25] Advocates of competition may applaud these state actions, yet they may still fall short of establishing a level playing field for fair competition.

Having a state law or PUC regulation that allows competitive local exchange carriers (CLECs) to provide service does not, by itself, constitute full and fair competition. Simply enacting a state law that allows competition may have no effect on local markets. Rather, the terms of competition determine whether or not prospective competitors can enter local markets and whether or not they can compete vigorously.

The Texas law enacted in 1995 serves to illustrate this point. The legislation allowed local competition but required that new entrants must commit to build a

---

[23] See Common Carrier Competition, CC Report No. 96-9 (Federal Communications Commission, Common Carrier Bureau, spring 1996).

[24] Laurie Itkin and Elizabeth McLaughlin-Krile, *State Telecommunications Reform Legislation Authorizing Local Competition Enacted During 1994 and 1995* (NCSL, Washington, D.C., 1995). According to this survey, Connecticut and Wisconsin enacted legislation in 1994 authorizing local competition, and in 1995, thirteen states did so: Colorado, Florida, Georgia, Hawaii, Iowa, Minnesota, New Hampshire, North Carolina, Tennessee, Texas, Utah, Virginia and Wyoming. Cautionary note: Some of the recent state legislation may be preempted by the Telecommunications Act of 1996; especially suspect are state laws that impose undue restrictions on prospective entrants in local telephone markets.

[25] Rabinovitz, "Competition to Begin for Local Phone Calls, Ending a Monopoly," *New York Times*, January 6, 1996, 24.

substantial network capacity over a period of years—an approach called "you pay to play." Most prospective competitors viewed these terms as so restrictive that they had little interest in entering local markets in Texas. They are likely to reconsider, however, if the FCC or the federal district court rules that the Texas law constitutes a barrier to entry, according to the Telecommunications Act of 1996.[26]

In fact, many firms seeking to enter local telephone markets have complained about barriers to entry erected by local exchange carriers. Existing telephone companies have historic advantages plus a functioning network with switches, lines and poles, and a residue of goodwill among their customers. They have been legally protected, state-regulated monopolies. Robert Crandall provides this summary:

> Long-distance companies complain that they cannot trust local companies to connect their calls on equitable terms if the local companies also offer long-distance services. Entrants into local services continually complain that these local telephone companies will not allow them to interconnect with their networks in an efficient manner.[27]

Some prospective competitors worry that local exchange carriers will use revenues from monopolistic services to cross-subsidize their competitive operations.[28] Hence, recent policy has emphasized "unbundling," which means disaggregating the costs of each service provided by local telephone companies to prevent cross-subsidization. MCI identified eight major barriers to local exchange competition: open entry, rights of way, number portability, interconnection/unbundling, mutual traffic exchange, pricing rules, universal service, and transitional regulation. (See Box IV-4.) Congress addressed these concerns in the 14-point "competitive checklist" in the Telecommunications Act of 1996. (See chapter five.)

It might be helpful to frame this discussion in terms of how supportive the state regulatory environment is in promoting vigorous competition. As of January 1994, approximately twenty states had a statutory or state constitutional provision that prohibited competition for local telephone service. Many of the remaining states allow

---

[26] On May 15, 1996, the Texas Public Utility Commission filed a petition with the FCC for an expedited ruling on whether provisions in the Texas law violate Sections 253(a) and (b) of the 1996 act and would be preempted. See "Washington Watch" (NECA, May 16, 1996). As expected, several petitions for a declaratory ruling were submitted to the FCC in late May asking the commission to preempt the enforcement of certain provisions of the Texas Public Utility Regulatory Act of 1995, pursuant to Section 253 of the 1996 Act. See "Washington Watch" (NECA, June 6, 1996).

[27] Robert W. Crandall, "Waves of the Future: Are We Ready to Deregulate Telecommunications?" *The Brookings Review* (winter 1996): 29. Also note the reporting by Leslie Cauley in the *Wall Street Journal*, March 20, 1995: "In the states already open to competition, Baby Bells routinely deny or slow access to their networks, price their services below cost, and invoke arcane statutes to protect their turf. Once rivals are up and running, the local Bell can force customers to dial complex access codes or to give up their phone numbers when they sign with a competitor."

[28] A summary of this view was written by Peter Passell, "Economic Scene: Turning the Baby Bells loose on the long-distance market," *New York Times*, June 8, 1995, D2:

> The worry is that the Bells would sell long-distance service below cost to gain market share and recoup their losses by overcharging local customers who do not have a choice. Indeed, it was just this logic that led the Justice Department to conclude that AT&T would have to divest itself of its local service in order to make long-distance competition viable.

partial competition in local exchange service, at least in theory. As stated, however, laws do not create meaningful competition; they only enable it. If the conditions are onerous or restrictive, firms will not contest local markets.

The state of Connecticut—by forcing the incumbent exchange carrier to sell its network capacity to all certified providers—has advanced the farthest toward achieving a level playing field for effective competition. (The Southern New England Telephone Company would not agree, given their protests about wholesale rates.) While the reform efforts of other states have been laudable, most will have to revisit this issue in light of the new Telecommunications Act, which preempts state authority on several points.

This definition from the National Association of Regulatory Utility Commissioners helps to clarify the issue: "The test of a competitive market is when consumers have the ability to choose among similar services offered by several firms and no firm or combination of firms has the ability to control the market prices of these services."[29] But there is still considerable room for interpretation. What is market power? When is it used to control prices?[30] State policymakers and PUC regulators will, no doubt, follow these debates closely in the years ahead.

Even on matters of general consensus, there may be very different interpretations of the kind of regulatory structure that will allow robust competition to evolve. For example, forty-two states have provisions requiring that open network architecture (ONA) tariffs be on file. ONA provides access to the local network by unbundling services so alternative providers can use the network in a manner that is technically efficient. As one might expect, ONA tariffs vary among states. Nevertheless, some regulatory requirement has been, and will continue to be, necessary.

This example illustrates an important paradox: promoting competition in a regulated industry may require more government rather than less. During the transition from regulated, monopoly telephone service to an environment with robust competition, government must provide a strong hand in establishing and enforcing fair rules for all providers. FCC Commissioner Susan Ness made this point in a speech just two weeks after passage of the Telecommunications Act of 1996:

> It may seem paradoxical that a law intended to reduce regulation will require some eighty rulemakings to implement. But remember the goal of these rules is to bring about competition that does not exist today. After all, 95 percent of telephone subscribers today are served by a monopoly provider. Cable companies still account for more than 90 percent of multichannel video programming subscribership.

> Our goal will be to craft rules that will facilitate the transition to competition in a way that best serves the public interest. It takes hard work to bring about fair competition. Wishing does not make it so.[31]

---

[29] Michelle L. Harris, "State Regulatory Commission Concerns Regarding the National Information Infrastructure" (Memorandum, National Association of Regulatory Utility Commissions, January 1994), 6.

[30] Allegations of market power, when the public suspects that one firm or a few very large firms dominate an industry, have been a prominent concern in this century. Note in recent years the allegations that Microsoft has used its market power to dominate the software industry, especially the development of operating systems for personal computers. See James Gleick, "Making Microsoft Safe for Capitalism," *New York Times Magazine*, November 5, 1995. According to Robert W. Crandall and Harold Furchtgott-Roth in *Cable TV: Regulation or Competition?* (Brookings Institution, Washington, D.C., 1996), 27: "A perfectly competitive market will yield a price no higher than marginal cost, and a contestable market will yield an equilibrium price no higher than average cost....Within a market, *market power*—the extent to which prices exceed marginal cost—is limited by competing sources of supply."

[31] From Susan Ness, "The New Telecommunications Marketplace: Radical Changes and Golden Opportunities" (Speech, Wharton School of the University of Pennsylvania, February 22, 1996.) See also Eli M. Noam, "Beyond Telecommunications Liberalization: Past Performance, Present Hype, and Future Direction," *The New Information Infrastructure* (Twentieth Century Fund, New York, 1995), 32. Noam makes an important distinction between liberalization, which he defines as "the entry into previously monopolized markets and the lowering of restrictions," and deregulation, which is "a reduction in government-imposed constraints on the behavior of firms." He observes:

> The experiences in the United States and the United Kingdom, two of the most liberalized markets, reveal that *more rather than less regulation emerged*, at least initially, after markets were opened. The process of partial liberalization tends to complicate matters and can lead to a more extensive set of rules to address new problems. *Partial liberalization requires that interconnection arrangements be set, access charges determined, and a level playing field secured. In some cases, cross-subsidization from monopolistic to competitive services must be prevented....*All of this leads to considerable regulatory complexity; no system is more lawyer intensive than partial liberalization. [Author's emphasis]

Below are three examples of innovative state policies that promoted competition for local telephone services prior to the Telecommunications Act of 1996.

New York PSC Smashes Prevailing Paradigm

In May 1989, the New York Public Service Commission issued a ruling that allowed competition in local exchange services. Based on this ruling, new entrants could petition to become common carriers and receive permission to provide interconnected local services. The ruling was a shock to most of the telecommunications industry. Although competition in the long-distance market had matured since the 1984 AT&T divestiture, few thought the local telephone monopoly would be broken. For most of the century, conventional wisdom held that local exchanges were natural monopolies.

Several firms had asked for permission to compete in providing local exchange services in New York. The PSC had to assess many conflicting factors. Could new firms provide services at better prices than New York Telephone? If so, would competition be limited to premium services for businesses, which might erode the revenue base of the incumbent telephone company and cause higher rates for remaining customers? Could interconnection rules be written fairly to both New York Telephone and prospective entrants? How should physical co-location rules be established? These were weighty issues for all parties.

The New York PUC followed the precedent of the 1989 ruling by continuing to encourage competition in private line, switched access, special access, local non-switched, and local loop. In 1994, the PSC approved MFS Intelenet's tariffs for residential local exchange service. (For some years prior, MFS provided interexchange access and local exchange services to businesses.) It was reportedly the first time such tariffs were approved in this country on behalf of a competitor to incumbent local exchange carriers. According to a NARUC publication, twenty-six companies had filed tariffs with the PSC to provide local exchange services in New York by August 1, 1995.[32]

These actions, and the sensible rules promulgated to implement these arrangements, cracked the Berlin Wall of local telephone monopolies in this country. The New York PSC most certainly blazed the trail for other progressive PUCs and deserves credit for guiding subsequent policy formulations, in particular, the sections relating to interconnection agreements in the Telecommunications Act of 1996.[33]

A major part of the New York story involves the interconnection agreements between NYNEX and competitive local exchange carriers (CLECs). In 1994, NYNEX agreed to interconnect with Teleport Communications. This action integrated the networks of both companies and facilitated the exchange of calls on a peer basis. The

---

[32] "NARUC Report on the Status of Competition in Intrastate Telecommunications," 91.

[33] Good rulemaking does not end conflict. As reported by Janet Lively, "PSC Tells Rochester Tel: Cut Costs to Competitors," *Democrat and Chronicle*, Rochester, New York, February 10, 1996, the New York PSC was drawn into a dispute over an AT&T petition regarding an open market experiment by Rochester Telephone. At issue are the terms and price of resale of network capacity to give competitors access to local residential customers. Lively quotes Lisa Roseblum, deputy chair of the PSC: "Moving from a monopoly to a competitive environment presents serious hurdles. There is a chance we could increase the discount." (*Discount* is the rate Rochester Telephone uses to sell network capacity to competitors, which the latter then use to sell services at retail to subscribers.)

agreement also included terms for mutual compensation for terminating calls on each other's networks.

NYNEX then signed an agreement with MFS Intelenet in January 1995 that addressed "arrangements for traffic exchange, interim number portability and reciprocal compensation." NYNEX also established an important precedent when it signed an interconnection agreement with Cablevision Lightpath, apparently "the first agreement between a BOC and a cable-TV company that recognizes the cable-TV company as a competitor."

If the New York PSC receives praise for innovation in promoting local competition, the incumbent local exchange carrier, NYNEX, must also be recognized for negotiating interconnection agreements with its new rivals, the CLECs.[34] As discussed in the next chapter, negotiating the terms of such interconnection agreements is a difficult but essential task in promoting competition in the local loop.

The Moderate Deregulation Approach in Wisconsin

Wisconsin Governor Tommy G. Thompson established a Blue Ribbon Telecommunications Infrastructure Task Force whose November 8, 1993 report outlined strategies and actions for state telecommunications policy. The forty-five members of the task force came from the Wisconsin telecommunications industry and included business and residential customers, educators, local and state government officials, and other citizens. The central objectives of the study were to:

- Manage the transition to a competitive communications marketplace. Whether competition exists is no longer a question. The question is how smoothly we make the change, and at the same time protect basic service for all.
- Remove barriers to competition and effective use of telecommunications. Let's bring down the walls that are no longer needed between the people who use technology, and between users, suppliers and regulators.
- Stimulate private sector deployment of enhanced telecommunications infrastructure. The benefits of infrastructure are many. Where development isn't as fast in bringing us these benefits as we need it to be, let's get moving.[35]

Wisconsin Act 496, the deregulation legislation, became effective in September 1994 and implemented five major recommendations of the Governor's task force. It merits attention because of these innovative features:

- Any of the state's ninety-five telephone companies that opts out of state protection of its monopoly status can shift to price caps instead of the traditional rate-of-

---

[34] Ibid, 92. Leslie Cauley in the *Wall Street Journal*, March 20, 1995, cites Richard Jalkut, president of telecommunications at NYNEX, as conceding that the New York Public Service Commission, one of the most pro-competition regulatory bodies in the United States, greatly influenced NYNEX's attitude toward competition. In fact, he says, "we weren't crazy about the idea at first."

[35] Introduction to "Convergence, Competition, Cooperation."

return rate structure; the price caps are intended to provide strong incentives for existing companies to reduce expenses and allow equal footing for new providers.

- Companies that invest in advanced technology and services, such as a system to hook up hospitals, schools and courts for easy information exchange, receive a reward of earnings 2 percent above the price cap.
- The Wisconsin Advanced Telecommunications Foundation was created as a non-profit corporation and will provide endowment funds for advanced application projects and consumer education on advanced telecommunications services.
- The law directed the PSC to "establish rules to protect the privacy of consumer medical records, Social Security numbers and other personal information that travels across telephone and computer lines."[36]

Two local exchange carriers, Ameritech and GTE, have sought price regulation under the terms of the new legislation and submitted their investment commitment plans to the state PUC. Also of note, AT&T has sought to become a certified intrastate telephone provider under the terms of the legislation, pending the adoption by the PUC of rules that "will ultimately create fair and open competition." Initial plans are to resell Ameritech and GTE services to provide local service to residential and business customers."[37]

Radical Liberalization of Local Telephone Markets in Connecticut

The state of Connecticut recently pioneered the most radical approach to competition in local telephone service. Legislation was enacted in 1994 that allows the PUC to authorize competing local networks and the sharing of local facilities and requires LECs to open their networks to competition. The legislation also authorized the PUC to establish an independent fund to support the provision of basic service by any provider.[38]

By the end of January 1996, businesses were to be given a choice of companies for local phone service. Within the next three years, residential customers throughout the state will also choose services from rival providers. The primary method for achieving competition was to require Southern New England Telephone (SNET) which enjoyed a statewide monopoly on local service to sell access to its network to competitors at discounted rates. SNET was not happy, however, with the rate DPUC established for network access, insisting it was far too low. A company spokesperson was quoted as saying, "We believe that the state's decision requires us to offer our services wholesale to big global concerns like AT&T and MCI at prices that are below our cost. We are in favor of competition, but we're being asked to subsidize our competitors."[39]

---

[36] Ellen Perlman, "Ringing in a New Era of Telecom Investment," Governing, November 1994, 59; and "NARUC Report on the Status of Competition in Intrastate Telecommunications," 145-49.

[37] USTA Weekly (United States Telephone Association, January 4, 1996).

[38] "NARUC Report on the Status of Competition in Intrastate Telecommunications," 18.

[39] Jonathan Rabinovitz, "Competition to Begin for Local Phone Calls, Ending a Monopoly," New York Times, January 6, 1996, 24.

The Connecticut precedent has exposed raw nerves in the debate over what constitutes a level playing field in local phone markets. Some argue that effective competition can evolve only when new entrants either build networks or purchase wholesale access to existing networks for resale. New networks are expensive, however; firms that make the investment only do so when they are confident there is sufficient demand for new capacity. In contrast, resale of network access enables any firm to compete for customers using existing network capacity.

Some expect that resale of existing capacity at PUC-determined rates will introduce effective competition, and that during this transition, some new entrants will invest in switches, fiber optics and co-location facilities to build their own networks. If successful, this approach will encourage competition in the price and quality of local phone services and would stimulate additional capacity.

The Connecticut experience highlights two major controversies that other states will encounter as they pursue similar approaches to competition:

- How does the PUC set wholesale rates? Setting them too low generates price competition but may undermine the financial stability of the local exchange carrier that built the existing network and must maintain it. Setting rates too high leaves resale margins so slight that little competition will result.
- Consumer advocates worry that competition will flourish only in urban markets and among business customers. They contend that this development will lead to higher residential rates, especially in rural areas.

Thomas M. Benedict, commissioner of the State Department of Public Utility Control and one of the architects of the wholesale-resale approach, predicted: "What you have in Connecticut right now is essentially what every state will have to go through. Connecticut is 18 to 24 months ahead of where most states will be if the telecommunications bill passes."[40]

Summary of State Innovation in Telecommunications Regulation

States were not passive in the period following AT&T's divestiture. The shock of major rate cases forced state regulators to react and also focused a spotlight on state regulation of telephone services. After the initial wave of rate requests, local telephone companies began to seek approval for ambitious infrastructure investments, and Governors started to realize the significance of modern telecommunications to state economic competitiveness.

Both developments increased the visibility of state regulation of telephone services. Many states responded by adjusting pricing, allowing entry into intraLATA markets, and experimenting with alternative forms of regulation. Price regulation, which gradually replaced rate-of-return methods, provided incentives to upgrade operations, reduce expenses, and improve the quality of services. Alternative forms of regulation encour-

---

[40] Ibid., 24.

aged infrastructure investment, which was considered essential to provide new and advanced forms of telecommunication.

State innovation in telecommunications policy made a contribution to the national debate on these issues. Henry Geller, former general counsel of the FCC, wrote this assessment:

> State regulation of intrastate telecommunications is desirable on a number of grounds—the so-called "grass roots" factor (i.e., the states are closer and more attuned to the particular facts in their jurisdictions than a centralized federal authority can be), and Justice Brandeis' apt point about the states as "laboratories" (i.e., the gains from substantial diversity in policy approaches among the states...). Thus, some states have been more innovative than the FCC in deregulatory approaches, such as with respect to intrastate tolls and in substituting price regulation for the traditional rate-of-return method.[41]

States also contributed to the national telecommunications policy debate by taking bold steps toward promoting competition in local and intrastate telephone markets. Early actions in New York and recent moves toward radical deregulation in Connecticut have blazed a trail to competition in the local loop.

For many years, would-be competitors argued for legislation to establish a level playing field in regulated markets. This concept proved to be elusive, but important state proceedings in Pennsylvania, Maryland, Michigan, and Illinois have sought to establish necessary conditions for the beginnings of local competition.[42] State actions establishing dialing parity, interconnection agreements, and resale rates have provided strong empirical evidence that states can play an essential role in ensuring that fair rules govern all players, and that consumers will benefit from a competitive environment. The congressional drafters of the Telecommunications Act of 1996, the topic of the next chapter, drew heavily upon these and other state experiments in telecommunications policy.

---

[41] Henry Geller, "Legal Issues in Preemption," *American Regulatory Federalism & Telecommunications Infrastructure* (Lawrence Erlbaum Associates, Hillsdale, New Jersey, 1995), 125.

[42] See Richard L. Cimerman and Geoffrey J. Waldau, "Local Exchange Competition: Alternative Models in Maryland," in *Toward A Competitive Telecommunications Industry* (Lawrence Erlbaum Associates, Mahwah, New Jersey, 1995), 119-135.

CHAPTER FIVE

THE TELECOMMUNICATIONS ACT OF 1996-MAJOR STATE ISSUES

After four years of tough congressional battles, new federal telecommunications legislation was enacted in the 104th Congress and signed into law by President Clinton on February 8, 1996. It was the first major rewrite of the 1934 Communications Act in sixty-two years and was intended to promote competition in telephone and cable services and partially deregulate much of the telecommunications industry. As expected, soon after passage, a flurry of mergers, acquisitions, and alliances within the telecommunications industry took place.

Key provisions of S. 652, the Telecommunications Act of 1996, will command the close attention of Governors and other state policymakers. The basic philosophy of this legislation is that regional Bell operating companies (RBOCs) that wish to enter the in-region interLATA (interstate) long-distance market should take a series of actions to enable competition to flourish in their own service areas first.

By allowing more competition in local and long-distance telephone markets (as well as in cable-TV services), the new legislation will create profound changes for states. These changes have already hit state regulators who are responsible for monitoring telephone service quality, affordability, and availability. Governors and state legislators will soon be drawn into contentious policy debates as well. They will have to consider how to create a level playing field for effective competition, and whether to create universal-service funds to ensure access to basic telephone services throughout their states.

This chapter presents a summary of this landmark legislation and emphasizes its impact on state responsibilities in regulating local and intrastate telephone services.[1] The first section highlights areas that are relevant to states. The second section describes the new framework for promoting competition and state roles during the transition period. It discusses the meaning of a level playing field for effective competition, the 14-point checklist in Section 271, and reasonable interconnection requirements. It also asks: How will resale rates for existing capacity be determined? What actions must public utility commissions (PUCs) take and when? And precisely how does federal legislation preempt state authority?

---

[1] Other provisions: allow television networks to own more stations; allow a TV station to own a cable company in the same area; give TV broadcasters first opportunity to obtain electromagnetic spectrum for digital broadcast; extend broadcast licenses to eight years; authorize the FCC to regulate satellite TV broadcasts; ban the dissemination of "indecent material" (cyberporn) on the Internet; and require that new television sets include V-chips, which would allow parents to screen out material they do not want their children to view. For one of the best summaries of this legislation, see Dan Carney, "Congress Fires Its First Shot in Information Revolution," *Congressional Quarterly* (February 3, 1996): 289-294.

The third section of this chapter treats the issue of universal service: How is universal service defined? What is the public benefit of providing universal access to established phone networks? At what price (and for whom) can geographic equity be achieved? If competition flourishes only in selective markets, does the state bear some responsibility to ensure that prices do not increase or that service levels do not decline in other areas?

HIGHLIGHTS RELEVANT TO THE STATES

The Telecommunications Act of 1996:

- *Ends local telephone monopolies by preempting state and local laws that bar competitors.* As expected, the long-distance companies (such as AT&T, MCI, and Sprint) have already entered most local markets quickly and aggressively. Also, cable companies and public utilities can now enter local telephone markets.
- *Allows RBOCs (regional Bell operating companies) to enter long-distance markets in their service areas after meeting the 14-point checklist in Section 271 for allowing prospective competitors to use their networks.* Most RBOCs have already announced that they intend to provide long-distance services out of their service territories. GTE can provide long-distance service immediately, without having to adhere to the checklist. Most RBOCs are moving quickly to meet conditions in the checklist, which must be approved by the FCC in consultation with the state PUC.
- *Directs the FCC to establish interconnection requirements, such as reselling services to competitors, keeping individual phone numbers when customers change services, making dialing simple for all customers, and giving competitors network access, including access to poles, conduits, and rights of way.* These conditions are intended to create a level playing field for effective competition. Some state PUCs may already have negotiated and approved some conditions, but major controversies are likely to arise in other cases. For example, local exchange carriers will claim they are meeting interconnection requirements, and new or potential competitors will claim they are not. To be sure, the terms and prices for interconnection agreements will be at issue. The FCC will promulgate essential ground rules for interconnection. Indeed, soon after legislative enactment, the FCC rapidly initiated rulemaking procedures on most of the issues identified. The state PUC has an important role in mediating, arbitrating, and approving interconnection agreements between the local exchange carriers (LECs) and prospective competitors. The FCC must consult with the state PUC on whether or not an RBOC meets the 14-point checklist before it allows the RBOC to enter the in-region interLATA (long-distance) market. State policymakers should expect to see "venue shopping" in this regard: firms with strong interests will seek to discuss these matters with Governors, friendly legislators, and state PUCs.

- *Requires that the FCC determine a minimum package of services for customers ("universal service"), which will evolve over time as the technology changes.* The FCC has already convened a joint board of federal and state regulators to set the federal standard for what types of services would be offered throughout the country. The joint board will report on November 8, 1996; a subsequent FCC ruling is expected in the spring of 1997. All service providers must contribute to the universal-service fund, which will provide subsidies to eligible companies with high fixed costs. States may establish universal-service funds that are consistent with the federal legislation.

- *Deregulates cable television and enables video programming by telephone companies.* Rates for cable-television services beyond the basic tier of local and educational channels will be deregulated after three-and-a-half years for major cable systems, and immediately for small systems (fewer than 50,000 subscribers).[2] Telephone companies will be able to provide video programming and can purchase smaller cable companies and up to 10 percent of the larger cable companies in their service areas.

What can state policymakers expect as a result of this legislation? They can anticipate that TV stations and cable systems will be bought and sold quickly;

---

[2] For more about cable regulation, see Robert W. Crandall and Harold Furchtgott-Roth, *Cable TV: Regulation or Competition?* (Brookings Institution, Washington, D.C., 1996).

telecommunications firms will form mergers and alliances; and every major firm will engage in unbridled competition and aggressive marketing. All of the principal players will seek to present their interests to Governors, state PUCs, and state legislatures. States may also expect telecommunications firms to argue for state and local tax equity and seek the elimination of discriminatory taxes and franchise fees.

THE SETTING: S. 652 BECOMES FEDERAL LAW

Before addressing key features of this legislation, it may be helpful to review some of the motivating factors that prompted a public policy shift. Since the 1984 AT&T divestiture, the local Bell operating companies, or seven RBOCs, were restricted from competing in long-distance services and video programming. In the last four years, the RBOCs lobbied hard for a deregulation law that would allow them to offer video programming to compete with cable-TV services, to enter the lucrative long-distance market, and to manufacture telephone equipment.

Long-distance companies resisted liberalizing legislation for two reasons: concern that local telephone companies would use their control of the local loop as a bottleneck and prevent access to prospective competitors; and concern that revenues from monopoly services would be used to cross-subsidize competitive services, providing an unfair advantage to local exchange carriers. Both telephone companies and cable-TV firms wanted to enter each other's markets. A final push came following recent advances in wireless and satellite systems, which have the potential to compete with wireline telephone and cable networks.

The final legislative product, naturally, did not please everyone. Most players responded as expected: the RBOCs were most pleased; long-distance companies swallowed their disappointment and vowed to compete aggressively in local markets; most cable companies were delighted to see the end of FCC-price regulation of all but basic cable services in 1999, and many accelerated their plans to enter the telephone business by installing switches on their coaxial cable systems. The greatest praise for this legislative product came from congressional leaders and officials in the Clinton Administration.[3]

A few dissenting views merit brief attention. Most consumer advocates praised the new law, believing that competition would lower costs and improve services. A few, however, expressed concern that inevitable rate restructuring at the state level would lead to higher phone bills for basic service in high-cost, rural areas. Leaders of state organizations were concerned that the federal law preempted state authority in several

---

[3] As quoted by Edmund L. Andrews, "Clinton Set to Sign Bill That Is Expected to Spur Competition," *New York Times*, February 2, 1996, A1. Representative Thomas J. Bliley, the bill's primary author:

> Today, we have broken up two of the biggest government monopolies left: the monopolies in local telephone service and in cable television. For the first time ever, Americans will be given choices. Besides lower rates and better service, the result will be innovative new products and services that will create thousands of new American jobs.

Also quoted was Vice President Al Gore, who—according to Andrews—effusively praised today's votes: "It's a bipartisan victory, a textbook example of how the White House and Congress can work together. Creativity that has bottled up for decades will be let out in a very constructive way."

areas.[4] Some economists found the legislation too timid and criticized it for not allowing more liberalization of markets and greater deregulation of the telecommunications industry.[5] Industry experts wondered how the FCC would manage to promulgate the new rules within the required six-month timetable. Most implementation rules are expected on August 8, 1996.

Despite these concerns, there was widespread support for federal legislation that would ensure a level playing field for fair competition in telephone and cable services. Below is a discussion of how the law seeks to establish a level playing field in what has long been a heavily regulated field. (Appendix B provides an excerpt from the NARUC summary of state responsibilities under this federal act.)[6]

FEDERAL LEGISLATION PROMOTES COMPETITION

An important provision of the new legislation is Section 253, Removal of Barriers to Entry. This section declares that "No State or local statute or regulation, or other State or local legal requirement, may prohibit or have the effect of prohibiting the ability of any entity to provide any interstate or intrastate telecommunications service."[7] This statement is significant because at the time of enactment, as many as twenty states had some regulation, statute, or constitutional provision that prohibited competition in local telephone service. Section 253 preempts state restrictions on local competition. Another paragraph grants broad authority to the FCC to preempt, after notice and a public comment, actions by state and local governments that are inconsistent with this section.

---

[4] State and local governments are concerned that the FCC will interpret the legislation in ways that preempt traditional authority in siting cellular towers and charging for access to public rights of way. According to the act, states and localities retain authority to manage public rights of way and collect fair and reasonable compensation for their use, as long as fees are applied on a "competitively neutral and nondiscriminatory basis." (This standard may prove difficult to reconcile with existing agreements with incumbent telecommunications providers.) For more information about local government concerns, see Anthony Crowell, "Local Government and the Telecommunications Act of 1996," *Public Management*, Vol. 78, No. 6 (ICMA, Washington, D.C., June 1996): 6-12. In contrast, NARUC commended the final version of the act because it retained substantial authority for state regulatory commissions. As a result of NARUC's extensive lobbying, the new legislation retains Section 152(b) of the 1934 Communications Act relating to state authority over intrastate matters.

[5] For one of the best short arguments of this position, see Robert W. Crandall, "Waves of the Future: Are We Ready to Deregulate Telecommunications," *Brookings Review* (winter 1996). Although published near the date of the enactment of S. 652, Crandall was quite critical of earlier legislative versions: "So far the revolutionary 104th Congress has done little more than nibble at the margins of a huge regulatory problem....If the Republicans in Congress truly believe that markets are superior to government controls in allocating resources, they could surely go much farther in dismantling telecommunications regulation than they are now prepared to do." Here is another key passage (29):

> The question is why we need federal regulation of voice, data, or video services at all when any of several companies can offer hundreds of video channels, local wireless telephone services, or long-distance voice and data services. Each new generation of technology can offer these services at a small fraction of the cost incurred by the previous one, built just a few short years ago. Monopoly power may exist in certain segments of the industry, particularly local telephony, but not for long under these conditions as long as regulators do not stand in the way.

[6] This chapter attempts to summarize and explain the most important concepts in the federal legislation to prepare state policymakers for the encroaching state telewars. Those seeking additional information about the new state role in telecommunications should begin with "Key Provisions of the Telecommunications Act of 1996" (National Association of Regulatory Utility Commissioners [NARUC], Washington, D.C., February 25, 1996) and obtain a copy of the federal legislation. See also Jay Kayne, "State Telecommunications Issues Following Enactment of the Telecommunications Act of 1996," (Issue Brief, National Governors' Association, Washington, D.C., May 23, 1996).

[7] Unless otherwise noted, all quotes in this section are from the Telecommunications Act of 1996, Pub. L. No. 104-104, 110 Stat. 56 (1996). This interpretation benefits greatly from a variety of analyses of the federal legislation; see especially, "Key Provisions of the Telecommunications Act of 1996" (NARUC).

Despite federal preemption of barriers to entry, the legislation maintains the authority of state regulatory commissions. This issue is addressed in a related paragraph: "Nothing in this section shall affect the ability of a State to impose, on a competitively neutral basis and consistent with section 254, requirements necessary to:

- Preserve and advance universal service;
- Protect the public safety and welfare;
- Ensure the continued quality of telecommunications services; and
- Safeguard the rights of consumers."

Hence, the FCC must ensure that state and local barriers to entry are removed. State commissions may continue to establish regulations and policies consistent with these four objectives, but must ensure that their actions not be interpreted as a barrier to entry. As one might expect, any firm that resists a PUC policy or regulation might well argue that it constitutes a barrier to entry. The federal preemption on this issue provides a new framework for local competition in telephony, but also poses challenges to state regulatory commissions.[8]

Another key provision is Section 251, which establishes different *interconnection* requirements on telecommunications carriers, local exchange carriers, and incumbent local exchange carriers. In effect, all telecommunications providers must "interconnect directly or indirectly with the facilities and equipment of other telecommunications carriers." To reinforce the general standard, Section 251 includes a prohibition against any telecommunications provider installing "network features, functions, or capabilities that do not comply" with established FCC guidelines and standards. All local exchange carriers must meet these requirements and many others. All incumbent exchange carriers must also meet these and other requirements.

The principle of interconnection is important to understanding how competition can be introduced to the local loop. *Interconnection* means, technically, the connection of a communications channel, facility, service, or piece of equipment with another from a different network. It is usually achieved by a physical connection between networks. In a practical sense, these requirements will enable prospective competitors to interconnect with the networks of incumbent local telephone companies, and with networks maintained by long-distance companies.

Interconnection requirements are essential to bring competition to the local loop and allow long-distance providers to interconnect their facilities with existing local networks. These requirements also make it possible for new, alternative networks to be integrated with wireline networks. Consider this hypothetical example: a firm has

---

[8] A group of state and local organizations, which included the National Governors' Association, National Conference of State Legislatures, National Association of Counties, National League of Cities, and United States Conference of Mayors, opposed this preemption language (Section 254(d) of Title II) in the summer of 1995, arguing that this was "an unwarranted preemption of state and local government authority." For more information about federal preemption, see Henry Geller, "Legal Issues in Preemption," *American Regulatory Federalism & Telecommunications Infrastructure* (Lawrence Erlbaum Associates, Hillsdale, New Jersey, 1995).

microwave capacity to transmit long-distance calls between New Orleans and Cleveland, but to sell these services, the firm needs to interconnect its facilities to local networks in both cities. The interconnection requirement allows this firm to link its facilities with local networks.[9]

The opportunity to compete in the local loop will entice cable-television companies to develop their coaxial cable systems as new networks for telephone services. Similarly, gas and electric utilities could modernize their networking infrastructure to provide local telephone services. As mentioned, wireless technologies already complement conventional wirelines. The new interconnection requirements will make it possible to integrate the distinct networks of all telecommunications providers and prospective competitors and allow them to function as one. Box V-2 below summarizes the interconnection requirements in Section 251.

Box V-2 Interconnection Requirements, Section 251

(A) **All Telecommunications Carriers** must interconnect directly/indirectly with other carriers, and not install network features, functions or capabilities that do not comply with requirements under Section 255 or 256.

(B) **All Local Exchange Carriers** must comply with requirements under (A) and not prohibit resale of its telecommunications services; provide number portability pursuant to FCC rules; provide dialing parity to competitors; permit nondiscriminatory access to telephone numbers, operator services, directory assistance and directory listings; afford access to rights-of-way to competitors on rates, terms and conditions consistent with Section 224; and establish reciprocal compensation arrangements for transport/termination of telecommunications traffic.

(C) **Incumbent Local Exchange Carriers** must comply with (A), (B), and negotiate in good faith (as must the requesting carrier); provide interconnection with the requesting carrier for transmission/routing of traffic, at any technically feasible point, of at least equal quality as provided to itself/affiliate, on just, reasonable and nondiscriminatory rates, terms and conditions in accordance with Sections 251 and 252; provide nondiscriminatory access to unbundled network elements; offer all retail services at wholesale prices to carriers; provide reasonable notice of changes in transmission/routing information; and provide for physical collocation unless a state commission approves virtual collocation.

Source: "Key Provisions of the Telecommunications Act of 1996" (NARUC, February 25, 1996).

---

[9] Recall the narrative in chapter three, which observed that states were first drawn into regulating telephone services, in part, because of the lack of interconnection requirements. Early in this century, competitive telephone companies built and maintained duplicate lines, phones, and equipment because these early networks did not interconnect.

As mentioned, the FCC is responsible for adopting appropriate rules to implement the interconnection requirements, along with many other key provisions, by August 8, 1996. While there is general consensus that some regulatory provisions are necessary to promote fair competition, one might expect controversy over the FCC rules that will govern this section of the law.[10] Unless FCC rules are explicit, state commissions will play a major role in interpreting them, especially those that relate to the costs of interconnection and resale. (See Box V-3 for divergent views about interconnection rules.)

Section 251(c)(3) requires that all local exchange carriers provide to any requesting telecommunications carrier *access* to its network elements (i.e, facility or equipment) on an unbundled basis, and on rates, terms, and conditions that are just, reasonable, and nondiscriminatory.[11] Although usually mentioned in the same breath, the difference between access and interconnection is important. Interconnection refers to how different networks can be linked together; access refers to the use of existing LEC network capacity, including lines, equipment and switches, by different carriers. Both interconnection and access are essential to achieve competition in the local loop. State commissions will be challenged to resolve the question of appropriate "rates, terms, and conditions that are just, reasonable, and nondiscriminatory."[12]

Similarly, states will need to determine appropriate interconnection charges. Section 252(d)(1) grants state commissions the authority to determine these rates. They are to be "based on costs (determined with reference to a rate of return or other rate-based proceeding) of providing the interconnection or network element (whichever is applicable), be nondiscriminatory and may include a reasonable profit."[13] Hence, the state commission may be challenged to determine, based on cost studies and industry data, the actual costs of providing interconnection to other carriers.

---

[10] The Notice of Proposed Rulemaking (NPRM) issued by the FCC on April 19, 1996 drew criticism from the National Association of Regulatory Utility Commissioners. In a press release issued May 2, 1996, NARUC President Cheryl Parrino said, "We are very concerned. States share the FCC's commitment to local telephone competition and are moving ahead to carry out the procompetition goals of the 1996 Act. However, this effort will be seriously impeded by a 'one size fits all' policy on all aspects of interconnection and unbundling. Further, we are disappointed with the apparent preemptive tenor and content of the FCC notice which goes well beyond the spirit and letter of the Act." For more on this controversy, see "Showdown on Interconnection Looms among Communications Heavyweights," DER No. 9 (Bureau of National Affairs, April 24, 2996), C-1-11.

[11] Section 251(c)(3) reads: "The duty to provide, to any requesting telecommunications carrier, for the provision of a telecommunications service, nondiscriminary access to network elements on an unbundled basis at any technically feasible point on rates, terms, and conditions that are just, reasonable, and nondiscriminatory in accordance with the terms and conditions of the agreement and the requirements of this section and section 252. An incumbent local exchange carrier shall provide such unbundled network elements in a manner that allows requesting carriers to combine such elements in order to provide such telecommunications service."

[12] Consider the controversy about the access charges paid by the long-distance companies since the 1982 MFJ. Long-distance companies need *access* to local exchange carriers (LECs) to originate and terminate these calls. In 1994, the long-distance companies paid an estimated $21 billion, or almost one-third of their gross revenues, to local exchange carriers in access charges. Some allege that these charges were set by regulators at levels higher than the actual cost of interconnection, which generated revenues that subsidized local telephone rates. Section 251(g) maintains the current policy toward access charges paid by interexchange services. This example suggests that granting access is not an issue. *What will be at issue are the terms and price of access.* Indeed, competition in the local loop is most likely to come, at least in the short term, from firms that purchase the use of existing network capacity and resell services to customers at lower prices than those of the incumbent local telephone company.

[13] A network element means "a facility or equipment used in the provision of a telecommunications service," a component of the network.

Box V-3 Divergent Views on Interconnection and Federal/State Roles

Alan Ciamporcero, vice president for federal regulatory relations at Pacific Telesis Group, says the FCC ought to let state regulators carry the main responsibility for implementing interconnection sections. He warns that long-distance companies want the FCC to put a "big, heavy boot on the necks of the states and the companies."

Bruce Cox, director of federal government affairs for AT&T, says it is technically feasible to unbundle at least eleven network elements of the LEC system. He says AT&T plans to become a facilities-based competitor of local phone companies, but says local phone companies have some big advantages in the early going, particularly in switching capacity.

Brad Stillman, senior legislative counsel for the Consumer Federation of America, says that without basic national policies, local competition will never materialize. The LEC push to give states the primary regulatory task "is a joke," he says.

Richard Metzger, general counsel for the Association for Local Telecommunications Services, says LEC fears of losing huge amounts of revenue through unbundling are unfounded. Even if new players get their way on access charges, the sky won't fall, noting that the joint board on universal service could fix any resulting imbalances. MFS Communications Company, Teleport Communications Group, and other CAPs have carved out a $1 billion niche by laying fiber connecting high-volume business customers directly to long-distance carriers, thereby bypassing LECs and access charges. They now want to become full-service providers.

Chris Savage, a cable lawyer for the firm Cole Raywid & Braverman, says that cable operators are mostly interested in securing fair interconnection terms because they already have many of the facilities they need to provide telephony. He says cable companies are likely to oppose long-distance arguments for establishing a big resale discount, arguing that such a discount could undercut their own nascent service.

Robert Blau, vice president of BellSouth, says LECs and their competitors should be able to negotiate interconnection agreements with minimal interference from the FCC. "If the commission gets so detailed in saying you will do this or do that, you get to the point where it's hardly worth negotiating anything," he says. "The whole thing...could become moot."

Andrew Regitsky, director of state affairs for the Competitive Telecommunications Association (CompTel), says that under the new law, competitors should be able to get cost-based access to LEC network elements, including for the purpose of offering long-distance service. "Interconnection is interconnection," he says.

Source: "Showdown on Interconnection Looms Among Communications Heavyweights," *Daily Report for Executives* (Bureau of National Affairs, No. 79, April 24, 1996), C1-2.

A related concern is resale. Section 251(b)(1) includes an obligation on local exchange carriers "not to prohibit, and not to impose unreasonable or discriminatory conditions or limitations on, the resale of telecommunications services." Any prospective competitor will need to purchase capacity from networks that are controlled by other companies in order to originate and terminate calls. What are the appropriate terms and costs of resale? Typically, the selling firm will seek the highest prices that can be defended through cost studies; firms that are purchasing capacity will argue for low prices so they can earn a profit on the resale through retail rates to the public. The state commission is the likely forum for resolving this dispute.

Section 251(c)(4) provides a better example of the same issue. It obligates incumbent local exchange carriers to offer telecommunications services for resale at wholesale rates. This is one of the most difficult provisions of the act and has a few important caveats. Purchasing existing network capacity at wholesale rates is essential for competition in the local loop, at least in the short term. Prospective competitors will seek the lowest wholesale prices for existing capacity and hope they can earn a profit by reselling directly to the public at competitive retail rates. Incumbent exchange carriers will defend higher wholesale rates; they will not be eager to sell capacity at rates that allow competitors to drain away sales and revenue. In the Connecticut example discussed in the previous chapter, the incumbent local exchange carrier bitterly contested wholesale rates established by the state PUC.

The state commission will have an extremely important role in determining appropriate wholesale rates for resale. An important exception in this section allows a state commission to "prohibit a reseller that obtains at wholesale rates a telecommunications service that is available at retail only to a category of subscribers from offering such service to a different category of subscribers." According to NARUC's interpretation of this language, the section allows the state commission to prohibit arbitrage in the resale market (e.g., to prohibit the resale of flat-rated residential service to business customers).[14]

The statute gives the state commission some direction in establishing appropriate wholesale rates. Section 252(d)(3) reads: "A State commission shall determine wholesale rates on the basis of retail rates charged, to subscribers for the telecommunications service requested, excluding the portion thereof attributable to any marketing, billing, collection, and other costs that will be avoided by the local exchange carrier." One interpretation is that it directs wholesale rates to be retail rates minus avoided costs. Wholesale rates are likely to be determined by the state commission after it conducts reliable cost studies.

---

[14] Section 251(c)(4) reads: "The duty (A) to offer for resale at wholesale rates any telecommunications service that the carrier provides at retail to subscribers who are not telecommunications carriers; and (B) not to prohibit, and not to impose unreasonable or discriminatory conditions or limitations on, the resale of such telecommunications service, except that a State commission may, consistent with the regulations prescribed by the Commission under this section, prohibit a reseller that obtains at wholesale rates a telecommunications service that is available at retail only to a category of subscribers from offering such service to a different category of subscribers."

State policymakers should be aware of an important exemption to the interconnection requirements in this section, related to rural telephone companies. Small local exchange companies, which are defined as having fewer than 2 percent of the nation's subscriber lines, may petition the state commission for a waiver or exemption from the interconnection requirements in Section 251(a) or (b). Similarly, rural local exchange carriers are exempt from the interconnection requirement in Section 251(c) until the state commission finds that interconnection is in the public interest and would not be "unduly economically burdensome."

In the latter case, the state commission must conduct an inquiry on whether to terminate the exemption once a request for interconnection is made to the rural telephone company. The rationale for these exemptions is self-evident: in general, small companies serve high-cost, scarcely populated rural areas. Allowing competition in these markets would drain essential revenues that are necessary to maintain basic telephone services at affordable rates. Lawmakers believed, as a practical matter, that few such markets would attract prospective competitors.[15]

The process for implementing interconnection requirements is described in Section 252 of the legislation. Voluntary agreements between incumbent local exchange carriers and other firms are encouraged and subject to the state commission's approval pursuant to Section 252(e). The state commission may only reject a voluntary agreement that "discriminates against a telecommunications carrier not a party to the agreement or (if) the implementation of such agreement or portion is not consistent with the public interest, convenience, and necessity."

The state commission may be asked to mediate these negotiations. Furthermore, if an incumbent local exchange carrier fails to negotiate in a timely fashion, the party seeking the negotiation may request that the state commission arbitrate any open issues. A state commission may reject an arbitrated agreement if it fails to meet the requirements of Sections 251 and 252(d), which describe the pricing standards for interconnection.

State regulators and industry representatives will soon master every nuance of Section 252. *State policymakers need to understand the underlying logic of the process as well. The legislation encourages voluntary agreements concerning interconnection agreements, which are the ground rules for allowing local competition in telephony. If negotiations fail, the state commission may mediate to reach an agreement. If mediation fails, the state commission may impose an arbitrated agreement.*

The FCC has two primary responsibilities: first, to adopt and implement the regulations specified in Section 251(d)(1); and second, to step into the fray if the state

---

[15] See Section 251(f)(1) "EXEMPTIONS FOR CERTAIN RURAL TELEPHONE COMPANIES" and the definition (47) "RURAL TELEPHONE COMPANY," added to Section 3, 47 U.S.C. 153; also see "Key Provisions of the Telecommunications Act of 1996" (NARUC). This introduces an important concept: common carriers, which are companies that have an obligation to provide services to any customer willing to pay for those services. Common carriers may not discriminate against any customer. See also the definition in the glossary.

commission fails to act in a timely fashion.[16] Judicial review of state commission actions on these agreements is available in an appropriate federal district court, according to Section 252(e)(6).

A major responsibility of the state commission will be to review the specific inter-connection requirements of any Bell operating company. As discussed, the RBOCs want to enter the long-distance market. The legislation allows them to do so only after they meet certain conditions that were designed to enable competition in their own markets. Section 271(c)(2) describes a 14-point competitive checklist, which is summarized below in Box V-4.

Box V-4 Section 271(c)(2): The 14-point Competitive Checklist

RBOCs must meet these criteria before they can provide in-region interLATA services:

1. Interconnection
2. Nondiscriminatory access to network elements
3. Nondiscriminatory access to poles, ducts, conduits, and rights-of-way
4. Local loop transmission from the central office to the customer's premises
5. Local transport from the trunk side of a wireline exchange carrier switch
6. Local switching unbundled from transport, local loop transmission, or other services
7. Nondiscriminatory access to 911, directory assistance, and operator call completion services
8. White page directory listings for customers of the other carrier
9. Nondiscriminatory access to telephone numbers
10. Nondiscriminatory access to databases and signaling necessary for call routing
11. Interim number portability
12. Nondiscriminatory access to services or information to allow the requesting carrier to implement local dialing parity
13. Reciprocal compensation arrangements
14. Telecommunications services available for resale

Source: "Key Provisions of the Telecommunications Act of 1996" (NARUC, Washington, D.C., February 25, 1996).

---

[16] Section 252(e) reads: "COMMISSION WILL ACT IF STATE WILL NOT ACT: If a State commission fails to act to carry out its responsibility under this section in any proceeding or other matter under this section, then the Commission shall issue an order preempting the State commission's jurisdiction of that proceeding or matter within 90 days after being notified (or taking notice) of such failure, and shall assume the responsibility of the State commission under this section with respect to the proceeding or matter and act for the State commission."

The state commission plays an important role in reviewing whether the RBOC complies with this checklist. For example, the state commission must approve interconnection agreements negotiated under Section 252. If no provider requests an interconnection agreement, then the Bell operating company may file "a statement of the terms and conditions that the company generally offers to provide such access and interconnection." This statement must be approved by the state commission. At that point, the RBOC may claim that it has met the conditions in the 14-point competitive checklist and petition the FCC for permission to enter the in-region InterLATA market (to sell long-distance services). The FCC must seek the opinions of two parties before it makes a determination on this request: the attorney general, who renders an opinion on whether the RBOC will gain undue market power, adversely affecting consumers, by entering the in-region long-distance market;[17] and the state commission, which verifies the compliance of the RBOC with the competitive checklist.

Most RBOCs are moving swiftly to comply with the checklist because they are eager to enter the in-region interLATA market. Meanwhile, many telecommunications carriers will be trying to negotiate interconnection agreements with incumbent local exchange carriers.[18]

Section 272 addresses concerns that RBOCs might use revenues from monopolistic operations to cross-subsidize competitive ventures, creating an unfair advantage to other firms. This section requires that RBOCs and their affiliate local exchange carriers maintain separate affiliates for manufacturing activities, providing in-region interLATA services, and interLATA information services. As one might expect, the law prohibits these affiliates from discriminating in dealing with other firms. They also must keep separate books. Every two years, a federal/state audit of affiliate operations will verify compliance and provide relevant information to both the FCC and the state commission about these activities.

---

[17] The key phrase in Section 271(d)(2)(A) is the last sentence: "The Commission shall give substantial weight to the Attorney General's evaluation, but such evaluation shall not have any preclusive effect on any Commission decision under paragraph (3)," which describes the criteria for determination. Historians may highlight this provision as one of the last-minute compromises made in the Conference Committee to reconcile different views and gain additional support for the legislation.

[18] Beginning in May 1996, the media reported a wave of interconnection agreements. *Communications Daily* (May 17, 1996) reported that BellSouth and MCI reached agreement on local interconnection, signing a two-year pact covering physical interconnection, reciprocal compensation, and interim number portability in five of BellSouth's nine states. Significantly, that agreement did not cover the terms of resale of local service.

On May 23, 1996, the *Wall Street Journal* (B3) reported that Ameritech and MFS Communications had signed a more comprehensive interconnection agreement. According to the article by Gautam Naik, "MFS will be able to lease Ameritech's copper phone lines to reach prospective customers without also having to lease other facilities owned by Bell, including expensive switching centers. Ameritech customers who choose to use MFS's service will be able to retain their phone numbers. The two carriers also agreed on rate parity: Ameritech and MFS will pay each other the same amount for local calls made on one company's network but ending in the other's." (*Communications Daily* reported the next day that Time Warner claimed that the Ameritech-MFS agreement did not satisfy the mandate in the act for "true facilities-based competition.")

On June 4, 1996, the *New York Times* reported that Bell Atlantic had negotiated an interconnection agreement with Jones Intercable in Virginia, and on June 5, that BellSouth and Time Warner had signed an interconnection agreement. In the June 5th article, Mark Landler summarizes: "The patchwork of deals underscores that neither the Bells nor their new competitors are a monolithic group. While MFS is angling for the business market, Time Warner is aiming at consumers. And while MFS and Time Warner are building their own networks to offer local service, AT&T plans to lease most of its capacity from the Bells." See also "AT&T Discounts Signal a National Price War," *Wall Street Journal*, May 30, 1996.

PRIMARY ISSUES IN PROMOTING COMPETITION
IN LOCAL TELEPHONY

To help policymakers understand major telecommunications issues in the years to come, a summary describes the state role as articulated in the new federal legislation.

1. Federal Preemption. Section 253 grants federal preemption of any state or local law or regulation that has the effect of "prohibiting any entity from providing telecommunications services." States may no longer prevent competition in the local loop. Furthermore, prospective competitors are likely to appeal to the FCC or legally challenge state legislation that imposes a barrier to entry into this market. In addition, state and local governments may retain the right to manage and require compensation for use of public rights of way, but must do so on a nondiscriminatory and competitively neutral basis. The FCC will provide appellate review of state policies in this area.

2. State Commission Approves Interconnection Agreements. Mediating, arbitrating, and approving interconnection agreements will be a huge responsibility for state commissions. The touchstone for state actions must be whether or not these agreements promote local competition. Also significant is the state commission's review of RBOC compliance with the 14-point competitive checklist. A key feature of both matters is the price of interconnection, especially the pricing of wholesale services, access, and other conditions. Federal legislation establishes the parameters for how the state commission should determine prices for interconnection. Since the state commission bears price-setting responsibility, state statutes that set wholesale prices arbitrarily may be subject to legal challenge.

3. Regulatory Forbearance. Section 401 directs the FCC to forbear from enforcing most provisions of this act if the FCC determines that they are not necessary to ensure just, reasonable, and nondiscriminatory rates; they are not needed to protect consumers; and forbearance is consistent with the public interest. Logically, states must forbear from applying a provision of the act whenever the FCC decides to forbear from applying it. NARUC suggests, however, that the FCC's decision to forbear should not diminish the state's authority to enforce its own regulations pursuant to state statutes or regulation. NARUC therefore anticipates that litigation may result from this potential conflict.[19] Other conflicts also may arise over state and local regulations that are considered inconsistent with the provisions of this act.[20]

---

[19] See "Key Provisions of the Telecommunications Act of 1996" (NARUC), 11.

[20] Many organizations representing states and local governments have continued to express their opposition to Section 704, Facilities Siting; (7) Preservation of Local Zoning Authority, which grants federal preemption on aspects of the traditional process of siting cellular towers. The act leaves most authority over facility siting with state and local governments, but here are three specific federal preemptions of traditional state and local authority:

1. State and local jurisdictions may not regulate cellular antenna siting on the basis of the environmental effects of radio frequency emissions, if the antenna facilities comply with FCC emission requirements. The FCC docket on this topic (ET Docket 93-62) will be completed on August 8, 1996.

2. State and local jurisdictions must act on siting requests within a "reasonable period of time." In addition, "any decision by a State or local government or instrumentality thereof to deny a request to place, construct, or modify personal wireless service facilities shall be in writing and supported by substantial evidence contained in a written record." The act also prohibits any state or local action that "unreasonably discriminates among providers of functionally equivalent services, of disallowing or having the effect of disallowing the provision of personal wireless services."

3. Affected parties may challenge state or local governments for actions inconsistent with this federal law, which a court must hear and decide on an expedited basis.

Will telewars break out in state capitols over these issues? Will state policymakers be drawn into debates about the state's role in allowing local competition? Will each telecommunications provider have its own interpretation of the federal law, FCC regulations, and the appropriate course of action by the state PUC? Will some firms seek state legislation that grants unfair advantage to them? Will industry representatives dance to and fro, from the state commission to the state legislature to the Governor's office, in pursuit of the most sympathetic response? Will industry lobbyists become creative in articulating the public interest to be served by certain state actions or interpretations?

Most state capitols will experience telewars—including gaming and venue shopping— because to put it crudely, a great deal of money is at stake. Although local telephone services constitute a rather large pie, both incumbents and competitors will seek big slices. Public concerns include the following: Who will benefit from competition? Will consumers receive, as promised, lower prices and better services? Can the quality of services be maintained or improved? Will the transition to competition be managed according to a fair process? What is the public interest in the new competitive environment?

Based on willing buyers and sellers, markets allocate most private-sector goods and services efficiently. Public goods, such as national defense, are available to everyone in society; that is, no one can be excluded from the benefits of public goods. Similarly, quasi-public goods, such as education and law enforcement, are distributed with more attention to equity. Individuals benefit from these services and so does society.

Should telephone service be treated as a private-sector commodity? Is basic phone service a public good that should be made available to everyone regardless of ability to pay? If so, should telephone stamps, similar to food stamps, be issued to low-income households and customers in high-cost areas, as AT&T and many economists suggest?[21] What about advanced telecommunications services or Internet access? Are these to be priced according to willing buyers and sellers? How should public policy distinguish between basic and advanced telecommunications services? The search for answers begins with an overview of universal service and how the Telecommunications Act of 1996 approaches these troublesome issues.

WHAT IS UNIVERSAL SERVICE?

Until recently, most historians traced the concept of universal service to T. Vail's corporate vision for AT&T or to the preamble to the 1934 Communications Act: "to make available so far as possible, to all people in the United States, a rapid, efficient, nationwide, and worldwide wire and radio communications service with adequate

---

[21] If coupled with the elimination of implicit subsidies through rate averaging, this remedy has the virtue of satisfying the equity objective at minimal social cost and price distortions.

facilities at reasonable charge."[22] One might think of basic universal service as the contemporary concept that all Americans have access to the national telephone network and to basic and defined services.[23]

When the 1934 Communications Act was enacted, only 40 percent of the nation's households had telephones, over half of these subscribers had party lines, and most calls, both local and long distance, were handled by operators.[24] Now, 94.3 percent of our households have telephone service—one of the highest penetration rates in the world—and only 1 percent of households lack single-line service. This impressive benchmark was achieved because most decisionmakers shared the common belief that "the value of telephone service is directly linked to the number of users on the system; the more people that can be accessed, the more valuable the service."[25]

Access to basic telephone services benefits individual consumers; access to virtually everyone benefits society.[26] Direct and cross-subsidies have been effective in expanding access to telephone service. Rural areas, with high operating costs, have received direct public subsidies to construct and maintain their local exchanges. For most of this century, FCC and state rate policies have provided cross-subsidies to keep residential rates affordable, although modest steps have been taken in the last twenty years toward more efficient pricing. In addition, most states have authorized special low-income assistance programs, mirroring the federal Lifeline program, to enable low-income households to afford basic telephone service.[27]

---

[22] Note the discussion in chapter three. Milton Mueller, "Universal Service as an Appropriability Problem: A New Framework for Analysis," in *Toward a Competitive Telecommunication Industry* (1995) argues that beginning in 1907 under Vail's leadership, the phrase *universal service* meant "interconnecting competing networks into an integrated monopoly, not putting a telephone into every home." Similarly, Mueller in *Universal Service: Competition, Interconnection, and Monopoly in the Making of the American Telephone System* (Cambridge, Massachusetts: MIT Press/American Enterprise Institute, 1996) argues that the preamble to the 1934 act was rhetorical. He contends that there was no legislative intent to promote universal service, as conventionally defined, in that act.

[23] John D. Borrows, Phyllis A. Bernt, and Raymond W. Lawton, *Universal Service in the United States: Dimensions of the Debate* (National Regulatory Research Institute, Columbus, Ohio, June 1994), 7. The authors also define *universal availability* as the "concept stressing the ubiquitous deployment of telecommunications capability with less emphasis on the actual utilization of the services by all potential customers." Many advocates seek both definitions of universal service to be met: essential services provided at affordable rates to all and the availability of advanced services to everyone regardless of how much they might be used. Defining universal service has been an exhaustive debate. One of the more expansive definitions was offered by California's Intelligent Network Task Force (Pacific Bell, 1988), which defined it "as affordable access for virtually all citizens to (a) the intelligent network and (b) a package of essential services that included touch-tone service, access to emergency services, access to public information services, access to educational services, services for customers not fluent in English, and services for persons with disabilities." *Left unresolved is what it costs to provide these services and who pays for them.* The above cited in Harmeet Sawhney, "Universal Service: Prosaic Motives and Great Ideals," in *Toward a Competitive Telecommunication Industry* (Lawrence Erlbaum Associates, Mahwah, New Jersey, 1995), 206.

[24] James Bradford Ramsay, "Building an Effective Information Infrastructure through Improved Technology Beyond Plain Old Telephone Service: REDEFINING UNIVERSAL SERVICE" (CSG/NCSL/NGA State Information Policy Consortium presentation, Washington, D.C., December 13, 1993), 3.

[25] Ibid.

[26] The first is called a *merit* good, i.e., the idea that all households should have basic telephone service to contact emergency services, seek employment, communicate with others, and participate in society. The second idea, called *positive externalities*, is that the more people are connected to the network, the more everyone connected to the network benefits.

[27] Federal universal-service support programs have been funded through charges to long-distance carriers. The act requires that all providers of telecommunications services should make an equitable and nondiscriminatory contribution to the preservation and advancement of universal service.

THE TELECOMMUNICATIONS ACT OF 1996 AND UNIVERSAL SERVICE

Following the strong legislative mandate to advance universal service, the FCC adopted a Notice of Proposed Rulemaking and an order establishing a joint board to consider universal issues. The joint board will conduct a thorough review of the present system of universal-service support and will report its findings to the FCC by November 8, 1996. Final FCC universal-service rules are expected in the spring of 1997. Below are some of the major questions the joint board will explore:

- What are the basic telephone services that consumers should have access to through existing networks?
- What provisions should be made to support small, rural, high-cost telephone systems?
- What provisions should be made to support low-income consumers?
- The Telecommunications Act of 1996 mandated special rates for schools, libraries, and health-care providers. How should that provision be structured?
- How should the costs associated with the new universal-service support mechanisms be divided between interstate and intrastate telecommunications carriers?

• Should the definition of what constitutes universal service evolve toward a higher standard of service as the technology improves and as the demand for these advanced services increases?

In addition, the FCC is seeking comment on a host of related questions: Should the subscriber line charge be increased? How should subsidy programs be calculated? What is affordability? What are reasonably comparable services? Who should administer universal support mechanisms?[28] Listed in Box V-6 is a brief summary of some of the current programs that promote universal service. The joint board will be reviewing each of these programs.

Box V-6 Current Explicit Subsidies to Promote Telephone Access

The Universal Service Fund is administered by the National Exchange Carrier Association (NECA) and funded by a charge against long-distance carriers; the USF provides support to customers in high-cost areas to keep local rates affordable. Factors that cause higher costs include geography, population density, and growth rates. Approximately 675 telephone companies receive USF funds.

Subsidized Capital for Rural Systems through the Rural Electrification Administration is provided through below-market-rate-interest REA loans to independent telephone companies and cooperatives in jurisdictions with fewer than 10,000 residents.

Lifeline Assistance Programs, authorized by FCC rules, and PUC rules in many states, provide a direct subsidy of the Subscriber Line Charge (SLC) for income-eligible households. By waiving all or part of the $3.50 federal subscriber line charge, this program keeps low-income subscribers on the network. As with the USF, this program is funded through a charge to the long-distance carriers and is administered by NECA.

Link-Up America, created by FCC, administered by NECA, and funded by the long-distance carriers, provides up to $30 to offset installation and connection charges for low-income subscribers. Approximately 2.2 million subscribers have benefited from this program since 1987.

Telecommunications Relay Service, also administered by NECA, was created by the FCC in 1993 and reimburses TRS centers for the cost of helping millions of Americans with speech and hearing impairments use the telephone.

Sources: *Keeping Rural America Connected: Costs and Rates in the Competitive Era* (Organization for the Protection and Advancement of Small Telephone Companies, 1994), National Exchange Carrier Association, and *Telecommunications: The Next American Revolution* (National Governors' Association, 1994).

---

[28] See "Washington Watch" (National Exchange Carrier Association, Washington, D.C, March 11, 1996). See also FCC's CC Docket 96-45, released March 8, 1996.

State policymakers need to understand four provisions in Section 254 of the federal law: 1. the Universal Service Principles (See Box V-7); 2. the priority given to ensure that schools, health-care providers, and libraries have access to advanced telecommunication services; 3. the provision to ensure that the rates for "interexchange telecommunications services to subscribers in rural and high-cost areas shall be no higher than the rates charged by each such provider to its subscribers in urban areas"; and 4. the provision that allows state authority to preserve and advance universal service provided that state actions "do not rely on or burden federal universal-service support mechanisms."[29]

Box V-7 Section 254(b) Universal-Service Principles

The joint board and the commission shall base policies for the preservation and advancement of universal service on the following principles:

(1) **Quality and Rates.** Quality services should be available at just, reasonable, and affordable rates.

(2) **Access to Advanced Services.** Access to advanced telecommunications and information services should be provided in all regions of the nation.

(3) **Access in Rural and High-cost Areas.** Consumers in all regions of the nation, including low-income consumers and those in rural, insular, and high-cost areas, should have access to telecommunications and information services, including interexchange services and advanced telecommunications and information services, that are reasonably comparable to those services provided in urban areas and that are available at rates that are reasonably comparable to rates charged for similar services in urban areas.

(4) **Equitable and Nondiscriminatory Contributions.** All providers of telecommunications services should make an equitable and nondiscriminatory contribution to the preservation and advancement of universal service.

(5) **Specific and Predictable Support Mechanisms.** There should be specific, predictable and sufficient federal and state mechanisms to preserve and advance universal service.

(6) **Access to Advanced Telecommunications Services for Schools, Health Care, and Libraries.** Elementary and secondary schools and classrooms, health care providers, and libraries should have access to advanced telecommunications services as described in subsection (h).

(7) **Additional Principles.** Such other principles as the joint board and the commission determine are necessary and appropriate for the protection of the public interest, convenience, and necessity and are consistent with this Act.

---

[29] Section 254(k) is important to state regulators. It directs the FCC and state commissions not to force universal service to bear "more than a reasonable share" of joint and common costs. See also footnote 34.

The joint board and the FCC have the unenviable task of trying to implement universal principles in the context of the overriding philosophy to promote competition in other sections of the Telecommunications Act. The decision rule is clearly stated in Section 254(c)(1):

> The Joint Board in recommending and the Commission in establishing, the definition of the services that are supported by Federal universal-service support mechanisms shall consider the extent to which such telecommunications services:
>
> (A) are essential to education, public health, or public safety;
> (B) have, through the operation of market choices by customers, been subscribed to by a substantial majority of residential customers;
> (C) are being deployed in public telecommunications networks by telecommunications carriers; and
> (D) are consistent with the public interest, convenience, and necessity.

It is difficult to speculate about the universal-service support mechanisms that the FCC will adopt in the spring of 1997. Given the uncertainty, the immediate challenge to state policymakers becomes even more vexatious. One might assume that current federal support programs—USF, Lifeline assistance, Link-Up America, and TRS—will continue and possibly be enhanced in some way. But note carefully the first two principles of Section 254(b), which now define what is meant by universal service: "Quality services should be available at just, reasonable, and affordable rates" and "Access to advanced...services should be provided to all regions of the Nation."

Will current support programs be adequate to meet these universal-service standards? If not, what kind of federal support program would be sufficient? These speculations are important to state policymakers, because the transition toward competition in local telephony could create a compelling argument for establishing a state universal-service fund to complement federal support programs.

Equally vexing for state commissions is the matter of granting special rates for schools, health-care providers, and libraries. Companies must provide advanced services to health-care providers in rural areas "at rates that are reasonably comparable to rates charged for similar services in urban areas of the State." The state would credit the difference in rates, if any, as part of a company's service obligation in the universal-service program. The provision that discounts advanced services to schools and libraries will rest with the state commission "with respect to intrastate services" and must be "appropriate and necessary to ensure affordable access to and use of such services by such entities."

The state commission has the responsibility to designate intrastate eligible telecommunications carriers (ETC); these are common carriers of services included in the federal universal support mechanisms. To date, only incumbent telephone companies serving high-cost areas have been eligible to receive assistance through universal-service funds. If found to be in the public interest, the state commission may designate more than one ETC in an area served by a rural telephone company, or in any other area it designates.

Many economists have noted the central conflict between promoting competition and the social objectives of universal service.[30] Theoretically, in a competitive environment, prices would be set by the market according to marginal cost (plus recovery of fixed investment). Not so in a regulated environment that seeks to promote universal service.

Section 254(g) serves as one example of this tension. The cost of providing long-distance is usually higher in rural areas than in urban areas (because of higher volumes and economies of scale). In a fully competitive world, companies would price services according to the marginal costs of providing them in different geographic locations. This will not happen, however, because Section 254(g) requires that "the rates charged by providers of interexchange telecommunications services to subscribers in rural and high-cost areas shall be no higher than the rates charged by each such provider to its subscribers in urban areas." *The statute has created a method of ensuring nationally geographically averaged toll rates* with the additional sentence:

> Such rules shall also require that a provider of interstate interexchange telecommunications services shall provide such services to its subscribers in each State at rates no higher than the rates charged to its subscribers in any other State.

Congress could have listened to dispassionate economists in considering this issue. They might have said that toll calls are usually discretionary expenditures, seldom made in response to emergencies, and, based on efficiency grounds, should be priced according to actual cost rather than being (nationally geographically) rate averaged. Nevertheless, when Congress adopted Section 254(g), it was endorsing the principle of universal service. Nationally geographically averaged toll rates provide affordable long-distance services to all Americans, regardless of their location, regardless of the high costs associated with providing long-distance services. Recall two arguments made for universal service: all households having access to basic services (including long-distance services) at reasonable rates is a *merit* good; and ensuring that more people are connected to the network does provide positive benefits to everyone else connected to the publicly-switched network.

Governors and other state policymakers may appreciate the political choice that Congress made on this issue. By promoting universal service through nationally

---

[30] Milton Mueller (1995) observes (227): "There is something a bit ridiculous about a policy regime that tries to undermine subsidies with one hand (by promoting competition) and save them with the other."

geographically averaged toll rates, it accepted an implicit cross-subsidy[31] and rejected unconstrained price competition that would have saved money for urban consumers.[32] As will be discussed below, state policymakers soon face similar tough choices between universal service and price competition as state rate structures are rebalanced due to the emergence of competitive forces.

STATE UNIVERSAL-SERVICE FUNDS

Several states already have universal-service funds. According to a recent report by the National Conference of State Legislatures, twelve states during 1994 and 1995 enacted provisions to ensure universal-service access, usually by requiring all telecommunication providers to contribute to a universal-service fund.[33] The Telecommunications Act of 1996 anticipated that many states without them would create their own programs.

Section 254(f) states: "A State may adopt regulations not inconsistent with the Commission's rules to preserve and advance universal service." All telecommunications carriers that provide intrastate services shall contribute, on an equitable and nondiscriminatory basis, in a manner determined by the state to preserve and advance universal service. The statute also enables states to adopt additional definitions and standards for universal service as long as the state regulations identify "specific, predictable and sufficient mechanisms" and "do not rely on or burden Federal universal-service support mechanisms." (See Box V-8.)

Among the telecommunications issues confronting state policymakers, this one is at the top of the chart. The FCC will define universal service and federal support mechanisms by the spring of 1997, although the joint board's report on November 8, 1996 is likely to reveal the general approach on these issues. As mentioned, states have the authority to adopt universal support programs consistent with the FCC's rules. Thus, a state may create a universal-service program to meet its own definitions and standards. Some states may wish to establish a higher standard of universal service than the federal one. Other states may have special needs that can be met through specific universal-service programs. States with unique demographics or terrain may conclude that federal support mechanisms simply leave pressing needs unmet. State universal-

---

[31] Allowing competition to price long distance according to actual cost would have increased the explicit subsidies directed to the eligible telecommunications carriers serving rural and high-cost areas. As Robert Kelley of Guam patiently explained to the author, Section 254(b) of the federal legislation establishes "access in rural and high cost areas" to services including long-distance services at rates "that are reasonably comparable to those services provided in urban areas" as one of the universal-service principles. To achieve that universal-service goal, explicit subsidies of substantial sums would have to be provided to all eligible telecommunications carriers providing long-distance services to customers in higher-than-average-cost areas. Whether implicit subsidies (via rate averaging) or explicit subsidies (to targeted populations) are used, the ratepayers pay ultimately for the costs of meeting society's universal-service objectives.

[32] Pricing policy based on geographic averaging instead of actual cost pricing is a substantial cross-subsidy. A study by the Telecommunications Industries Analysis Project estimated that the effect of shifting from a geographic averaging basis for local and toll calls to full cost would lower the bills of the average urban customer by $77 annually while raising the rural customer's bill by $316 annually. See Carol Weinhaus et al, "What Is the Price of Universal Service? Impact of Deaveraging Nationwide Urban/Rural Rates" (Presentation to NARUC, July 26, 1993).

[33] Laurie Itkin and Elizabeth McLaughlin-Krile, "State Telecommunications Reform Legislation Authorizing Local Competition Enacted During 1994 and 1995" (NCSL, Washington, D.C., 1995). According to this September survey, the following states enacted legislation in 1994 and 1995 relating to universal service: Colorado, Connecticut, Florida, Georgia, Hawaii, Iowa, Minnesota, North Carolina, Tennessee, Texas, Wisconsin, and Wyoming.

Box V-8 Section 254(f) State Authority

A state may adopt regulations not inconsistent with the commission's rules to preserve and advance universal service. Every telecommunications carrier that provides intrastate telecommunications services shall contribute, on an equitable and nondiscriminatory basis, in a manner determined by the state to the preservation and advancement of universal service in that state. A state may adopt regulations to provide for additional definitions and standards to preserve and advance universal service within that state only to the extent that such regulations adopt additional specific, predictable, and sufficient mechanisms to support such definitions or standards that do not rely on or burden federal universal service support mechanisms.

service funds could provide assistance to supplement federal support mechanisms to meet these service needs.

The last sentence of this provision also merits close attention. It appears to constrain states slightly in their efforts to preserve and enhance universal-service objectives. Note that authority is granted to states "only to the extent that such regulations adopt additional specific, predictable, and sufficient mechanisms" and to the extent they "do not rely on or burden Federal universal-service support mechanisms." This sentence appears to protect the federal support mechanisms from being overtaxed by state actions. Which state actions might be considered burdensome to federal universal-service support mechanisms? The answer is likely to be determined through trial and error.

Hence, the constraint on state universal-service programs may be rather modest. It is not likely to be an economic constraint, because the volume of intrastate calls in any state would generate substantial revenue even at a very small charge per call. (Alternatively, a surcharge of a few percent on monthly bills would generate substantial resources). *The constraint is largely a political one: How much would state policymakers want to charge all consumers of local and intrastate telephone services to achieve universal-service objectives?*

State policymakers might be tempted to wait until the FCC rules on universal-service standards and programs in the spring of 1997 before assessing the requirements for a state universal-service fund. The reason this may become a pressing concern for Governors and state legislatures is that competition in local loop may well force a major price restructuring, which may then affect the affordability of essential telephone services.

COMPETITIVE PRICING OF LOCAL TELEPHONE SERVICES

The intent of the Telecommunications Act of 1996 was to promote competition in the telephone and cable industries. New competitors will enter new markets. Local telephone companies, after meeting the FCC's test for providing a level playing field for prospective competitors, will provide long-distance services. Long-distance companies will seek entry to many local markets. Cable-TV systems will invest heavily in modern switches and equipment to provide telephone services.

Introducing competition in local telephony represents major threats to local telephone companies as well as opportunities for consumers. Some day consumers will be able to choose among telephone providers and perhaps enjoy the benefits of lower prices and better services.

From a public policy perspective, there is just one likely short-term threat to incumbent exchange carriers: that new entrants will capture some of the high-margin business in local services and leave incumbent carriers burdened with low-margin services and the high cost of basic infrastructure maintainence. Indeed, Crandall and Waverman make this point:

> Unfortunately, little attention is given to the fact that competition will immediately undercut the distorted rate structure erected by state regulatory officials. The RBOCs are in the difficult position of being forced to open up their local networks to competition without being allowed to reprice services immediately. If competition develops under these conditions, the RBOCs (and other local-exchange companies) will suffer an immediate loss of their high-margin business while being saddled with the nonremunerative services.[34]

Initially, the strongest competition will probably occur in discrete markets, such as large businesses and select urban areas, whose services have been priced above marginal costs. For a very long time, the cross-subsidies embedded in most state rate structures were justified as a strategy to promote universal service. Two cross-subsidies are significant: business rates are usually twice as high as residential rates (and much higher than the actual costs for business services). This cross-subsidy keeps residential rates affordable at the expense of businesses.[35] The other cross-subsidy results from rate averaging.

---

[34] Crandall and Waverman, *Talk is Cheap*, 217.

[35] For an important dissenting view, see David Gabel, "Pricing Voice Telephony Services: Who is subsidizing whom?" *Telecommunications Policy*, Vol. 19, No. 6 (1995): 453-464. From Gabel's abstract:

> Local exchange companies (LECs) have argued that, because of entry, they will no longer be able to subsidize residential exchange service. The available economic data show that residential service is not subsidized. This finding casts doubt over the need for entrants to contribute to a universal service fund that would be used to subsidize residential service. Since 1984 there has been a radical decline in the cost of providing voice services. The failure of the LECs to adjust their rates to reflect the cost decline explains in part why competitive access providers have entered the market.

Gabel also concludes (454): "The evidence shows that residential exchange service is priced above its relevant incremental costs and is, therefore, not subsidized. Many state regulatory commissions have considered this issue and reached the same conclusion."

Paying for the local loop represents a major policy issue for state commissions, in particular, how the costs of maintaining it will be shared. Individual services can be priced based on marginal cost (using a formula such as total service, long-run

This definition explains:

Rate Averaging: When local telephone companies file tariffs with the state public utilities commission they must retain the same rate for residences located throughout large geographic areas. Therefore, customers living many miles from switching offices pay the same price for service as customers next door. This policy reallocates the actual costs across all consumers and helps to lower the costs of service for customers living in the more remote areas.[36]

A possible sequence of events might be as follows: first, the actual cost of serving business and urban consumers is below current rates; second, aggressive competition begins in these selected markets and erodes the basis for rate averaging; third, the local carriers lose revenue from price competition and may be forced to revisit the rates they charge for all other customers. If the prices for businesses and urban markets are driven down by robust competition, then—according to this logic—the incumbent local exchange carrier may be forced to recoup lost revenues by raising rates for all other customers.

Many analysts anticipate that rates will be fundamentally restructured as a result of competition in local and intrastate services. Consumer advocates fear that residential rates will rise as business rates fall. Rural advocates fear that pricing schedules tied to actual cost will dramatically increase rates for phone service in high-cost areas. Here is one assessment of the policy challenge posed by competition in the local loop:

The current system of affordable and widely adopted telephone service is based on rate averaging and cross-subsidies among routes, users, and locations. Competing networks undermine this support system because they are able to undercut the incumbent's prices in routes and services that are generating the surpluses, still benefiting from access to the areas controlled by the incumbent. This kind of

---

incremental cost [TSLRIC]), but how much of the cost should be included in essential services, and how much from all other services including toll calls?

This issue is so contentious that Section 254(k) of the Telecommunications Act directed the FCC and the state commissions not to force universal service to bear "more than a reasonable share" of joint and common costs. Some analysts argue that because all services use the same basic equipment and local exchange network, all services should contribute. Local exchange carriers (LECs), however, are concerned that their revenues cover their extensive fixed investment as well as current operational expenses. They argue that subsidies are needed to maintain access to voice services at affordable rates.

Long-distance companies, however, are not fond of paying access charges to the LECs to use the local loop to complete toll calls. They contend that access charges are many times higher than the actual cost of completing toll calls.

Consumer advocates, for their part, contend that costs for the local loop should be recovered from all services, not just from local exchange services. For example, if the local loop is considered a "joint and common cost" (shared by toll calls and all other services), the actual cost of local exchange services need not be subsidized by other revenue sources. This interpretation has been expressed in recent rulings by state commissions in Colorado, New Hampshire, Florida, Pennsylvania, and Kentucky, as cited in Gabel.

[36] As quoted in "Special Report on Telecommunications," No. 47, NADO News, Vol. 17, No. 34 (National Association of Development Organizations, Washington, D.C., August 25, 1995). Ironically, at the time this was written, U S West was filing for a rate increase in Washington State that included requesting a higher rate for rural customers, due to the higher cost of service, than for urban customers. See footnote 39.

"cream-skimming competition" will inexorably lead to unbundling of the routes and services of the public network and a deaveraging of the rates associated with each service component. As this happens, many end users, forced to bear the "full cost" of their particular network components, will not be able to afford it.[37]

If conventional wisdom is valid, state regulators will not have an easy time navigating between the shoals of emerging competition and the rocks of universal-service goals. The National Regulatory Research Institute, the research arm of NARUC, uses a similar metaphor: "Regulators are like the captain of a ship with a universal service engine propelling the ship in one direction, while a competition engine pushes the ship in another direction."[38]

A report of the Governor's Telecommunications Policy Coordination Task Force in Washington State, released in April 1996, includes a good summary of the policy challenge ahead. In the section on recommendations, "Review current telecommunications subsidies to ensure competitive neutrality," this fine discussion appears:

A variety of subsidies have evolved with the telecommunications industry. Enhanced 911, the Telephone Relay Program for the hearing impaired, the Telephone Assistance Program for low-income residents, and universal-service pools are explicit subsidies. Others are implicit, such as the use of statewide average rates and toll access rates to even out the cost of service among customers. While some of these subsidies have helped provide essential public services and should continue in force, *other subsidies have been called into question by increasingly heated competition. It may no longer make sense for some ratepayers to defray the costs of providing services to other ratepayer groups. The WUTC needs to review these subsidies and determine whether these subsidies are being applied in a competitively neutral manner. The WUTC should report back to the Governor, Task Force and Legislature with recommendations for rationalizing or eliminating these subsidies.* [Author's emphasis][39]

---

[37] Milton Mueller (1995), 225. Mueller used the quoted paragraph to summarize "the conceptual framework that now dominates the policy debate over universal service," although the balance of the article criticizes that conventional analysis.

[38] As quoted in Christopher R. Conte, "Reaching for the Phone," *Governing*, July 1995, 32. Conte offers this advice: "It requires a painstaking inquiry into just who gets universal service subsidies and who pays for them-an inquiry that requires both wading through an accounting swamp and risking political storms."

[39] Governor's Telecommunications Policy Coordination Task Force, *Building The Road Ahead: Telecommunications Infrastructure in Washington State* (Department of Revenue, Olympia, Washington, April 29, 1996), 5-6. This report also includes a summary of a recent U S West rate case (Docket No. UT-950200), which has received some attention by industry analysts because the company had sought a higher rate for its rural customers. From this report (6) is the following excerpt: "WUTC determined the following:

    1. Residential rates are priced above cost....2. An average statewide rate is not inconsistent with a competitive market....Evidence in the case showed that it does cost more to service rural areas, however, neither the cost difference nor the level of competition were significant enough to justify a rate differential....3. Other services (toll and business) do not subsidize residential service....U S West was ordered by the Commission to substantially lower business, toll and toll access rates."

U S West has appealed the order in court.

Allen Hammond, a New York Law School professor, is quoted in *Governing* as saying: "The universal-service debate is transplanting the debate over health and welfare to telecommunications and it has a good chance of becoming just as fractious." Consider these anecdotes as well:

- Many telecommunication firms support the idea of explicit fees that are paid by all service providers to a universal-service fund, but there is great debate over who should get these subsidies and why. Andrew Lipman of MFS Communications, a competitive access provider in several large cities, offers this perspective: "No other commodity or service offered in the marketplace is sold at subsidized prices based solely on geography—even those that are most essential to human life, such as food, health care, electricity, or gasoline."

- Despite the trend of creating state universal-service funds, the public sometimes rejects explicit subsidies. A case in point: in 1991 the Illinois state legislature rescinded a 15-cent monthly surcharge approved by the Illinois Commerce Commission to help reduce the cost of providing telephone services to low-income families.

- Universal-service advocates are committed to keeping local basic rates low and naturally argue that rate increases will prevent low-income households from maintaining phone service. A counter-intuitive case in point: Massachusetts regulators approved a local rate increase from $2.50 per month to $10.00 per month (and lower intrastate toll rates), and yet the chair of the Department of Public Utilities claims that "the effect on universal service has been nil."[40]

A TARGETED APPROACH TO UNIVERSAL SERVICE

For most of the century, the United States aspired to achieve Plain Old Telephone Service (POTS) at affordable rates as the standard for universal access. Now many contend that single-line "touch tone" should be provided as part of the basic, affordable service. At least two states—Wisconsin and Vermont—have defined basic services that include: affordable rates, touch-tone dialing, access to long-distance carriers, and 911 emergency services. "Advanced services," according to Wisconsin law, "are also supposed to be accessible in some way, but not necessarily to every home or subsidized as heavily as basic services."[41] Vermont's broad universal-service fund is financed by a 1.25 percent surcharge on customers' bills and collected by all service providers. It generates financial support for a Lifeline program, a state high-cost fund, telecom relay service, and a statewide E-911 system to be completed by July 1997.[42] (See Box V-9.)

---

[40] Conte, "Reaching for the Phone," 36-7. An economist might ask: What is the price elasticity of demand?

[41] Conte, 36.

[42] *NARUC Report on the Status of Competition in Intrastate Telecommunications* (National Association of Regulatory Utility Commissioners, Washington, D.C., October 4, 1995), 156.

A targeted approach to universal service would include a definition of basic, affordable service and focus resources on two discrete populations: low-income households and customers in high-cost areas. Expanded Lifeline programs would increase the number of low-income households that have telephones. This group has the lowest penetration rates, partly because of the cost of basic service. Also, these households have trouble controlling telephone use and often lose their phone service because they are unable to pay long-distance charges.

One response to this problem is to require the local telephone company to provide only local service, at the request of a low-income household. This procedure, in effect, blocks long-distance calls, but allows local service to continue. Another option is to allow the household to choose a predetermined amount for long-distance calling each month, beyond which toll calls are blocked.

Some states allow telephone companies to charge high installation fees or require large deposits for households that have lost service because of outstanding charges. A policy of blocking or limiting long-distance calls and lowering installation charges might increase the number of low-income households with local telephone services, including for emergencies. Pennsylvania is one state that prevents phones from being disconnected for failure to pay toll call charges.

In November 1994, the Ohio PUC approved a settlement in an Ameritech rate case that provides some guidance on this issue. The settlement included a universal-service assistance (USA) program that assured low-income households of basic telephone service without having to pay either a deposit or connection charge. Participants in this program may request free toll restriction, including blocking 900 and 976 toll calls. The limitations on participants are reasonable and modest: they cannot have deluxe or custom calling services; nor can they have other telephones in their households.[43]

Another targeted approach relates to the geographic service areas for most rural areas. Rural consumers value being able to call family and friends in the next town as part of basic service, but a disproportionate number of their toll calls are made to reach services only available in the nearest large town. If the old concept of value-of-service pricing is applied, rural basic rates would be very low because the geographic service area is so limited. State commissions have experimented with alternative and expanded geographic service areas that enable rural customers to access nearby towns and villages as part of their basic rates and not as toll calls. (By way of comparison, the value of service for urban consumers is very high since the basic rate provides access to so many services.)

Within the past decade, the Colorado PUC ordered a plan for county-wide extended area service (EAS); the Georgia PUC ordered a county seat plan; the Louisiana commission established a local option service "that caps rates on toll calls made within twenty-two miles of a parish (county) calling area"; and in 1990 the Washington Utilities and Transportation Commission "adopted rules to identify and expand local calling areas where customers must rely excessively on toll service to meet basic calling needs."[44]

STATE VIRTUAL VOUCHERS

California has been one of the leading states in providing Lifeline assistance and direct subsidies to small companies in high-cost, rural areas to ensure universal-service objectives. The California PUC has also broken new ground in thinking about alternative ways to achieve universal-service goals. It may be the first state PUC to implement the idea of a virtual voucher (which Congress rejected in consideration of the federal legislation) if its proposal is enacted by the state legislature. (See Box V-10.)

NECA, on behalf of the FCC, distributes approximately $737 million in high-cost funds to keep the cost of basic services affordable for customers in high-cost areas. Cost

---

[43] Ellis Jacobs, "Expanding Low-Income Communities' Access to Telecommunications Technology," *Clearinghouse Review* (July 1995): 275. For more on this topic, consult with the National Consumer Law Center, Washington, D.C.

[44] Edwin B. Parker and Heather E. Hudson, with Don A. Dillman, Sharon Strover, and Frederick Williams, *Electronic Byways: State Policies for Rural Development Through Telecommunications* (Boulder, Colorado: Westview Press, 1992), 74-75. Here is their explanation:

> In major cities most telephone calls are local. Businesses can reach customers and suppliers elsewhere in the city with local calls. Residents can make appointments, call the school, talk with merchants, call government offices and otherwise conduct their personal business with local phone calls....In rural areas, however, a much higher percentage of calls for the identical purposes are long distance. Businesses in outlying areas are also at a disadvantage if their customers must make long distance toll calls to reach them.

> The appropriate, financially feasible response is EAS, a tariff that lets rural residents make unlimited calls within an extended area for a flat monthly rate. This policy helps reduce the disparities between rural and urban subscribers.

studies for defined areas determine eligibility for these funds. For some time, economists have criticized the idea of providing direct subsidies to the companies serving these high-cost areas because, they argue, it provides an insufficient incentive for them to improve operations and lower costs.

Box V-10 The California PUC Proposal for a High-cost Voucher Fund

In its proposal, the California PUC suggests that customers living in a designated high-cost area will receive a credit ("virtual voucher") on their bill to keep their rates affordable. If there is more than one local telephone company serving the high-cost area, consumers will receive a credit regardless of which telephone company they choose as their provider. The credit represents the difference between the cost of providing service to the consumer and the rate he or she pays. To receive the subsidy, a company must accept the obligation to serve all customers in an area. This mechanism is called "the high-cost voucher fund." The voucher mechanism under consideration is compatible whether the PUC uses an auction or cost study to determine subsidy amounts on an ongoing basis.

Source: "CPUC Report to Legislature on Maintaining Universal Service in Competitive Local Phone Market" (California Public Utility Commission [R.95-01-020, I.95-01-021], December 20, 1995).

A virtual voucher would provide compensation to any carrier that provides services to a customer in a high-cost area. The amount of the voucher would be calculated using a methodology similar to current small-area cost studies. The voucher would go directly to the carrier chosen by the customer and would be valued at the difference between the actual cost of providing service and an average price set by the PUC. For example, a customer living in a high-cost area where the actual cost of basic service is $50 would chose any carrier; if the average monthly cost of basic service in the state was $25, then the chosen carrier would receive the difference ($25 in this example) as a voucher from the state universal fund.

In a report to the state legislature, the California PUC explains the current policy as well as the rationale for adopting a "high-cost voucher fund":

> In areas that are expensive to serve, rates have been kept low in three ways. First, the California High-Cost Fund (CHCF) reduces rates for customers of small telephone companies by providing funds to some rural high-cost companies. All telephone customers currently contribute to the CHCF through a small charge on their monthly telephone bill. Second, by requiring large telephone companies to

charge a single rate for basic service within their territory, rates are kept at reasonable levels in high-cost areas. Third, local exchange carriers charge access and toll rates which are priced above cost; these revenues may enable basic service to be priced below cost. These three mechanisms are only available to existing local exchange carriers.

In a competitive environment, prices for services which provide revenue, like toll, will gradually be driven down. In addition, competitors will enter high-revenue, low-cost areas, putting pressure on large carriers to offer different rates in different areas. With local exchange competition, the Commission must develop a funding mechanism which targets high-cost areas throughout California, not specific telephone companies. This funding should be competitively neutral and available to all companies that provide basic service within the high-cost area.[45]

There are substantial advantages, at least in theory, to the idea of using a virtual-voucher system instead of direct subsidies to maintain small companies in high-cost areas. The California PUC and other states face a major challenge in their efforts to design and implement such a system. The voucher idea also may attract prospective carriers that want to provide "one-stop shopping" (i.e., one bill for all telephone services including long-distance). Governors and state legislators should carefully consider this innovative approach to universal service, which has the distinct advantage of providing greater consumer choice.[46]

AN EXPANSIVE DEFINITION OF UNIVERSAL SERVICE

An alternative approach to universal service would be to create a state definition and standard higher than that articulated in the federal law or implemented by the FCC. In recent years, the political debate has drawn attention to the "information-haves" and "information-have-nots."[47] Most states will want advanced telecommunications services, including information services, to be available to all consumers. The semantics are

---

[45] "CPUC Report to Legislature on Maintaining Universal Service in Competitive Local Phone Market" (California Public Utility Commission [R.95-01-020, I.95-01-021], December 20, 1996). For more on the virtual voucher idea, see "Defining and Funding Basic Universal Service: A Proposal of MCI Communications Corporation" (July 1994).

[46] Under the Telecommunications Act of 1996, customers in high-cost areas could have a choice of a provider if the state commission approved another company as an eligible telecommunications carrier. One doubts that most state regulators would be eager to approve another company as an ETC, thereby becoming eligible to receive universal-service subsidies, for fear that customers and revenue would be lost to the incumbent rural company. For more on this, see Section 251(f).

[47] Frequently cited is Vice President Al Gore's speech on January 11, 1994:

> As the information infrastructure expands in breadth and depth, so too will our understanding of the services that are deemed essential. This is not a matter of guaranteeing access to play video games. It is a matter of guaranteeing access to essential services. We cannot tolerate nor in the long run can this nation afford a society in which some children become fully educated and others do not; in which some adults have access to training and lifetime education, and others do not. Nor can we permit geographic location to determine whether the information highway passes by your door.

According to the "Current Population Survey: Computer Use in the United States" (U.S. Bureau of the Census, October 1993): Seventy-four percent of families making more than $75,000 own at least one computer; only 15 percent of families with incomes less than $20,000 own a computer.

important to the policy debate. Having access to advanced services, which are purchased at cost, is one policy option. Quite a different option is to include advanced services as part of a state's definition of universal service. Advocates of this non-incremental approach should be aware that the social cost of doing so may be extraordinarily high. (See Box V-11)

Many public advocates argue that advanced telecommunications services should be included in the definition of universal service. For example, a coalition of public interest groups petitioned the FCC to prevent telephone companies from excluding poorer neighborhoods from their video dialtone systems, essentially, alternative cable-TV services. The petitioner made this argument:

> Increasingly, information means economic, social and political power. If substantial segments of the population, particularly those of lower-income or minority status, are denied access to advanced networks, America will be divided into the technologically wealthy and a technologically disadvantaged underclass, and we will all suffer for it.[48]

---

[48] As quoted in Christopher R. Conte, "Reaching for the Phone," *Governing*, July 1995, 36. Here is the "Goal: Advanced Universal Service" adopted by the Alliance for Public Technology, Washington, D.C.:

> To make available as far as possible, to all people of the United States, regardless of race, color, national origin, income, residence in rural or urban area, or disability, high capacity two-way communications networks capable of enabling users to originate and receive affordable and accessible high quality, voice, data, graphics, video and other types of telecommunications services.

Although the rhetoric is impassioned, the cost of providing everyone with the capacity to send and receive voice, video, and data transmissions is astounding. According to the Telecommunications Industries Analysis Project at the University of Florida, the cost of creating such a switched, broadband network could be more than $400 billion.[49] The question that state policymakers must ask is: What will the public be willing to pay to provide advanced telecommunications services to those who cannot pay for them?

As shown in chapter four, consumer advocates consistently oppose major infrastructure investment to provide services for which demand has not been demonstrated, because ratepayers will get stuck with higher rates. Similarly, consumer groups have opposed mandating advanced telecommunications services as part of the definition of universal service because they fear that ratepayers will be burdened with the cost of providing two-way video services, which are of dubious social value and for which market demand is unproved. Daniel Pearl, writing in *The Wall Street Journal* quoted Bradley Stillman, legislative counsel of the Consumer Federation of America, "I don't want to be forced to pay for the interactive video games or movies on demand of my neighbor down the street." According to Pearl, "telephone companies promote a broad definition of universal service because it allows them to lay miles of fiber-optic wire at customers' expense. His group has the support of the powerful American Association of Retired Persons, which wants to ensure that rates for basic telephone service aren't raised to subsidize more speculative services."[50]

HARD QUESTIONS FOR STATE POLICYMAKERS

State regulators understand acutely that basic telephone services can be priced in roughly three ways: (a) by competitive markets (based on actual cost and including the recovery of fixed investments such as switches); (b) by rates determined by the commission that use implicit cross-subsidies or rate averaging; or (c) by rates that include explicit universal-service subsidies (which taxes all services to fund specific services for specific populations). *The price competition and rate rebalancing that will result from local competition will thrust these difficult policy choices before the Governors and state legislatures.* Below are some preliminary questions that Governors' policy advisors may wish to ask prior to encroaching legislative debates:

What is the social and economic value of providing universal access to basic telephone services? What constitutes basic services? Should direct subsidies be limited to low-income households and handicapped consumers? Should direct subsidies be provided to any company that serves high-cost areas to keep basic telephone services affordable for customers in those areas? (Note that if competitive markets set prices in high-cost areas, some customers will discontinue

---

[49] *Ibid.*

[50] Daniel Pearl, "Debate Over Universal Access Rights Will Shape Rules Governing the Future of Communications," *Wall Street Journal*, January 14, 1994, A12.

telephone service.) Will the public continue to support universal-service goals if, as a result of competition, cross-subsidies are slashed from the rate structure and are replaced by explicit subsidies for targeted populations? Will urban households and consumer advocates rebel at having to pay surcharges on their local phone bills to fund a state universal-service fund supplementing federal universal-service programs?

In the forthcoming debates on universal-service provisions and their inevitable tension with competition, state policymakers should think about these questions:

- How will the competition in telephone service alter the rate structure and affect the affordability of residential rates?
- If robust competition emerges in selective markets—for example, among business users or urban dwellers—what might be the impact of rate restructuring on remaining areas of the state, especially suburban and rural areas?
- If cross-subsidies are squeezed out of the rate structure because of robust competition, will the public continue to support universal service by paying surcharges and taxes for explicit subsidies to targeted populations?
- Should the definition of universal service evolve toward a higher standard of service as technology improves and the demand for advanced services increases?
- Should states create a definition of universal service higher than that articulated in the law and implemented by the FCC? Or should the states adopt programs that supplement federal support mechanisms to meet its definition of universal service?

The major telecommunications battle of the coming decade will be between establishing fair rules to promote competition and preserving universal-service goals. In the short term, the challenge for state policymakers will be how to ease the transition to rates that reflect the actual costs of telephone service, ensure access to basic telephone services, and promote fair competition. In most states, the PUCs will have the authority to resolve these contentious issues, within the parameters of the Telecommunications Act of 1996.

It is the state legislature, of course, that creates the state commission in the public interest, and defines, clarifies, and amends its statutory authority. Notwithstanding the fine performance of these commissions, broad policy issues often find their ways into Governors' offices and state legislative chambers. If they don't naturally flow to these locations, sometimes they are pushed. Because of the substantial business revenues at stake, one might expect that telecom providers will seek support for their positions in all three places: the PUC, state legislature, and Governors' offices. Governors may wish to frame the debate by developing a policy position on universal service and demonstrating leadership on these issues.

ANTICIPATING THE FUTURE

Johann Gutenberg's invention of movable type in 1453 has been widely acknowledged as the beginning of the modern era of social communications. Books became the medium that allowed information to be transmitted over distance, and they served to transform society. Social communication over distance, however, still required the physical transport of people or tangible objects, whether drawn, written, or printed.

The origins of telecommunications, as commonly defined, can be traced to early nineteenth-century inventions in the field of electricity. These enabled the development of other media for transmitting information. First came the telegraph, a product of several inventors including Samuel Morse, who wrote the code that made the invention practical. Soon afterward, experiments with sound inspired Alexander Graham Bell to invent the telephone. Theoretical work by James Clerk Maxwell on electromagnetic waves became the foundation for successful experiments using wireless radio to transmit sound waves as well as Morse signals.[1]

The subsequent history of telecommunications is almost anticlimactic compared to earlier inventions. At the beginning of this century, electric signals were used to send messages (telegraph) and sound (telephone) through wires. Even more astonishing, the air became the medium for transmitting wireless telegraph, now called radio. People could transmit information over distances instantaneously. To paraphrase Samuel Morse, "What, indeed, hath God wrought?"

Telecommunications have transformed modern economy and society, for good or ill, first through telephony, then broadcast radio, then television, and now through a convergence of technologies. Aided by the revolution in microelectronics, massive quantities of information—in the form of voice, pictures, data, and text—can be transmitted quickly and reliably through fiber-optic cable.[2] As suggested in Box VI-1, the rate of progress may be accelerating. Some suggest that digital radio (wireless) will soon provide the "on-ramp" to the information superhighway.

Using our rich past as a guide, the future holds both promise and uncertainty. This chapter reviews some of the most promising telecommunications technologies currently being developed. It speculates about the future and summarizes the major challenges to be faced by state policymakers.

---

[1] See Joel Mokyr, *The Lever of Riches: Technological Creativity and Economic Progress* (New York: Oxford University Press, 1990), 143-4.

[2] For a fascinating account of the microelectronic revolution, see George Gilder, *Microcosm* (New York: Simon & Schuster/Touchstone, 1989).

THE FUTURE IS NOW

Prior to passage of the Telecommunication Act of 1996, most states did not allow competition in local telephone exchanges. But in the increasing number of states that did, competitive access providers (CAP) grew rapidly to capture lucrative business customers.

In 1993, an estimated 41 percent of the revenues of local exchange carriers came from commercial customers. This is the preferred market of CAPs, which currently operate in 222 cities. CAPs target their switched and special access services to high-volume business customers. CAP investment in local networks was more than one billion dollars in 1993, according to one study. CAPs also are forming alliances with cable-television and long-distance companies to extend their networks. In short, CAPs are "cream-skimming"—draining off revenue from local exchange carriers, which have an obligation to serve all customers.[3]

Competitive access providers may be the most immediate threat to incumbent local exchange carriers, but they represent the tip of iceberg in terms of future competition. Here is the prognosis of three telecommunications experts:

- Gas and electric utilities will deploy optical fiber and wireless technologies to exploit their extensive rights of way, which reach virtually every home and office.

---

[3] Robert G. Harris, Gregory L. Rosston, and David J. Teece, "Competition in Local Telecommunications: Implications of Unbundling for Antitrust Policy" in *Toward a Competitive Telecommunications Industry* (Lawrence Erlbaum Associates, Mahwah, New Jersey, 1995), 70-1.

- Cable systems operators will deploy new digital technologies to significantly increase the capacity of cable systems, and enable two-way communications over these systems.
- Cellular personal communications services (PCS) carriers will deploy digital technologies that will dramatically increase capacity and reduce costs and prices so that cellular service will compete directly with wireline.
- Satellite-based communications services, including VSAT, DBS (direct broadcast satellite), and LEOS (low earth-orbiting satellites) will expand rapidly with digital technology.[4]

Facing the onslaught of competitive forces, it is small wonder that RBOCs want to enter other markets such as video programming and long-distance services. The potential for acquisitions, mergers, joint ventures, and strategic alliances between and among these technology firms is overwhelming. Some experts observe that "the revolution in telecommunications...is not just a story of escalating competition [but] also a story of complementarity and cooperation."[5]

Others write about the future in terms of a network among networks. Eli M. Noam argues that "the central institutions of future telecommunications will not be carriers but systems integrators that mix and match transmission segments, services, and equipment, using various carriers....The new issues will be those of integrating the emerging 'network of networks'"[6]

PROMISING TECHNOLOGIES

The GAO report on the Information Superhighway identifies five innovative technologies that will facilitate the delivery of many advanced capabilities on the information superhighway. They are: narrowband ISDN; advanced signaling and intelligent networks; B-ISDN; personal communication networks; and broadband in the local loop. They are described briefly below.[7]

The Narrowband ISDN. ISDN is an abbreviation for Integrated Services Digital Network. It is an end-to-end digital network that replaces the current analog connection to the central office switches. Because it provides transmission speeds of 144,000 bits per second or higher, ISDN will enable customers to send and receive different forms of information, including conventional voice, computer transmissions, and other high-speed transmissions. Although ISDN had implementation problems because of poor interoperability, the industry has adopted national standards to improve reliability. Some expect ISDN to be in broad use by the turn of the century, replacing many

---

[4] *Ibid.*, 68.

[5] *Ibid.*

[6] Eli M. Noam, "Beyond Telecommunications Liberalization: Past Performance, Present Hype, and Future Direction," *The New Information Infrastructure* (Twentieth Century Fund, New York, 1995), 31.

[7] This section draws heavily on "Appendix III: Description of Advanced Technologies," *Information Superhighway* GAO/AIMD-95-23 (General Accounting Office, Washington, D.C., January 1995).

analog connections in the local loop and providing users with faster, more extensive communications services.[8]

Advanced Signaling and Intelligent Networks. The telephone industry is developing common channeling signaling networks based on the Signaling System 7 (SS7) protocol. This protocol provides a packet-switched communications network that transports call control and signaling messages. An SS7 network is a dedicated high-speed data network, separate from existing voice or data communications networks. As such, it facilitates the development of advanced intelligent networks (AIN). In short, an AIN can be programmed to interrogate remote processors, databases, and mobile communications devices. The technology provides tremendous opportunities for greater customer control of advanced telecommunications services and provides the tools for the creation of virtual private networks.

B-ISDN Technologies. These technologies provide transmission speeds of up to 2,488 mbps. They use Asynchronous Transfer Mode (ATM)/Synchronous Optical Network (SONET) optical fiber networks. SONET is the international standard for optical carrier networks, which operate at tremendous speed, many between 156 and 622 mbps. Future SONET circuits are expected to operate at up to 2,488 mbps (2.488 gbps). ATM standards are being defined by the industry, the Advanced Research Projects Agency, and the National Science Foundation. SONET, using ATM standards, will provide one of the high-speed transmission systems required by the information superhighway.

Personal Communications Networks. Some envision a ubiquitous, tetherless meta-network that integrates cellular and satellite communications systems, supplemented by wireline networks. The PCN has two distinctions: it would provide person-to-person mobility, since it would use cellular technologies; and it would integrate analog and digital communications by using all existing networks, including cellular systems, mobile satellite systems, paging, and local area networks. The boldest version of PCN integrates digital wireless communications and the B-ISDN networks, and combines both with space-based cellular type services.

Broadband in the Local Loop. The "last mile" refers to the distance between the home and the central office switch. Current technology and equipment limit the capacity of the last mile, which prevents customers from using advanced telecommunications services and broadband transmissions such as video programming. The telephone industry is developing several technologies to cope with this bottleneck in the local loop, the so-called "on-ramp to the information superhighway." One approach is the asymmetrical digital subscriber line, which uses a single copper wire to transmit both video and telephone signals. Fiber-to-the-curb architecture would provide switched digital services

---

[8] "ISDN Basic Service is opening up the world of high-speed digital communications to thousands of students, consultants, home-based business people and telecommuters who could never have afforded it before. ISDN lets you talk, receive and send data, and transmit video or images all on one line-at the same time. And because it transmits information digitally, it's extremely accurate. It's also far faster than a modem and traditional telephone line. ISDN Basic provides two 64,000 bit-per-second (bps) channels to carry communications. They can be bundled to transmit at 128,000 bps." Quoted from a bill insert sent by NYNEX.

to optical network units serving multiple residences. Optical network units would convert optical signals to electrical impulses and distribute them to individual homes. In addition, new or rebuilt cable systems use a hybrid fiber optics/coaxial cable architecture (called fiber trunk feeder), which is capable of supporting all digital, fully switched ATM/SONET services. These are just two of the fiber-to-the-curb architectures that could be developed to deliver broadband services to subscribers.

Understanding what the public wants in broadband services is at least as important to telecommunications providers as overcoming the technological challenges of building the on-ramp to the information superhighway.

PREPARING FOR TELEWARS IN THE STATES

Along with contentious battles over interconnection, unbundling, and resale rates will come rapid changes in industry structure. State policymakers—burdened with establishing fair rules that allow local competition while preserving universal-service goals—can take some comfort from the challenges that face industry leaders in this turbulent time. The millions of dollars invested in promising technologies pale compared to the billions of dollars of private-sector resources wagered on acquisitions, mergers, and alliances. In hindsight, some of these bet-the-company deals will look brilliant; many will not. But in any event, the leaders of telecommunications firms have access to tremendous resources and information with which to make their corporate decisions.

Two important observations flow from this summary. First, the wisdom of corporate decision making will have a profound effect on the future development of telecommunications in this nation. Second, lobbyists and corporate executives will not be shy about communicating with state policymakers on issues that concern them, and state legislative sessions may become a forum for intensive lobbying efforts.

In an April 12, 1996 letter to its customers, AT&T attempted to explain the telecommunications reform bill and announced, "There's a marketing scramble on the horizon such as you've never seen. Competing companies from near and far—some familiar, some not—will approach you in the months ahead with offers claiming convenience, savings, and who knows what else." The analog of this public marketing campaign is the anticipated lobbying of state capitols for favorable treatment on all matters related to competition. These include the 14-point competitive checklist in Section 271, resale prices, interconnection agreements, and universal-service definitions. Continuing the analogy, AT&T's letter advises its customers: "It's important to understand that sweeping reforms will come, but not overnight. You'll need to carefully consider your choices." So too, Governors and other state policymakers will need to consider their choices if, as expected, telecommunications issues come to dominate the state policy agenda.

To help prepare for state telewars, here are a few possible strategies the telecommunications industry might adopt:

- Aggressive marketing to customers and state procurement agencies.
- Multiple alliances among firms to provide different products and services (especially during this experimental period).
- Rapid deployment into wholesale/retail arrangements to establish a high-profile presence in the most lucrative markets, which might be called "quick but shallow" competition.
- A deliberate, artfully designed strategy to build selected facilities, which will add to network capacity and form the basis of "real and sustainable competition."
- The establishment of RBOC subsidiaries that offer one-stop shopping to the public by combining long-distance and local services. The Rochester/Frontier model, approved by the New York PSC, is the precedent for this approach. Ameritech sought regulatory approval of a similar approach in 1995.[9]

QUESTIONING THE CONVENTIONAL WISDOM

One view about telecommunications ten years from now is as follows. Four or five major telecommunications giants compete aggressively on price and service in most markets and in every form of telecommunication—local and long distance voice, data, video, and so on.[10] The role of government is to ensure that networks interconnect and systems are interoperable; that fair rules are enforced; and that neither public nor private-sector actions constitute barriers to entry.

At the household level, people own their telephone numbers and often carry hand-held phones that can send and receive voice and data. To supplement federal universal service programs, all states provide assistance to ensure that all households have basic services. Most states, as part of their universal-service programs, continue to provide direct subsidies to companies serving high-cost areas. A few states use "virtual vouchers" to allow all customers—regardless of location—to choose their companies. Most states are content to allow the market to determine advanced telecommunications services. Some progress is made toward achieving tax equity for the telecommunications industry and privacy protection for consumers.

Although this view of the future is plausible, every assumption is suspect. No one can predict the future development of promising technologies, nor can they know whether economies of scale will continue in telephony, how successful cable systems

---

[9] See Crandall and Waverman, *Talk is Cheap*, 47.

[10] An excellent source of conventional wisdom is the *New York Times*. Read everything written by Edmund L. Andrews. For example, in "From Communications Chaos, Order?" June 16, 1995, Andrews projected these long-term (five- to ten-year) effects from national deregulation of the telecommunications industry:

Cable TV Rates May Eventually Fall in some areas as more cable monopolies face competition from phone companies and direct satellite broadcasters.

Local Phone Rates May Decline in Real Terms as more telephone monopolies are challenged by cable TV companies. Consumers in many markets may be offered one-stop shopping for local, long-distance and cable services by more than one company.

Some Areas Would Never Benefit because they are too small or expensive to attract a challenger to an entrenched local cable or phone company. Rates in those areas would remain high.

will be in providing local telephone services, whether personal communications networks will advance at an unprecedented rate, how Governors and state legislators will respond to political pressures, and so on. Consider three examples that demonstrate the inadequacies of conventional wisdom:

- When AT&T negotiated the consent decree with the Department of Justice, leading to the Modified Final Judgment (MFJ) in 1982, it eagerly sought to enter the computer business. It expected to achieve a wonderful synergy between telephony and computers, but *the synergy failed to develop*. At the end of 1995, AT&T announced it was splitting into three parts, like ancient Gaul, separating its long lines business from computer operations and telephone equipment manufacturing (now called Lucent Technologies).
- After the MFJ, the RBOCs and other telephone companies sought to repeal the prohibition on providing information services. The newspaper industry felt threatened by the prospect that LECs might provide information electronically. Although the courts removed this restriction in the fall of 1991, the LECs have been slow to compete. Firms that dominate the field include America Online, Compuserve, Prodigy, Delphi, a cluster of smaller operations, and the software giant, Microsoft. Some industry observers are surprised the LECs have fared so poorly, considering their inherent advantages and eagerness to develop services in a growing market.
- Similarly, the LECs have fought hard for permission to provide video programming in their own service areas, competing directly with cable television. The technology to do so has lagged, complications developed, and initial forays into this field have been stymied. (Perhaps the LECs have simply had a slow start. Pacific Telesis, NYNEX, and Bell Atlantic had invested $100 million in Tele-TV, a programming venture using wireless cable technology, by the spring of 1996 and still had not signed up a single viewer. Some executives were said to be impatient.)[11]

These examples should provide a sobering perspective on future developments in the industry. To frame some of these uncertainties, here are a few additional questions:

- Can the new ground rules for fair competition be sustained or will the incumbent exchange carriers act in a predatory fashion toward prospective competitors?
- Will wireless technologies develop so rapidly and cheaply that they can compete effectively against existing wireline networks?
- Will new (e.g., satellite, wireless, or cable) networks capture so much revenue from the publicly switched network that universal-service objectives are threatened?

---

[11] Mark Landler, "A Sticking-to-Their-Knitting Deal," *New York Times*, April 23, 1996, D8; and Edmund L. Andrews, "Why Fix Phones that Aren't Broken?" *New York Times*, December 24, 1995, E5.

- Will cyber-communications (specifically, electronic mail via the Internet) threaten the wireline networks? Will voice messages via the Internet be regulated in the future by the FCC?[12]
- Will the FCC, emboldened with markets, act to liberate the radio spectrum by auctioning its use?[13]
- Are there unforeseeable clouds on the horizon that state policymakers should consider during the transition to competition in telephony?

Below are three immediate challenges that Governors' policy advisors face as they navigate the turbulent seas of change.

TAX EQUITY

For most of this century, telephone companies were regulated monopolies. As such, they and other public utilities were convenient sources of revenue for state and local governments. Indeed, regulators generally allowed taxes on public utilities to be passed through to ratepayers. State and local taxes had little incidence on corporate profits, because regulators were using rate of return (not unlike a cost-plus approach) to set telephone and utility rates. This was a sweet deal for state and local administrators. Few companies protested very long or very hard, because most of the tax burden was simply passed along.

The era of local telephone companies as regulated monopolies is about to end, but has not ended quite yet. As competition begins, state governments will need to think about establishing alternative tax structures. (See Box VI-2.) Karl E. Case, economics professor at Wellesley College, has written an excellent monograph on the subject, *State and Local Tax Policy and the Telecommunications Industry*, published by CGPA in 1992 and addressing the current challenge for state policymakers. Here is Case's summary:

In the past two decades, changing technology and deregulation have blurred the boundaries of the telecommunications "industry," and firms face intense competition for both their traditional markets and newly emerging ones.

These changes create two problems for the states. First, tax administrators find it more difficult to determine which firms or parts of firms in the industry should be

---

[12] The March 6, 1996 issue of "Washington Watch," published by the National Exchange Carrier Association, included this item: "The American Carriers' Telecommunications Association (ACTA), which represents small long-distance companies, filed a petition with the FCC asking it to regulate rates for long-distance telephone calls over the Internet. ACTA proposed three steps for FCC action: issue a declaratory ruling asserting its authority to regulate; order companies to stop providing unregulated Internet phone services; and initiate a rulemaking on how such services should be regulated. According to the FCC, access to the Internet has been considered enhanced services, which are not subject to regulation under the agency's 1983 access charge order. ACTA estimated that computer calls can average 3.3 cents per minute, one-seventh of the average residential long-distance price." See the Washington Telecom Newswire (3/5/96) as the original source for this information.

[13] See Michael L. Katz, "Interview with an Umpire," in *The Emerging World of Wireless Communications* (Annual Review of the Institute for Information Studies, The Aspen Institute, Queenstown, Maryland, and Nortel North America, Nashville, Tennessee, 1996). See also Eli M. Noam, "The Airwaves as a Toll Road," *New York Times*, February 11, 1996.

taxed as "telecommunications providers." Second, because most of the firms in the industry no longer enjoy state-provided privileges and protection from competition, the rationale for special tax treatment is gone. States are finding that the industry is no longer complaisant. Faced with increasing competition from many quarters, firms in the industry are lobbying heavily for a "level playing field." They argue that special taxes are outdated and put them at a competitive disadvantage:

> Clearly, competition has become the single most important factor in the provision of telecommunications services. In response to this, all information movement and management companies have become enterprises no different in virtually all substantive respects from other types of service or product providers in today's markets. Under such circumstances it is not reasonable for traditional differentiated taxing schemes, based essentially upon factors incompatible with competition, to be continued. (AT&T, 1986)[14]

Box VI-2 Information Highway State and Local Tax Study Group Recommendations

Taxes applying only to transactions on the information highway, only to revenues earned by providers of services on the highway, or only to property of companies on the highway are inequitable because they bias investment away from the information highway infrastructure and raise the cost of telecommunications and information technologies relative to all other products and services, and they should be eliminated.

Tax policies that result in inequitable treatment among providers or functionally equivalent transactions or property of providers are anticompetitive and are obstacles to the achievement of a level playing field, and need to be modified.

Tax policies intended to encourage innovation and investment in the information infrastructure should include taxes, tax credits, and tax exemptions for taxpayers serving the information highway that are at least as favorable and comparable as the taxes, tax credits, and tax exemptions available to general taxpayers.

In short, the telecommunications industry should be taxed in the same manner and at the same level as other commercial and industrial businesses. Moreover, participants in the telecommunications industry should be taxed on an equivalent basis with one another. Taxes that discriminate against the industry or within the industry should be eliminated.

Source: "Supporting the Information Highway: A Framework for State and Local Taxation of Telecommunications and Information Services," *State Tax Notes* (Information Highway State and Local Tax Study Group, July 3, 1995).

---

[14] Karl E. Case, *State and Local Tax Policy and the Telecommunications Industry* (CGPA, Washington, D.C., 1992), 1.

Reforming state and local tax policies and procedures to achieve tax equity for the telecommunications industry is a challenge that cannot be understated. Two public policy problems are timing and reality. Although no time is a good time if a major shift in tax policy is not revenue-neutral, some have argued that tax reform should be advanced after robust competition develops in local telephone markets. In other words, moving from a regulated utility model of taxation to a competitive model before competition has been established simply provides a windfall to incumbent exchange carriers. A rival to the RBOCs might argue that premature action constitutes an unwarranted public gift to the regulated monopolies. Utility taxes on local monopolies should continue for now, runs the argument, and tax policy should be reformed for all firms operating in a neutral, fair, competitive environment.

Richard McHugh, an economist who has studied telecommunications taxes in several states, addresses this question: "should the differential treatment of LECs be maintained?"

> There is no absolutely right or wrong answer to this question, but the trends in the market put a higher weight on the side of the argument that the switch should be made. In...making these decisions, one must keep in mind that decisions on tax policy, particularly during an exercise in fundamental or basic tax reform, can be durable. Consequently, the decision should be made with an eye toward future developments, specifically whether the local exchange market will be more competitive over time than it is now.[15]

One problem in achieving equity is the long-standing practice whereby local governments assess and tax the property of telephone companies at a higher rate than other property. (Twenty-nine states use classification systems for assessing property, but even that approach may be subject to legal challenge in the future.) (See Box VI-3.) Ending this practice reduces the property tax revenue of local taxing jurisdictions and shifts tax burdens to all other taxpayers. Neither result will be popular. Local officials will protest the loss of property tax revenue, and local property owners may threaten to rebel.

Ohio is one of the first states to take steps toward tax equity for the telecommunications industry. Its experience may prove helpful to other states.[16] Ohio's approach is to compensate in part for the loss of property tax wealth during a transitional period. Utah, Georgia, Washington, and New Jersey have begun to study some of the state and local tax changes that must be made if, as expected, competition emerges in local telephony to replace the regulated utility model.

---

[15] Richard McHugh, "The Taxation of Telecommunications," in *Taxation and Economic Development: A Blueprint for Tax Reform in Ohio*, Roy Bahl, ed. (Columbus, Ohio: Battelle Press, 1996), 802.

[16] *Ibid.*

Box VI-3 MCI Challenges Ohio Property Tax

Ohio taxed tangible personal property of public utilities, including telephone companies, at 100 percent (today 88 percent) of its true value. Tangible personal property of resellers, however, was treated as general business property and taxed at only 31 percent (today 25 percent) of its true value. MCI sought to have the scheme invalidated on equal protection grounds. The court ruled that the scheme's discriminatory treatment was unconstitutional.

Source: "Supporting the Information Highway: A Framework for State and Local Taxation of Telecommunications and Information Services," *State Tax Notes* (July 3, 1995), footnote 26.

Most states have some form of educational funding formula that provides assistance to local school districts with some sensitivity to local need. In general, the state provides assistance in inverse proportion to community wealth, so the poorest school district receives far more in state aid than the richest district. This kind of funding formula mitigates efforts to equalize local property tax assessments of telephone company property, since reducing the local property wealth of a school district means that district would receive more in state educational aid. States may consider amending the state aid formula with a "hold harmless provision" to help local school districts achieve property tax equity during the transition period.

Policymakers will have to address many different aspects of state and local taxation as they strive to achieve tax equity for the telecommunications industry. Case observes in his earlier study that "No good economic logic now justifies singling out telecommunications firms for special taxation." He concludes:

The time has come for states to treat telecommunications firms as they do other businesses. First, the boundaries of the industry have become ambiguous and are likely to become more so. With new products and services and rapid technological change, it is difficult to distinguish telecommunications firms from firms in related industries, such as information management and data processing, which has made special taxes difficult to administer. Then, differential taxes on telecommunications firms are not neutral with respect to economic choices; they distort both consumption and investment decisions, which leads to misallocation of society's valuable resources. High telecommunications costs owing to high taxes may also retard a state's economic development. Finally, the burden of special state and local taxes on telecommunications firms appears to fall disproportionately on lower-income households.[17]

---

[17] Case, *State and Local Tax Policy and the Telecommunications Industry*, 14-16. Because of its importance to states, CGPA plans to commission and publish a monograph on this topic in the future.

A tax reform study group representing a cross-section of telephone, cable, wireless and information provisioning companies argued that "the telecommunications industry should be taxed in the same manner and at the same level as other commercial and industrial businesses." Equity should be sought within the industry as well. All providers "should be taxed on an equivalent basis with one another."[18] In addressing these issues, Governors and other state policymakers should heed these broad considerations:

Economic Development. Telecommunications firms make some investments that are location-neutral and discretionary. States with burdensome taxes on this industry will be less attractive locations for this investment. In addition, telecommunications services are a very important cost for businesses. States that are pursuing a strategy of economic competitiveness should not burden important business inputs, such as telecommunications, with onerous taxes.[19]

Equity across All Providers of Similar Services. Are cellular calls taxed the same as local calls? Are resellers taxed the same as local exchange carriers? Are all providers of the same service subject to the same taxes? And the correlative, are different services taxed differently? For example, are paging services taxed the same as cellular calls? Are long-distance calls taxed?[20]

Tax Incidence. Who bears the burden of telecommunications taxes? Does it fall disproportionately on lower-income households? What are fair tax burdens across incomes? Do state and local taxes apply to all telecommunications providers? As required in Section 253 of the federal legislation, are the requirements concerning compensation for use of public rights-of-way applied in a nondiscriminatory and competitively neutral basis? Are local franchise fees and taxes appropriate and applied to all other businesses?

Administrative Efficiency. Can taxes be easily and fairly collected? Is taxpayer compliance easy? Can tax evasion be minimized?[21]

---

[18] Information Highway State and Local Tax Study Group, "Supporting the Information Highway: A Framework for State and Local Taxation of Telecommunications and Information Services," *State Tax Notes* (July 3, 1995), 57.

[19] McHugh, "The Taxation of Telecommunications," offers this assessment (803):

> While for some types of investment, the location of the investment will not matter much for the quality of telecommunications services, for others it is clearly important. For example, the profitability of investment by the CAPs can be influenced by tax policy and the willingness of these firms to provide their services in one area versus another will be impacted. The decision by a "Baby Bell" on where to install fiber-optic lines next is another example of a decision in which the location of the investment can have important regional economic development implications.

[20] Of the forty-five states with sales taxes in 1995, forty taxed telephone services. Two states without general sales taxes imposed special taxes on telephone services. Of this group of forty-two states, thirty-six tax long distance services as well as local service (nineteen states tax intrastate and interstate long distance calls; seventeen states tax intrastate, but not interstate, long distance calls. See McHugh, "Taxation of the Telecommunications Industry in Georgia: Problems and a Prelude to Difficulties with other Public Utilities" (Unpublished paper, Policy Research Center/Georgia State University, Atlanta, Georgia, March 1996).

[21] *Ibid.* See also "Prop 13 Meets the Internet: How State and Local Government Finances are Becoming Road Kill on the Information Superhighway" (Center for Community Economic Research, Berkeley, California, http://garnet.berkeley.edu:3333/budget/tax-internet.html); and Catherine Yang, "New Tolls on the Info Highway?" *Business Week*, February 12, 1996. Finally, McHugh, in "The Telecommunications Industry in Utah and Its Implications for General Sales Taxation" (Policy Research Center/Georgia State University, January 15, 1996) offers this important observation (28):

> As use of 800 numbers and the Internet grows for the purposes of ordering tangible goods, greater shares of total purchases escape taxation. Mail order purchases are growing tremendously and, given several recent court rulings, are escaping any state sales taxation. The expansion of the sales tax base to include telecommunications services may, in the end, prove to be just an offset to this already eroding tax base.

Complicating this task is Section 601 of the Telecommunications Act of 1996, which preempts the local taxation of direct-to-home satellite service. Note, however, that (c) of this section does not *prevent taxation of a provider of direct-to-home satellite service by a State or to prevent a local taxing jurisdiction from receiving revenue derived from a tax or fee imposed and collected by a State.* [Author's emphasis]

PRIVACY

The quality and privacy of telephone calls using cellular systems are less reliable than calls made through wireline networks. It would appear that the advantages of mobility are greater than the disadvantages for many millions of users.[22] Yet, the public is concerned with the integrity of electronic communications and with a host of privacy issues as well: being able to block caller-ID, the right to keep a phone number from being disclosed, the right to avoid unwanted communications, and the concern about personal data being used or sold by telecommunication providers.

Privacy concerns include the possibility of accessing personal information in computer systems and broadly distributing it through the networks. Information privacy has been defined as "the claim of individuals to determine what information about them is disclosed to others and encompasses the collection, maintenance, and use of identifiable information."[23] Indeed, one expert observes that "privacy—both as it concerns the right to withhold oneself from others and the right to control one's communications—is both a personal and an economic concept."[24]

In any case, privacy is an important concept that must be balanced with other rights, including those in the First Amendment. Privacy need not be in conflict with the needs of law enforcement interests and other social objectives. Nevertheless, there are competing interests that states may be called upon to balance and clarify. In fact, states have been active in this area. (See Box VI-4.)

---

[22] The integrity of private communications is highly valued, of course. Consider the embarrassment of the British royal family when this private call, made on a cellular phone, was inadvertently intercepted (As quoted in James Gleick, "The Telephone Transformed—Into Almost Everything," *New York Times Magazine*, May 16, 1996, 28):

> CHARLES: "Oh, God. I'll just live inside your trousers or something. It would be much easier."

> CAMILLA: "What are you going to turn into, a pair of knickers?...Oh, darling, don't be silly. I'd suffer anything for you. That's love. It's the strength of love. Night night."

[23] Charles M. Firestone and Jorge Reina Schement, eds., *Toward an Information Bill of Rights & Responsibilities* (The Aspen Institute, Queenstown, Maryland, 1995), 137. For a discussion of the equally important topic of public access to information, see Ronald L. Plesser and Emilio W. Cividanes, *Serving Citizens in the Information Age: Access Principles for State and Local Government Information* (Information Industry Association, Washington, D.C., July 1993). Plesser and Cividanes cite the following from a 1822 letter by James Madison: "A popular government without popular information or the means of acquiring it, is but a Prologue to a Farce or a Tragedy or perhaps both. Knowledge will forever govern ignorance, and a people who mean to be their own Governors, must arm themselves with the power knowledge gives."

[24] Daniel Brenner, "What About Privacy in Universal Telephone Service?," in *Universal Telephone Service* (Institute for Information Studies, The Aspen Institute, Queenstown, Maryland, 1991), 47. Brenner suggests that subscribers should be asked their permission before personal data about them is used or sold by telephone companies; he also argues that people should be paid for the commercial use of information about them. See Alan Westin, *Privacy and Freedom* (New York: Atheneum, 1967), 324-25 for the argument that personal information "should be defined as a property right with all the restraints on interference by public or private authorities and due process guarantees that our law of property has been so skillful in devising."

Box VI-4 Constitutional Antecedents to Information Policy

Rights related to information and communication are not new in the American civic consciousness. In the Constitution, the founders promoted a view of government as a necessary collector, processor, and disseminator of information by instituting a decennial census (Article I, Section 2) and establishing a Congressional record (Article I, Section 5). The founders also paid special attention to the information infrastructure by granting Congress the power "to establish post offices and post roads" (Article I, Section 8). And they envisioned government as a supporter of new knowledge, as well as a protector of the intellectual property generated by scientists, inventors, and authors (Article I, Section 8).

The Bill of Rights
With the ratification of the First Amendment, eighteenth century Americans registered their anxieties that speech, association, and belief deserved special protection. When, in the Fourth Amendment, they underscored their concern for protecting the privacy of citizens, they singled out papers as meriting special protection from "unreasonable searches and seizures." It is, therefore, misleading to imply that any awareness of the importance of information rights and responsibilities stems from the arrival of an "information society."

Source: Firestone and Schement, *Toward an Information Bill of Rights & Responsibilities*, (The Aspen Institute, Washington, D.C., 1995), 2.

In response to the telemarketing campaigns of the 1980s, most states enacted statutes that prohibited harassment by telephone with the intent to annoy. By 1986 fifteen states had restrictions on the use of automatic dialer and recorded message players (ADRMPs). Because states did not have authority over interstate calls (which telemarketers used), Congress was compelled to enact the Telephone Consumer Protection Act of 1991. The act prohibits "any telephone call to any residential telephone line using an artificial or prerecorded voice to deliver a message without the prior express consent of the called party." Regrettably, there are two loopholes in the legislation: for charitable solicitations and political purposes. Relief is within reach: the act explicitly assures that "state laws requiring more restrictive intrastate behavior will not be preempted by the federal rules."[25]

---

[25] See Anne Wells Branscomb, *Who Owns Information? From Privacy to Public Access* (New York: Basic Books, 1994), 33-4.

In recent years, states have been active in addressing other privacy issues as well. Several states have modified caller-ID to protect those who needed their numbers blocked (e.g., victims of domestic violence and harassment, or certain categories of personnel, such as law enforcement officers, therapists, or psychiatrists). Pennsylvania blocked caller-ID, rejecting the service entirely as unconstitutional. Connecticut was one of the first states to pass a law that prohibits unsolicited facsimiles.

Anne Wells Branscomb, a communications and computer attorney, raises questions that are relevant to state policymakers as consumers appeal to the states to protect their privacy rights:

- Privacy versus privacy. The caller can achieve anonymity, but the called may choose to block all anonymous calls. Who should be required to pay for this privilege?
- Disclosure of information that is generated via a telephone number. The value of this information (called *transaction-generated information*, or TGI) is rather high. "Regulation of TGI is a legal nightmare waiting to happen. The more computer networks come on line, the more likely the public is to become aware of how their personal data is being gathered and used for business interests. With this awareness will come a greater demand for more personal autonomy over such information."
- Who owns the telephone number? "How telephone numbers are issued, used, protected, and marketed will come increasingly to the forefront of public debate, as users become increasingly agitated about their deployment."[26]

Guam has the answer to Branscomb's first question. It solved the privacy problem by providing all caller-ID services, including incoming call block, anonymous call block, per call block, incoming call accept, as a basic telephone service. The Guam Telephone Authority adopted this progressive measure in November 1994; it became effective on January 1, 1995. Other states and territories may wish to follow Guam's example, which protects the privacy of both callers and the called.[27]

In response to Branscomb's third point, Section 251(e) of the Telecommunications Act authorizes the FCC to create or designate "one or more impartial entities to administer telecommunications numbering and to make such numbers available on an equitable basis."[28] Indeed, the FCC has already chartered the North American Numbering Council to administer a neutral numbering system.

---

[26] *Ibid*, 47-52.

[27] The author appreciates the assistance of Robert F. Kelley, Jr., advisor to Guam Governor Carl T.C. Gutierrez, for information about this important precedent in privacy protection.

[28] The author thanks Tim Totman of GTE for citing this provision.

Box VI-5 From Privacy to Public Access

1. Secrecy: the right to prevent disclosure of information.
2. Privacy: the right to prevent unwelcome and unauthorized intrusions.
3. Confidentiality: the right to release information with restrictions, to prevent others from obtaining the information without the subject's consent.
4. Publicity: the right to release information into the public domain at a time and place of one's own choosing.
5. Commerciality: the right to sell information for fair value.
6. Accessibility: the right to obtain information.
7. Reciprocity: the right to receive value in exchange for value given.
8. Integrity: the right to control the accuracy and reliability of information.
9. Interoperability: the right to transparency in the transfer of information.
10. Responsibility: the duty to act responsibly.
11. Liability: the right to have grievances redressed.
12. Commonality: the right to share information in the public domain.
13. Equity: the right to have no wrong go unrighted.

Source: Anne Wells Branscomb, *Who Owns Information?* 181.

As mentioned in chapter four, Wisconsin has a statute that provides privacy protection to consumers who use advanced telecommunications services.[29] The law directed the Wisconsin Public Service Commission to "establish rules to protect the privacy of consumer medical records, Social Security numbers, and other personal information that travels across telephone and computer lines." Other states, no doubt, will follow Wisconsin in protecting the privacy of personal data. Indeed, Utah and California were the first to enact state statutes granting legal protection for digital signatures, i.e., specially coded messages that accompany electronically transmitted contracts and other legal documents.[30] Clearly, protecting individual privacy will become a major state responsibility in the future regulation of telecommunications and the administration of its internal data and communications networks.

---

[29] See *Privacy and the NII: Safeguarding Telecommunications-Related Personal Information* (National Telecommunications and Information Agency, U.S. Department of Commerce, October 1995). This excellent white paper observes that the dramatic growth of computer and telecommunications services poses a major threat to personal privacy. Existing privacy laws do not apply uniformly to various media—telephony, video, and other services—thus "concerns about safeguarding privacy will likely grow." Also note that the Clinton Administration has supported an encryption standard called the *clipper chip* that would allow federal law enforcement agencies, with sufficient cause, to monitor traffic on the information superhighway for evidence of wrongdoing. If enacted, a federal statute of this nature would probably preempt state statutes protecting individual privacy.

[30] See Alan Sherwood, "Digital Signature Law Inked," *Government Technology* (February 1996), 18-19; and David Bollier (rapporteur), *The Future of Electronic Commerce* (The Aspen Institute, Queenstown, Maryland, 1996).

COMPETITION, UNIVERSAL SERVICE, AND THE PUBLIC INTEREST

Not so many years ago, Governors had a limited role in charting state telecommunications policy. A primary responsibility for most was to appoint the members of the state public utility commission. (Fewer than a dozen states have publicly elected PUC members.) The PUCs set rates and tariffs, regulate telephone companies, and monitor basic telephone services. In addition to regulation, state governments have had two other policy levers for shaping telecommunications: state legislation that establishes boundaries for competition and taxation of the industry; and state procurement, since states are often the largest consumer of telecommunication services. In addition, many Governors convened special commissions or task forces to promote infrastructure investment, foster state economic development, develop public-private initiatives, and implement state policies to enhance telecommunications services.

The intensity of future policy challenges contrasts sharply with the placid image of the "good old days." Indeed, the PUCs were created to take rate requests and service monitoring out of the political arena. Consequently, many Governors and state legislators have chosen to avoid controversy over major rate cases. Setting basic policy, however, has been one of the primary responsibilities of state elected officials.

In the course of future state telewars, the most common question will be: *"Why mess with the best telephone system in the world?"*[31] The short answer is that introducing competition into regulated industries trucking in 1978, the airlines in the early 1980s, and now electric utilities stimulates innovation, increases efficiencies, and speeds the development of superior products and services. Evidence also exists that liberalizing long-distance services beginning in the 1980s resulted in lower consumer prices.[32]

Many observers point to the consumer benefits from competition in the long-distance telephone business. Vice President Al Gore, in a January 1994 speech, offered this example:

> To understand why competition is so important, let's recall what has happened since the breakup of AT&T ten years ago this month. As recently as 1987, AT&T was still predicting that it would take until the year 2010 to convert 95 percent of its long distance network to digital technology. Then it became pressed by competition. The result? AT&T made its network virtually 100 percent digital by the end of 1991. Meanwhile, over the last decade the price of interstate long distance service for the average residential customer declined over 50 percent.[33]

---

[31] That question is familiar because it was asked repeatedly following the 1982 Modified Final Judgment that forced the 1984 divestiture of AT&T. The reason the best telephone system in the world was reorganized then was because the Department of Justice contended that AT&T violated Section 2 of the Sherman Antitrust Act by monopolizing the long-distance and telephone-equipment business.

[32] See Eli M. Noam, "Beyond Telecommunications Liberalization: Past Performance, Present Hype, and Future Direction" in *The New Information Infrastructure*.

[33] Vice President Al Gore, speech to the Academy of Television Arts and Sciences, Los Angeles, January 11, 1994.

Liberalizing the telephone and cable-television markets was a major goal of the Telecommunications Act of 1996. Regardless of how well the FCC performs in promulgating rules to implement this legislation, many will be critical. Many telecommunications providers will feel that the rules are unfair to them, while granting advantages to their competitors. Public advocates will be disappointed that federal universal-service support mechanisms are insufficient to achieve a laudable, egalitarian vision of universal service.[34] The public will wonder: "Why does it cost me more to call half-way across the state than it costs to call across the country?"[35]

Governors need to think about conflicting objectives in state telecommunications policy. The central dilemma is to reconcile competition in the local loop with universal service objectives. Unleashing competition in telecommunications also forces a serious reevaluation of state and local tax structure. It threatens incumbent common carriers and provokes difficult pricing issues and tax equity problems. These are tough issues. The state role will be to define the public interest in a turbulent environment; promote competition and preserve universal service; deregulate and ensure quality services; promote infrastructure investment and protect ratepayers; promote tax equity and protect the privacy of citizens.

Encroaching telewars in the states may follow the rough contours of the congressional debates of the past four years: major battles between incumbent local exchange carriers and prospective competitors will capture newspaper headlines, frustrate the patience of state regulators, and even find their way into state legislative chambers. Also important will be the

---

[34] There are four reasons that the FCC will be criticized for its role in implementing the Telecommunications Act of 1996 even if it were to do an outstanding job:

First, FCC faces a major contradiction in implementing the Act's two primary goals promoting competition and preserving universal service. *USTA Weekly*, February 23, 1996, reported that FCC Chairman Reed Hundt is acutely aware of this contradiction. Soon after the act was enacted, Hundt explained at a public meeting that the FCC must decide in the next fifteen months how to balance universal service goals with "real world economics." Attempting such a balance puts the FCC "in tension with the first goal because it tells us we need to have rules which interfere with pure competition," said Hundt. Specifically, interpreting the universal service provisions will be most controversial: if the advocates are not disappointed then surely a large part of the industry will be.

Second, the political hyperbole that accompanied congressional enactment raised consumer expectations about lower prices for telephone services because of ensuing competition. Whether or not this may happen, consumer advocates wasted little time in alleging that phone companies were planning to raise their rates. (See Mike Mills, "Phone Firms Seek Higher Local Rates," *Washington Post*, May 7, 1996.) Of interest, the basis of these allegations by the Consumer Federation of America, Consumers" Union, and the American Association for Retired Persons was testimony submitted by the companies to the FCC that "local rates would have to rise to pay for universal service subsidies." See above paragraph.

Third, Albert R. Karr reporting in the *Wall Street Journal*, April 22, 1996, recorded the displeasure of state regulators and RBOC officials at the proposed FCC rules "for opening up local telephone service to competition." State regulators felt that their authority had been pre-empted by the strong national rules; RBOCs, according to Karr, "want vague FCC guidelines to give them greater flexibility in the states, where they have sizable political clout." So strong national rules upset the states and the RBOCs, but weak rules may not ensure sufficient opportunities for competition, frustrating prospective competitors.

Fourth, the rush to implement complex rules may result in highly visible mistakes that will lead to public criticism by congressional leaders and others. Also, the fast-track of FCC's implementation schedule is so extraordinary that Washington law firms will have too little time in which to bill their telecommunications clients for their valuable legal services.

[35] At the risk of disappointing Congressman Thomas J. Bliley, Jr. (R-Virginia) (of whom Mike Mills, in his May 7 *Washington Post* article, wrote, "It drives him crazy that today it costs more to place a phone call from Richmond to Norfolk than it does from Richmond to Los Angeles") intraLATA and intrastate competition may not change pricing enough to alter that anomaly.

battles between public advocates who want to include advanced telecommunications services in a state's definition of universal service, and consumer advocates who wish to protect the public. States will face other battles as well: how to achieve state and local tax equity for the telecommunications industry and protect the privacy of consumers.

This book was written for Governors' policy advisors to address some of the more contentious issues in the years ahead. Will the states rise to these challenges? Will they continue to serve the nation as policy laboratories for telecommunications? At the beginning of this century, states began to regulate telephone companies to protect the public and require that competing companies interconnect with each other. Over most of this period, state regulation of telephone services has received more criticism than praise.

In recent years, many states have adopted innovative price regulation methods to replace rate of return. Several states have taken the lead in establishing a level playing field for competition and encouraging private-sector investment for advanced telecommunications services. As shown, many of these actions preceded efforts at the national level by the FCC and Congress in the Telecommunications Act of 1996.

Most state governments will succeed, and a few will excel, in meeting these policy challenges. At the risk of being polemical, states and territories will manage telecommunications policy issues at least as well as the federal government.

SUMMARY OF MAJOR THEMES

"For those who never have time to read anything for more than ten minutes!"

CHAPTER ONE: CONVERGENCE AND COMPETITION IN TELECOMMUNICATIONS

The digital convergence of computers and telecommunications has increased the capacity of existing networks to transmit voice, data, and video. We once used wires to transmit voice and the air to broadcast sound (radio) and pictures (TV). The gradual trend in telecommunications is shifting toward using the air to transmit voice (via cellular and PCS) and using wireline and cable networks to transmit more sound and video.

Convergence in the telecommunications industry has brought mergers, acquisitions, and alliances among communications, information, and entertainment firms. Competition has spurred technological innovation that will allow alternative networks (wireless, cable, and satellite) to supplement and perhaps compete with the traditional wireline network.

The telecommunications industry is characterized by many large corporations that compete in large markets. Local telephone service generates $90 billion in revenues. Long-distance service, regulated by the FCC, generates $70 billion and home video, an estimated $74 billion. Firms seeking to enter these lucrative markets have not been reticent about expressing their corporate views on public policy issues. Nor will they be reticent in the future.

New federal legislation promotes competition in local telephone and cable services. States have new responsibilities under this legislation, and they will continue to be important venues for making public policy decisions about the cost and quality of local and intrastate telephone services. Firms that are eager to enter liberalized markets will lobby the states aggressively.

CHAPTER TWO: THE IMPORTANCE OF STATE TELECOMMUNICATIONS ISSUES

Quality telecommunications are essential to states' economic competitiveness. Firms that compete in regional, national, or international markets are severely disadvantaged if they lack advanced telecommunications services.

Emerging telecommunications applications can give citizens ready access to public information (via kiosks and web sites) and essential services (such as distance learning, telemedicine, and job placement), often in ways that are more efficient than traditional ones.

Advanced telecommunications services and related information technologies also have tremendous potential to improve state government management of people, programs, and data.

CHAPTER THREE: A SHORT HISTORY OF TELEPHONY

Governments have regulated telephone companies because they were monopolies. In 1907 states began regulating telephone service to protect consumers and force competing networks to interconnect. States shared regulatory authority with the federal government until the Communications Act of 1934. This legislation established the FCC, which was granted the authority to regulate long-distance toll calls between states. States continued to regulate local and intrastate telephone services.

AT&T emerged as the dominant company in the early development of telephony, because the firm pioneered long-distance technology that connected calls between local exchanges. It also aggressively acquired local exchanges and promoted a corporate philosophy of "One System, One Policy, Universal Service."

The Modified Final Judgment in 1982 led to the divestiture of AT&T. At the same time, twenty-two Bell operating companies were organized into seven Regional Bell Operating Companies (RBOCs) to provide local telephone services. They were restricted, however, by the MFJ from entering other telecommunications markets. Passage of the Telecommunications Act of 1996 eases these "line-of-business" restrictions for RBOCs once specific conditions are met.

CHAPTER FOUR: TWELVE YEARS OF POLICY INNOVATION IN STATE TELECOMMUNICATIONS REGULATION

The divestiture of AT&T thrust a tangled web of pricing and competition issues on state public utility commissions. States rose to these challenges through innovations in regulatory policy.

In the twelve years between the 1984 AT&T divestiture and the Telecommunications Act of 1996, states first *reacted* to immediate rate requests, then *retrenched*, and then *restructured* how they regulate. States adopted alternatives to rate-of-return regulation (e.g., incentive plans, price caps, and rate deregulation). They allowed competitive entry in intrastate long-distance services and began to establish rules for allowing competition in local telephony. *Many of these innovations preceded similar regulatory reforms made by the FCC at the federal level.*

CHAPTER FIVE: THE TELECOMMUNICATIONS ACT OF 1996- MAJOR STATE ISSUES

The Telecommunications Act of 1996 preempts state and local barriers to competition in local telephone and cable services. States have new responsibilities under the act, such as approving interconnection agreements between local exchange carriers and prospective competitors. The terms and prices for interconnection will be contentious.

Under the act, RBOCs must meet a 14-point competitive checklist before they are allowed to enter the in-region interLATA (toll calls between states) long-distance markets.

Competition in local telephone services will force rate rebalancing. If robust competition comes first to urban consumers and businesses, the rates for all other customers may be affected. Rate deaveraging will add to the political pressure on Governors and state legislators to create universal-service funds. States may choose to create these funds to ensure that access to basic telephone services is available to low-income households and customers in high-cost areas.

CHAPTER SIX: ANTICIPATING THE FUTURE

Media convergence, industry consolidation, and rapid technological progress will complicate states' regulatory responsibilities. For example, states must prepare for making major changes in state and local tax policy. Current taxes on telephone companies, based on the prior model of taxing regulated monopolies, cannot be sustained in a competitive environment. Difficult choices await state policymakers concerning which services should be taxed and how. Also, consumers who value privacy will look to the states for additional protection.

In summary, encroaching state telewars may follow the rough contours of the congressional debates over the past four years. Major battles between incumbent local exchange carriers and prospective competitors will capture newspaper headlines, frustrate the patience of state regulators, and find their way into state legislative chambers. Also important will be the battles between public advocates who want advanced telecommunications services as part of a state's definition of universal service and consumer advocates who are interested in protecting consumers. States will face other public policy battles as well: how to achieve state and local tax equity for the telecommunications industry and how to protect consumer privacy.

NARUC'S SUMMARY OF STATE RESPONSIBILITIES UNDER THE TELECOMMUNICATIONS ACT OF 1996

STATE COMMISSION RESPONSIBILITIES

Consider requests for virtual collocation. State Commissions may allow virtual collocation if the LEC demonstrates that physical collocation is not practical for technical reasons or because of space limitations. [251(c)(6)]

Consider bona fide requests by competitors for Section 251(c) items (interconnection, unbundling, resale) from rural telcos. State commissions are to grant the request within 120 days if it is not unduly economically burdensome, is technically feasible, and is consistent with universal service requirements in Section 254. [251(f)(1)]

Consider petitions from LECs with fewer than 2% of national access lines for modification of application of Section 251(b) or (c) items (interconnection, unbundling, resale, number portability, dialing parity, rights-of-way, reciprocal compensation). State Commission shall grant petition within 180 days if applying the sections would be unduly economically burdensome or technically infeasible and if the petition is consistent with the public interest. [251(f)(2)]

Determine rates and terms for interconnection, unbundled network elements, reciprocal compensation, and wholesale services consistent with standards in Section 252(d).

Upon request at any time, mediate any differences in negotiations between incumbent LECs and other carriers for Section 251 items. [252(a)(2)]

Upon request between the 135th and 160th day, arbitrate any open issues in negotiations between incumbent LEC and other carriers for Section 251 items. Must resolve each issue in arbitration petition within 9 months after LEC received request to negotiate. [252(b) and (c)]

Consider incumbent LECs' interconnection agreements, including those negotiated before the date of enactment, which must be submitted for approval [252(a) and (e)]:

May reject a negotiated agreement only if it discriminates against a carrier not a party to the agreement or it is not consistent with the public interest. May reject an arbitrated agreement if it does not comply with Section 251, including FCC regulations, or the pricing standards in Section 251(d).

State Commission must act on negotiated agreement within 90 days and on arbitrated agreement within 30 days. If State Commission doesn't act, FCC preempts. Court review is to be at Federal district court level only.

Consider filings that the BOC may submit regarding general terms it offers to comply with Section 251 and the standards in Section 252. The review, including reconsideration, must be completed within 60 days unless the BOC agrees to an extension. Alternatively, the Commission may allow the filing to become effective within the 60 days, but subject to later review. [252(f)]

May not prohibit the ability of any entity to provide interstate or intrastate telecommunications service. [253(a)]

Advise FCC on BOC requests for in-region interLATA service [271(d)(2)] regarding whether the BOC has complied with 271(c). In addition to the competitive checklist for 271(c)(2), the State commission may address whether the BOC has entered into binding agreements for access and interconnection, under which an unaffiliated provider is serving residential and business customers, or whether providers have failed to negotiate in good faith or not failed to comply with implementation schedules. [271(c)(1)]

Biennial audits of BOC/affiliate relationships will be submitted to the FCC and State Commission, which shall make the results available for public inspection and allow parties to file comments. [271(d)]

Ensure that universal service is available at reasonable and affordable rates. [254(i)]

Determine the discount of intrastate services offered to educational providers and libraries under the definition of universal service. [254(h)(1)(B)]

For intrastate services, establish rules to ensure that universal services bear no more than a reasonable share of joint and common costs. [254(k)]

Designate common carriers as an eligible telecommunications carrier for universal service funding. The State Commission shall designate more than one eligible telecommunications carrier in an area, except that a public interest finding is required in rural areas. [214(e)(2)] The requirements for an eligible carrier follow:

(A) It must offer the services supported by the Federal universal service support mechanisms, either through its own facilities or through a combination of facilities and resale. (B) It must advertise the availability of its service through media of general distribution. [214(e)(1)]

If no carrier is willing to serve an area, the State Commission, for intrastate services, may designate a common carrier to serve the unserved area, by determining which carrier is best able. [214(e)(3)]

Permit an eligible carrier to discontinue service to an area which is served by more than one eligible telecommunications carrier, but shall ensure that all customers of the exiting carrier continue to be served by the remaining eligible telecommunications carrier(s). [214(e)(4)]

Determine whether electric or gas assets can be sold to an affiliated telecommunications company. [34(h)]

PERMISSIVE STATE ACTIONS

May prohibit resellers from offering a service to a different category of subscribers than the category to which the corresponding retail service is offered, consistent with FCC regulations. [251(c)(4)]

FCC shall not preclude State regulations for access and interconnection that are consistent with Section 251. [251(d)(3)]

FCC may delegate jurisdiction over numbering to the State Commissions or other entities. [251(e)(2)]

May impose, on a competitively neutral basis, requirements necessary for universal service, public safety and welfare, quality communications, and consumer protection. [253(b)]

May, along with local governments, manage public rights-of-way and require compensation from providers for their use, on a competitively neutral and nondiscriminatory basis. [253(c)]

May require a company wanting to provide telephone exchange or exchange access service in a rural area to meet requirements in 214(e)(1) for designation as an eligible telecommunications carrier. [253(f)]

May adopt universal service regulations not inconsistent with FCC rules, including additional definitions and standards, such that Federal funding sources are not used to support the additional definitions and standards. [254(f)]

May enforce slamming rules for intrastate services. [258(b)]

May enforce regulations prescribed prior to the date of enactment to further competition that are not inconsistent with this Act or the FCC's regulations to implement this Act. [261(b)]

May impose requirements for intrastate services that further competition and that are not inconsistent with this Act or the FCC's regulations to implement this Act. [261(c)]

MISC. NOTES

LECs shall continue to provide exchange access, information access, and exchange services until existing restrictions and obligations are superseded by FCC regulations. [251(g)]

FCC shall forbear from applying any provisions of this Act to a carrier or service in a geographic market if forbearance is in the public interest. States may not continue to apply provisions that the FCC has decided to forbear. [10(a)-(b)]

FCC will hold biennial reviews, and repeal or modify any regulation no longer in the public interest. [11(b)]

Source: "Overview of Federal and State Responsibilities: Telecommunications Act of 1996" (National Association of Regulatory Utility Commissioners [NARUC], Washington, D.C., February 25, 1996).

GLOSSARY OF BASIC TELECOMMUNICATIONS TERMS

accelerated depreciation is a change in accounting that reduces the number of years over which an asset will be amortized.

access gives a user the ability to reach or communicate with someone else. From an individual customer's perspective, access is the ability to communicate with the outside world through the telephone network. From a long-distance carrier's perspective, access is the ability to interconnect with local telephone companies to originate and terminate long-distance traffic, thereby reaching all customers in a geographic area.

access charges are imposed on long-distance carriers to compensate local telephone companies for connecting to the local network. Some contend that regulators have set the access fees artificially high to subsidize local telephone service. Access charges can also refer to the monthly *subscriber line charge* customers pay for access to the local telephone network. (See below.)

access lines connect customers to the local switching network. The connection between the customer's phone and the facilities at the telephone central office is also called the *local loop*.

acoustic coupler is a special type of modem that allows a standard telephone handset to transmit and receive data. It may be used to connect with a computer, or to enable people with hearing or speech impairments to communicate over the phone with a telecommunications device for the deaf (TDD).

address is a sequence of bits or characters that identifies the destination and the source of transmission.

advanced intelligent network, or AIN, is a network design (an evolving architecture) being developed at Bellcore laboratories that will allow third parties and telephone customers to customize their own telephone services.

aggregators are businesses other than telephone companies that lease phone lines and resell them at locations such as hotels, motels, hospitals, and airports. Aggregators are not common carriers.

analog refers to any device, usually electronic, that represents values by a continuously variable physical property, such as voltage in an electronic circuit. An analog device can represent an infinite number of values within the range the device can handle. In contrast, *digital representation* maps values onto discrete numbers, limiting the possible range of values to the resolution of the digital device. A layperson's definition of analog is "something that corresponds to something else; in computers, a device that computes by measuring one object by its relation to something else." (Shurkin, 1996.)

analog communications is a format in which information is transmitted by modulating a continuous signal, such as a radio wave. Voice and video messages originate in analog form since sound and light are wave-like functions. Converting them into digital messages enables them to be transmitted along digital communications formats or media.

architecture is a general term referring to the structure of all or part of a computer system. The term also covers the design of system software, such as the operating system, as well as the combination of hardware and basic software that links the machines on a computer network. Computer architecture refers to an entire structure and to the components needed to make it functional. Thus, computer architecture covers computer systems, chips, circuits, and system software, but typically does not include applications, which are required to perform a functional task but not to make the system run.

ascii stands for the American Standard Computer Interchange, which is the standard seven-bit binary representation for letters, numbers, and other keyboard and control characters.

asynchronous operation is a function that proceeds independently of a timing mechanism, such as a clock. In communications, two modems communicating asynchronously rely upon each one sending the other start-and-stop signals to pace the exchange of information.

asynchronous transfer mode (ATM) is a digital protocol for transferring data in the form of packets. Each message includes an address, allowing the information to be routed automatically without using switches. It is a fast-packet technology; current ATM standards allow it to scale from speeds of 155 megabits per second (mbps) to 622 mbps over fiber networks. ATM appears to be the best alternative for multimedia applications in which data are mixed with voice, images, or full-motion video.

automated information service allows a caller to access a computer database on one or more computers by using a telephone keypad.

automatic number identification (ANI) is a service that transmits and displays the phone number of the caller to the person being called. Also known as calling number identification or caller ID. See the discussion in chapter six on privacy.

backbone refers to the high-density portion of the communications network.

bandwidth is the width of an electrical transmission path or circuit, in terms of the range of frequencies it can pass, i.e., a measure of the volume of communications traffic that the channel can carry. For example: a voice channel has a bandwidth of 4,000 cycles per second, while a TV channel requires about 6.5 megahertz. In computer networks, greater bandwidth indicates the capacity to transfer more data in the same or less time.

Nicholas Negroponte in *Being Digital* provides a good explanation (16):

> The number of bits that can be transmitted per second through a given channel (like copper wire, radio spectrum, or optical fiber) is the bandwidth of that channel. It is a measure of how many bits can get down a given pipe. That number or capacity needs to be matched carefully with the number of bits needed to render a given type of data (voice, music, video): 64,000 bits per second is more than ample for high-quality voice, 1.2 million bits per second is more than ample for high-fidelity music, and 45 million bits per second is terrific for rendering video.

barriers to entry, according to George Stigler, are the costs on entrants that are not present for incumbents. According to Spulber (1995), "Sunk costs are said to be barriers to entry if entrants must make irreversible investments in capacity, expenses that incumbents have already incurred. Government regulation that takes the form of rules applying unequally to incumbents and entrants can create additional costs for entrants, potentially restricting market entry entirely."

basic exchange digital radio service (BETRS) is a rural communications service that transmits digitized communications using radio signals rather than wire or cable.

basic service refers to the minimum level of service necessary for connecting to the publicly switched network. In the past, only local telephone companies provided basic service, which was priced below cost using subsidies from access, long-distance, and other services.

baud is commonly defined as the speed of transmission in bits per second (bps) in a binary (two-point) telecommunications transmission. (It is named after Emile Baudot, the inventor of the asynchronous telegraph printer.) Typical baud rates are 2400 and 9600 bps. Example: using a baud rate of 14,400 bps, the manuscript for this book was transmitted over the telephone lines from Brooklyn to Washington, D.C. in thirteen minutes.

Bell operating companies (BOCs) are the twenty-two local companies that were organized into the seven regional Bell operating companies (RBOCs) following the 1982 Modified Final Judgment, which forced the divestiture of AT&T. The MFJ also forbid the BOCs from providing long-distance services or video programming, and from manufacturing telephone equipment. At divestiture, the RBOCs (sometimes referred to as regional holding companies, or RHCs) and their respective BOCs were as follows:

Ameritech: Illinois Bell, Indiana Bell, Michigan Bell, Ohio Bell, Wisconsin Bell.

Bell Atlantic: Chesapeake & Potomac (C&P) telephone companies of the District of Columbia, Maryland, Virginia, and West Virginia; Diamond State Telephone; New Jersey Bell; and Bell of Pennsylvania.

BellSouth: South Central Bell, Southern Bell.

NYNEX: New England Telephone, New York Telephone Company.

Pacific Telesis: Pacific Bell, Nevada Bell.

Southwestern Bell: Now known as SBC Communications.

U S West: Mountain Bell, Northwestern Bell, Pacific Northwest Bell.

Two other local companies-Cincinnati Bell and Southern New England Telephone-were licensees of, but never wholly owned by, AT&T, so they remained independents.

billing and collection refers to the service by local telephone companies of billing customers and collecting revenues from long-distance charges on behalf of other companies.

binary refers to a numbering system using two digits, usually a 1 and a 0, the most common system used in computers.

bit is a binary digit with values of zero or one, or yes and no. In a communications system, a bit is represented by the presence or absence of an electronic pulse. In processing and storage, a bit is the smallest unit of information handled by a computer. In groups of eight, bits become the familiar bytes used to represent various types of information, including letters of the alphabet and numbers.

bits per second is the basic measuring unit of the speed of digital transmission. It is the number of information bits that can be sent between one facility to another in one second. Kbps is kilobits (or 1,000 bits) per second; mbps is megabits (or a million bits) per second; and gbps is gigabits (or a billion bits) per second.

broadband refers to digital technologies that provide simultaneous voice, high-speed data, and video-on-demand to customers through a single facility at rates of 1.544 megabits per second or higher. Fiber optics and coaxial cables can carry broadband communications, while the copper wires traditionally used by telephone companies cannot.

broadband carriers are the high capacity transmission systems—provided by coaxial cables, microwave radio systems, or optical fibers—used to carry large blocks of telephone channels or one or more video channels

bulletin board system (BBS) is the online version of a bulletin board, used to share information. Government agencies at all levels have begun to post information using a BBS, which anyone with a computer, modem, and phone line can access. Also, individuals, businesses, and corporations can run a BBS (sometimes called electronic bulletin board).

bypass occurs when an entity avoids using the local exchange company network, such as when a corporate customer connects directly into the long-distance network or buys a direct line between offices instead of using the publicly switched network. Service bypass refers to the use of local exchange, company-provided dedicated access facilities as an alternative to switched access facilities. Facilities bypass refers to the use of services other than those provided by the telephone company, such as cellular radio, two-way cable TV, short-haul microwave, or direct satellite to rooftop antennae.

byte is normally a cluster of eight binary digits, or bits (see above) processed together. Sixteen-bit and 32-bit bytes also are becoming more common.

cable television (CATV) is the transmission of television signals, including signals that originate at over-the-air television stations, to subscribers on a wired network.

caller ID: See automatic number identification.

calling party pays is a service for cellular companies that bills airtime charges to the person calling a cellular phone, instead of the person being called.

carrier is any company that is authorized by regulatory agencies to provide communications.

carrier of last resort is a common carrier required to provide services to all customers within a service area. A carrier of last resort may receive subsidies for serving all of the customers in uneconomic, high-cost areas.

cell is the smallest geographic area in a cellular system for mobile communications systems.

cellular systems are mobile telephony systems that operate within a grid of low-powered radio sender-receivers. As a user travels to different locations on the grid, the signal is passed along to different receiver-transmitters automatically to support the message traffic. Cellular telephone calls are connected into publicly switched networks, for which the cellular providers compensate local exchange carriers.

centrex is a service offered by telephone companies that provides business customers with direct inward dialing on their internal lines. Centrex allows businesses greater control over their internal telecommunications systems.

circuit is a communications path.

circuit switching is a method of opening communications lines, as through the telephone system, and creating a physical link between the initiating and receiving parties. In circuit switching, the connection is made at a switching center, which physically connects the two parties and maintains an open line between them for as long as needed. Circuit switching is typically used in modern communications on the dial-up telephone network, and it is also used on a smaller scale in privately maintained communications networks.

coaxial cable is metal cable that can carry broadband signals by guiding high-frequency electromagnetic radiation. It is a high-capacity medium that can transmit dozens of TV channels or several thousand voice conversations. The cable consists of two conductors: a center wire inside a cylindrical shield that is grounded. The shield is typically made of braided wire and is insulated from the center wire. The shield minimizes electrical and radio-frequency interference. Signals in a coaxial cable do not affect nearby components, and potential interference from these components does not affect the signal carried on the cable.

co-location is a direct connection to a telephone company central office that allows another company to provide transport services. Both long-distance companies and competitive access providers need co-location with the local exchange carrier to interconnect with the local network. Co-location provides, in essence, a link between the networks of several different companies. Physical co-location occurs in the central office of a local telephone exchange that houses modern switching equipment. Virtual co-location occurs when the interconnection between networks is near but not in central office locations. The FCC in 1993 mandated physical co-location, but the courts vacated that order in 1994. Hence, the term *virtual co-location* refers to the provision of transmission facilities for the exclusive use of another carrier to facilitate the connection of that carrier's network to the local telephone company's network.

common carrier is an entity licensed by the Federal Communications Commission (FCC) or state Public Utility Commissions (PUCs) to supply communications services to all users at established prices. A common carrier may not discriminate among users. Vietor (1994) traces the rights and obligations of the common carrier to Blackstone in 1768: "If a ferry is erected on a river, so near another ancient ferry as to draw away its custom, it is a nuisance to the owner of the old one. For where there is a ferry by prescription, the owner is bound to keep it always in repair and readiness for the ease of all the king's subjects; otherwise he may be grievously amerced."

common costs are best defined by Alfred Kahn as cited by Gabel (1995): "When the same equipment can be used to make products A and B, and when producing A uses capacity that could otherwise be used to supply B, then we speak of their costs as common instead of joint."

common line-loop/carrier common line charge refers to the usage-based access charge paid by long-distance companies to local exchange carriers for access to, or use of, the local loop.

Communications Decency Act is a provision of the Telecommunications Act of 1996 that regulated the communication of obscene materials through the Internet. On June 12, 1996, a panel of three judges in the U.S. Court of Appeals ruled that the CDA was unconstitutional because it infringed on First Amendment rights.

communications protocol is a set of rules or standards designed to enable computers to connect with one another and exchange information with as little error as possible. The word *protocol* is used to refer to the multitude of standards affecting different aspects of communication. The standards govern anything from hardware connections to data transmission, file transfer, and the methods by which messages are passed around the stations on a local area network. Taken as a whole, these various and sometimes conflicting protocols represent attempts to facilitate communication among computers of different makes and models.

competitive access providers (CAPs) are companies that compete with incumbent local exchange carriers by providing access to long-distance carriers and offering local communications services.

compressed video is a television system that requires less bandwidth than commercial television standards; it is often used in business and educational settings.

compression is the process of condensing audio or video signals or other digital information into fewer bytes, which minimizes storage and facilitates transmission at narrower bandwidth.

computer network is a group of computers and associated devices that are connected by communications facilities. A network can involve permanent connections, such as cables, or temporary connections made through telephone or other communications links. A network can be as small as a local area network (LAN) consisting of a few computers, printers, and other devices, or it can consist of many small and large computers distributed over a vast geographic area (wide area network, or WAN). Small or large, a computer network enables users to locate, communicate, and transfer information electronically. Some types of communication are simple user-to-user messages; others, often called distributed processes, can involve several computers and the sharing of workloads to perform tasks.

computer terms: See John A. Barry, *Technobabble* (Cambridge, Massachusetts: MIT Press, 1993) and Alan Freedman, *The Electronic Computer Glossary* (Computer Language Company, Philadelphia).

convergence is the confluence of distinct communications technologies into a single, electronic, computer-driven environment, specifically, the blending of telecommunications and computers. According to George Gilder ("Life After Television, Updated," *Forbes ASAP*, February 23, 1994), "What is driving the "telefuture" is not any convergence of films and TVs, consumer electronics and publishing, computers and games. What is driving it is the onrush of computer technology, which is invading and conquering all these domains. The computer industry is converging with the television industry in the same sense that the automobile converged with the horse, the TV with the nickelodeon, the word processor with the typewriter, computer-aided design with the drafting board, and digital desktop publishing with the Linotype machine and the letterpress."

copper wire is the medium that conventionally carries most telephone conversations. A standard 3-inch-thick copper cable contains 1,200 pairs of copper wires, which can carry over 14,000 phone conversations. Today, most telephone companies are phasing out copper cable in favor of fiber-optic cable.

cost of service pricing refers to the method of pricing according to the actual costs of a particular service.

cream skimming occurs when a company attempts to sell to the most profitable customers, or offers only those services that generate the best profit margin. One might think of Federal Express and UPS as skimming the cream from the U.S. Postal Service, for example.

cross-subsidy is financial support for one service from the revenues generated by another service.

customer premises equipment (CPE) refers to equipment such as a telephone set or facsimile machine located in a home or business that connects to the publicly-switched network.

customer proprietary network information (CPNI) is data about calling patterns or the use of the telephone network that could prove valuable to marketing companies. Telephone providers generally cannot sell or reveal this information.

data compression reduces a given amount of information to facilitate computer storage or transmission. It is a key technological advance leading to the convergence of media, computing, and telecommunications.

dedicated line is a private line for the exclusive use of the subscriber.

depreciation is an accounting term that represents the difference between the first cost of a capital item and its estimated net salvage value at the end of its expected life. For tax purposes, this amount is treated as an expense to offset revenues over the years of the expected life of the asset.

dialing parity enables customers to access their preferred long-distance carrier by dialing "1" plus the area code and number. Without dialing parity, customers would first have to dial several digits to access their preferred long-distance carrier.

digital describes a function that operates in discrete steps using binary (on-off) forms (in contrast to the continuous analog function). Digital communication is the transmission of information using discontinuous, discrete electrical or electromagnetic signals that change in frequency, polarity, or amplitude. In computing, digital is virtually synonymous with binary because the computers familiar to most people process information coded as combinations of binary digits, or bits. One bit can represent at most two values—0 or 1. Two bits can represent up to four different values—00, 01, 11, and 10. Shurkin (1996) defines digital as the use of digits, usually 0 and 1, to measure discrete numbers.

digital signature is a cryptographic method by which the recipient of a message or any third party can verify the identity of the message's sender and the integrity of the message. It works using "public-key cryptography" (see below). Basically, a sender creates a digital signature for a message by transforming it with his or her "private" key. The recipient, using the sender's "public" key, applies a corresponding transformation to the message, thereby verifying the digital signature.

digital switch is a telecommunications switch that operates with digital signals (rather than analog).

direct broadcast satellite (DBS) is a satellite system designed with sufficient power so that inexpensive earth stations (such as a receiving antenna of eighteen inches in diameter) can be used for direct residential or community reception.

divestiture is the legally sanctioned breakup of a large company, such as the breakup of AT&T into many separate operating companies in 1984 as a result of the 1982 Modified Final Judgment. Prior to divestiture, AT&T was the world's largest corporation.

dual party relay service is a state service established to enable hearing-impaired persons to communicate with others with the assistance of an interpreter who operates a telecommunications device for the deaf (TDD). The hearing-impaired person types a message and sends it to a relay center via the TDD; an interpreter at the center calls the requested party and conveys the message by voice; the interpreter then types the party's response and sends it via the TDD to the hearing-impaired caller. The Americans with Disabilities Act of 1990 mandated dual party relay service, also called *telecommunications relay service.*

earth station is a communications terminal on the ground, which is designed to receive and transmit radio signals through an orbiting communications satellite.

electronic bulletin board: See bulletin board system (BBS).

electronic data interexchange (EDI) is the use of computer and telecommunications technologies to process common transactions electronically (instead of using paper documents). EDI protocols have improved the efficiency and effectiveness of data operations, including invoices, shipping notices, and billing.

electronic mail (e-mail) is correspondence, including both text and data files, that takes place by interconnecting computers, online information systems, and telecommunications systems.

electronic redlining refers to new telecommunications providers seeking the most lucrative customer groups, but failing to serve those offering lower returns. The term *redlining* was first used to describe bankers who drew red lines on city maps around lower-income neighborhoods to indicate areas loan officers should avoid in making home mortgages.

encryption is the transformation of data into a form readable only by using the appropriate key, held only by authorized parties. The key rearranges the data into its original form by reversing the encryption.

enhanced 911 service is a service usually run by a local government agency that expedites a person's call for help after dialing 911. Enhanced 911 refers to the information stored in the computer (such as the caller's telephone number, location, and other important information) to facilitate a prompt response.

equal access: See dialing parity. Note that some use the phrase "equal access" to refer to measures in the Telecommunications Act of 1996 that require incumbent exchange carriers to interconnect and unbundle in order to enable local competition.

ethernet is a high-speed network used by corporations. Its top speed is 10 million bits per second, fast enough to deliver two copies of *Moby Dick* every second.

exchange area is the area in which all calls are considered local.

extended area service (EAS) is a broadening of the area within which no long-distance charges are assessed, usually to include communities of interest.

facility refers to any equipment or media that form part of the complete end-to-end telephone connection, such as transmission lines, switches, and central offices.

facility-based competition occurs when a provider builds its own network elements (such as lines, equipment, and switches) for delivering telecommunications services. This type of competition is increasing. In the past, most new competitors purchased capacity from incumbent common carriers and then resold those services to the public. Most of the firms in the long-distance market, for example, purchase existing capacity (at wholesale rates) and then resell services to the public. Only four long-distance companies-AT&T, MCI, Sprint, and LDDS-have their own networks and facilities.

Federal Communications Commission (FCC) is an independent federal agency, created by Congress in 1934, that regulates interstate and international communications by radio, television, wire, satellite, and cable. (Local and intrastate telephone services are under the jurisdiction of state public utility commissions.) The FCC consists of five commissioners appointed by the president and confirmed by the U.S. Senate. The FCC's Notices of Proposed Rulemaking (NPRMs) to implement the Telecommunications Act of 1996 may be accessed at its Web site: [http//www.fcc.gov].

fiber optics is a method of transmitting light beams along optical fibers. A light beam, such as that produced by a laser, can be modulated to carry information. A single fiber-optic channel can carry significantly more information than most other means of information transmission. Optical fibers are usually thin strands of glass.

firewalls are protective systems designed into data networks to prevent unauthorized users from accessing restricted files and data bases. For example, a firewall checks traffic from the extended world to the internal system and only admits traffic that has been deemed acceptable. (See, for example, encryption and intranet.) See also James Evans, "Internet Security: Imperfect, But Improving," *Government Technology*, February 1996.

flat rate is a method of pricing local telephone service so that customers pay a fixed charge each month for an unlimited number of local calls.

forbearance is a term that relates to regulatory flexibility by the FCC. In the Telecommunications Act of 1996, forbearance means that the FCC may refrain from enforcing certain regulations in a geographic area or on a particular telecom provider if the FCC believes that this forbearance will promote competition in the public interest.

frame relay is a type of fast packet technology using variable length packets called *frames*. By contrast, a cell relay system, such as ATM, transports user data in fixed-sized cells.

frequency is the number of recurrences of a phenomenon during a specified period of time. Electrical frequency is expressed in hertz, which are cycles per second.

frequency spectrum is the range of frequencies of electromagnetic waves in radio terms. The range of frequencies useful for radio communication is from ten hertz (Hz) to 3,000 gigahertz (GHz). (A gigahertz is one billion cycles per second.)

gateway is the entrance to and exit from a communications network. In data communications, it is the node on a network that connects two otherwise incompatible networks. (See interoperability, below.)

giga is a prefix for one billion (10^9) times a specific unit.

gigabyte (GB) is specifically, 1,073,741,824 bytes. Generally means 1000 megabytes.

hardware is the electrical and mechanical equipment used in telecommunications and computer systems.

HDTV is high definition television.

hertz is the frequency of an electric or electromagnetic wave in cycles per second, named after Heinrich Hertz who detected such waves in 1883. One kilohertz equals one thousand cycles per second; one megahertz equals one million cycles per second; one gigahertz equals one billion cycles per second. Frequency measurements in hertz are used to define the bands of the electromagnetic spectrum for communications, and to define the bandwidth capacity of a transmission medium.

independent telephone company is a local exchange carrier that is not part of the Bell system. GTE is the largest independent telephone company providing local exchange services.

information superhighway is a popular term for the emerging global broadband digital metanetwork. Also known as the national information infrastructure, infobahn, or global grid. This phrase has been attributed to a 1991 *Scientific American* article written by then U.S. Senator Al Gore.

integrated services digital network (ISDN) is a set of standards for integrating voice, data, and image communication. ISDN enables a telephone customer to talk, receive and send data, and transmit video or images all on one line—at the same time. Several local companies are marketing ISDN basic service, which includes two 64,000 bits-per-second (bps) channels to carry communications, which can be bundled to transmit at 128,000 bps. The goal of ISDN is to replace the current analog telephone system with totally digital switching and transmission facilities capable of carrying data ranging from voice to computer transmissions, music, and video.

intelligent network is a telecommunications network that uses computers to provide customized services to consumers.

interactive means to operate in a back-and-forth, almost conversational manner, as when a user enters a question or command and the system responds immediately.

interconnection is the linking of a communications channel, facility, service, or piece of equipment with another from a different network. The failure to interconnect limits the value of any one network; it can only transmit from one point to another within that one network. Interconnection enables a call originating on one network to terminate on a telephone connected to a different network. The prices charged for interconnection are hotly debated because prospective competitors need affordable access to existing networks while incumbent exchanges would prefer higher charges.

interexchange carrier (IXC) is a long-distance company such as AT&T, MCI, or Sprint, which is authorized to carry calls between local access and transport areas (LATAs). IXCs are authorized by the FCC to carry interLATA, interstate traffic, and by the state public utility commissions to carry interLATA, intrastate traffic. The distinction between IXC and LEC, the local exchange carrier, has been important since the AT&T divestiture in 1984. It will become less important, however, because the new federal legislation will allow LECs to provide long-distance service after they have fulfilled the requirements of the 14-point competitive checklist for allowing competition in their local service areas.

interface is a device that operates at a common boundary of adjacent components or systems and that facilitates the transfer of information between or among them. (Never to be used as a verb.)

interLATA means a call originating in one local access and transport area (LATA) and terminating in another LATA or internationally. The Modified Final Judgment in 1982 restricted interLATA transmissions to the long-distance carriers.

internet is a widely used public message network that links various networks, allowing users on different systems to communicate with one another throughout the world. The Internet was initiated in the 1970s by the Defense Advanced Research Project as a means of providing a secure linkage of selected computers, and to facilitate the transfer of data and research. As it evolved into an international network of networks, it received support from several federal agencies, including the National Science Foundation, the National Aeronautics and Space Administration, and the Department of Energy. As a technical communications term, internet means a set of computer networks (possibly dissimilar) joined together by means of gateways that handle data transfer and the conversion of messages from the sending network to the protocols used by the receiving network (with packets if necessary).

interoperability is the ability of two or more systems or components to exchange information and to use the information that has been exchanged.

intranets are internally secure networks, which are being rapidly developed by many large corporations, using the same protocols as the Internet. As defined by the *Open Forum* (NYS Forum for Information Resource Management, April 1996), "The intranet is an internal Internet that allows organizations to deliver information to employees' desktops with minimal time, cost and effort. An internal intranet structure is similar to an external Internet structure. It utilizes the TCP/IP protocol and manages documents in the Web's HTML format. Although the intranet infrastructure is the same as for the Internet, the intranet is only open to those inside an organization. One of the strongest points of the intranet is that it strives to slash the need for paper in an organization. The intranet web browsers run on any type of computer which enables information to be electronically viewed by any employee." See also Amy Cortese, "Here Comes the Intranet," *Business Week*, February 26, 1996.

joint board is the body consisting of three FCC commissioners and four state public utility commissioners to investigate regulatory issues that affect both inter- and intrastate jurisdictions. As directed by the Telecommunications Act of 1996, the joint board, formed in the spring of 1996 to investigate universal-service issues, also includes a consumer representative.

joint costs occur when "the products can only be economically produced in fixed proportions (e.g., cotton and cotton seed)." From Alfred Kahn as cited by Gabel (1995).

kilo is a prefix for one thousand (10^3) times a specific unit.

last mile is the popular term for the last segment of the connection between the communications provider and the customer. A captivating topic in recent years has been how to provide broadband services in the last mile or from curb to home.

lexicon: See Tom Bonnett, *A New Vocabulary for Governing in the 1990s: A Lexicon for Governors' Policy Advisors* (Washington, D.C.: CGPA, 1994).

Lifeline is a federal program that waives the monthly subscriber line charge to ensure access to telephone service for low-income subscribers; most states have matching Lifeline programs.

Link-Up America Program is a program that helps low-income subscribers become connected with the telephone network by reducing the cost of the initial installation. States must have their Link-up programs approved by the FCC.

local access and transport area (LATA) is a regional telephone service area, usually following metropolitan area boundaries. LATAs were created as part of the Modified Final Judgment in 1982 to designate the local service areas of the Bell operating companies and other independent telephone companies. Telephone calls between one LATA and another were generally carried by long-distance companies (IXCs). The federal legislation to deregulate the telecommunications industry will enable the regional Bell operating companies (RBOCs) to enter the long-distance business after meeting certain conditions specified in the federal legislation, subject to the approval of the FCC.

local area network, or LAN, is a group of computers and other devices dispersed over a relatively limited area and connected by a communications link. LANs commonly include a variety of computers and shared devices such as printers and large hard disks. LANs usually use coaxial cable or fiber optics.

local competition refers to the opening up of an exclusive franchise to permit more than one company to provide local telephone service.

local exchange carrier (LEC) is a telephone company that provides service within a LATA, a defined area (see above). After meeting the conditions set by the Telecommunications Act of 1996 and interpreted by the FCC, a LEC may enter the in-region long-distance business.

local loop is the link that extends from a central telephone office to the telephone instrument. An overhead view of the local loop would look like a star pattern with the central office switch in the center. The coaxial cable in a broadband or CATV system that passes by each building or residence on a street and connects with the trunk cable at a neighborhood node is called the subscriber loop. That loop looks like the travel pattern of a city bus that only goes in one direction.

market power, as conventionally defined, describes a company that exploits its large market share to administer prices. Economists define market power as pricing higher than marginal cost.

medium is the message is the classic phase of Marshall McLuhan in his 1964 book, *Understanding Media*. In the first chapter, McLuhan begins: "In a culture like ours, long accustomed to splitting and dividing all things as a means of control, it is sometimes a bit of a shock to be reminded that, in operational and practical fact, the medium is the message." He was also the first to observe, "As electrically contracted, the globe is no more than a village."

mega is a prefix for one million (10^6) times a specific unit.

megabyte (MB) is 1,048,576 bytes.

memes (rhymes with schemes) "are ideas that alter the ways in which we think. They hold on and don't let go unless displaced by rival memes," according to Edward Rothstein, ("Technology," *New York Times*, June 10, 1996, D5). Rothstein cites the work of Richard Dawkins, an evolutionary biologist at Oxford University, to explain: "Just as genes propagate themselves in a gene pool by leaping from body to body via sperm and eggs, so memes propagate themselves in the same pool by leaping from brain to brain."

memory is one of the basic components of a central processing unit (CPU). It stores information for future use. "Computer people never die, they just lose their memory."

message telecommunications service (MTS), also known as message toll or long-distance service, is a method of charging subscribers based on the time, duration and distance of the call.

microwave refers to high-frequency radio transmitters that radiate over air waves (rather than through wires or cables) to beam voice, data, and video signals. Microwave transmitters must be in "line of sight" with receivers.

modem is the short name for modulator/demodulator, which translates digital information into an analog signal for transmission over analog phone lines, and then back again into digital format. (See also baud.)

Modified Final Judgment (MFJ) was the ruling by Judge Harold Greene in 1982 that settled an antitrust suit by the U.S. Department of Justice against AT&T. The MFJ forced the 1984 divestiture of AT&T, which resulted in the creation of the regional Bell operating companies and the establishment of various business restrictions.

monopoly exists when one provider can produce a good or service cheaper than two or more firms produce the same good or service. John Stuart Mill in 1848 may have been the first political economist to write about the problem of wasteful duplication of transmission facilities that can occur in utility services, as cited in Spulber, 1995. Utilities, including the telephone companies, were considered monopolies because they had very high fixed investments (transmission lines and equipment), the incremental cost of adding another customer was close to zero, and the positive externalities of the network increased the value of it as more users joined it.

multimedia is the popular term to describe the integration of different types of information in a single format; for example, an electronic document may contain text, embedded voice, video, and/or images.

nanosecond is one billionth of a second.

narrowband communication is a system capable of carrying only voice or relatively slow speed computer signals.

National Association of Regulatory Utility Commissioners (NARUC) is an organization based in Washington, D.C. that serves the representatives of state regulatory agencies. It is an excellent source of information on state telecommunications issues.

National Education Technology Funding Corporation is a group authorized by Section 708 of the Act to leverage resources in education technology infrastructure.

National Exchange Carrier Association (NECA) is an organization created by a FCC order to file interstate access tariffs on behalf of local exchange carriers, to manage the various access revenue pools, and to participate in FCC and court proceedings. NECA collects and distributes revenues in the Universal Service Fund, the Lifeline Assistance Program, and the Telecommunications Relay Service.

national information infrastructure (NII) was the Clinton administration's 1993 initiative to create "a seamless web of communications networks, computers, databases, and consumer electronics that will put vast amounts of information at users' fingertips. Development of the NII can help unleash an information revolution that will change forever the way people live, work, and interact with each other." Below are the principles and objectives of the NII initiative:

> Promote private sector investment; extend the "universal service" concept to ensure that information resources are available to all at affordable prices; act as catalyst to promote technological innovation and new applications; promote seamless, interactive, user-driven operation of NII; ensure information security and network reliability; improve management of the radio frequency spectrum; protect intellectual property rights; coordinate with other levels of government and with other nations; and provide access to government information and improve government procurement. (From *The National Information Infrastructure: Agenda for Action*, September 15, 1993.)

Negroponte switch: See uncommon laws.

network is a system for connecting various devices. George Gilder ("Issaquah Miracle," *Forbes ASAP*, June 7, 1993) has argued that the most powerful technology is not computers, but computers joined in networks: "Explaining the magic of networks, Booker asks you to imagine a car plumped down in the jungle. Checking it out, you might find it a very useful piece of equipment indeed. A multipurpose wonder, it would supply lights, bedding, radio communications, tape player, heat, air conditioning, a shield against arrows and bullets, and a loud horn to frighten away fierce animals. In awe of the features of this machine, you might never realize that the real magic of a car comes in conjunction with asphalt."

node is the point at which terminals, computers, or telecommunications equipment link to the transmission network.

number portability is the ability to change to a different local service provider and keep the same phone number. Prospective competitors in providing local telephone service have argued that consumers should be allowed to "take their numbers with them" as a condition of establishing fair local competition.

oligopoly, according to *Webster's*, is "a market situation in which each of a few producers affects but does not control the market." Despite the presence of hundreds of small resellers, many analysts have called the long-distance market an oligopoly since the three largest companies earn about 90 percent of the total revenues.

open network architecture (ONA) are standards that allow different telecommunications vendors to interconnect with a network. The FCC adopted these regulatory standards to provide prospective competitors with the equivalent functionality to the networks of the Bell operating companies and GTE as their affiliates currently have.

open video is the term used in the section of the Telecommunications Act of 1996 that establishes requirements and safeguards specific to the operating of open video systems, including non-discrimination among video program providers, limits on carriage offered by other providers, network non-duplication, and open video system fees.

online is being actively connected to a network, computer system or information service. Usually being online enables one to exchange data, commands, and information with the other system.

on ramp is a popular term for a digital broadband connection linking a subscriber to the information superhighway. (See local loop and last mile.)

optical fiber is a thin flexible glass fiber the size of a human hair that can transmit light waves capable of carrying large amounts of information (and bandwidth). An optical fiber consists of two different types of glass, core and cladding, surrounded by a protective coating. The core is the light-guiding region of the fiber, while the cladding ensures that the light pulses remain within the core. One mile of fiber, capable of transmission speeds of 2,500 megabits per second (2.5 gigabits per second) weighs about 1/7 of a pound. A copper cable with the same information-carrying capacity would weigh 33 tons.

other common carriers (OCC) are companies, which include specialized carriers, that compete with established common carriers.

packet switching is a technique of switching digital signals with computers by consolidating the data into packets during transmission and then reassembling them in the correct sequence at the destination. Although each packet may travel along a different path, and the packets composing a message may arrive at different times or out of sequence, the receiving computer reassembles the original message. Packet-switching networks are considered fast and efficient.

paging refers to the service that delivers a message to a customer whose exact location is unknown. These services use radio signals to activate a receiver carried by the individual being paged.

personal communications network (PCN) is an emerging technology that consists of advanced cellular communications and the internetworking of both wire and wireless networks, which together are expected to offer new communications services via very small, portable handsets. This network will use microcellular technology—many low-power, small-coverage cells—and a common channel signaling technology to provide a variety of services in addition to basic two-way telephone services. It will use a short-range, low-power digital radio link for voice and data terminals that can be accessed through one's personal user number. It will provide portability in local areas and can be coded to travel with the user to other areas as well. PCN operates on a digital frequency while cellular networks can operate on both analogy and digital frequencies. Recent FCC auctions for PCN licenses will enable new entrants in the telecommunications industry and additional competition with existing cellular and publicly-switched networks.

personal communications service (PCS) is the next generation of cellular service. PCS will be a smaller, less expensive mobile device that will provide both voice and data communications, using only digital technology. PCS will use higher radio frequencies and smaller "cell" sites than current cellular technology.

plain old telephone service (POTS) refers to traditional voice-based telephone service.

point of presence refers to the access facility of a long-distance carrier located within the service area of a local telephone company.

point-to-point service is a dedicated private line between two locations.

POTS is the acronym for plain old telephone service.

price cap is an alternative to rate-of-return regulation that sets the maximum price that telephone companies can charge for general services. The price cap changes over time, usually escalating at a rate based on the inflation index.

price regulation has been used increasingly in the past decade to focus on a regulated company's prices and quality of services instead of the traditional emphasis on rate of return, which focused on earnings, profits, and return on investment.

private branch exchange (PBX) is a telephone switching system, usually on a customer's premises, that is connected to a common group of lines from a central office and provides telephone service to many individual stations.

privacy, as defined by legal scholar Alan Westin, is the ability of people to determine "when, how, and to what extent information about them is communicated to others." David Brenner, a communications scholar, says privacy-"both as it concerns the right to withhold oneself from others and the right to control one's communications-is both a personal and an economic concept."

private line is a dedicated line, provided to a single customer and used exclusively by that customer between specified points without connecting to central office switching equipment. Usually customers lease a private line for high-volume voice, data, audio or video transmissions.

private network is a privately owned and operated system that uses its own telephone facilities, lines, and switches to transmit communications within that network.

public access refers to the requirement that telecommunications providers offer services to schools, hospitals, and libraries at special, affordable rates. It is also a broad concept that contends that network operators should be obligated to make the platform available to diverse service providers among the public. This argument was developed as municipalities granted franchise rights to cable companies. In some cities, a condition of the franchise was that the public had access to producing community programming on selected channels.

public key cryptography is a system involving the use of matched keys to encode and decode messages such as a digital signature (see above). The system works by assigning users a pair of keys, one of which is private, and one that is posted in a public directory.

publicly switched telephone network is the commercial telephone network in this country. It is a privately-owned, nationwide, interconnected, publicly regulated telephone network that all customers can access. Not included in this publicly switched network are the private networks used by large corporations (see above).

public utility commission (PUC) is the state entity that has the responsibility for regulating public utility services, including local telephone service, and setting rates for various services. In some states, it is called corporation commission or department of public service.

rate base is the total amount of investment made by a company. It is the denominator in the rate-of-return formula used to calculate an allowed rate of return.

rate case is a regulatory proceeding by the state public utility commission for adjusting or reviewing the rate structure for local and intrastate telephone service.

rate of return (ROR) is the percentage net profit that a regulated company is authorized to earn, measured by calculating net earnings against net plant.

really big numbers: (Original source: National Institute of Standards and Technology) As reported by Stephen Beck, "Yottabytes Are a Lotta Bytes," The *New York Times* (June 10, 1996), D5:

Prefix	Power of 10	Units	Number
Kilo	3	thousands	1,000
Mega	6	millions	1,000,000
Giga	9	billions	1,000,000,000
Tera	12	trillions	1,000,000,000,000
Peta	15	quadrillions	1,000,000,000,000,000
Exa	18	quintillions	1,000,000,000,000,000,000
Zetta	21	sextillions	1,000,000,000,000,000,000,000
Yotta	24	septillions	1,000,000,000,000,000,000,000,000

really small numbers: (same source as above)

Prefix	Power of 10	Units	Number
Milli	-3	one thousandth	.001
Micro	-6	one millionth	.000001
Nano	-9	one billionth	.000000001
Pico	-12	one trillionth	.000000000001
Femto	-15	one quadrillionth	.000000000000001
Atto	-18	one quintillionth	.000000000000000001
Zepto	-21	one sextillionth	.000000000000000000001
Yocto	-24	one septillionth	.000000000000000000000001

real-time system is a system that responds to events as they occur.

regional Bell operating companies (RBOCs) are the holding companies that AT&T formed at divestiture to manage the twenty-two Bell operating companies. The seven RBOCs are Ameritech, Bell Atlantic, BellSouth, NYNEX, Pacific Telesis, Southwestern Bell Communications or SBC Communications (formerly Southwestern Bell), and U S West.

resale is the sale of existing capacity by one provider to a prospective competitor, which will then package these services and resell them directly to the public. Determining appropriate resale rates will be one of the most contentious battles in state telecommunications policy during the coming decade. Incumbent local exchanges will prefer reselling existing capacity at high rates. Prospective competitors will seek low rates so that they can make profits on the margins.

reseller is a common carrier whose services are purchased wholesale from another company and then sold to customers.

security: See firewalls and encryption.

shared tenant service is an arrangement that allows a business customer to resell local phone service to individuals or companies residing on the customer's premises.

signaling is the process of sending messages between network switches and/or control points that convey information about circuit status, traffic loads, call routing, and other aspects of network operations. Signaling occurs when a modem shakes hand with another modem and before it transmits data.

signaling system 7 (SS7) is a control system for the publicly switched network that enables computers to communicate directly with each other about routing calls and using signaling circuits.

synchronous optical network (SONET) is an international standard for transmitting information over optical fiber at high speeds.

subscriber line charge (SLC) is a monthly access charge that subscribers pay to local exchange carriers. The SLC is a maximum of $3.50 for residential and single-line business subscribers and $6 for multi-line business subscribers. Local exchange carriers levy this flat monthly charge on local subscribers to compensate for the non-traffic sensitive costs of providing local access and maintaining the local network infrastructure.

SLC waiver programs are state assistance programs, approved by the FCC, that reduce the monthly subscriber line charge of $3.50 (either by 50 percent or in total).

switches are the machines and computers that direct telephone traffic. Switches sort through thousands of possibilities to match the caller with the party being called. Modern switches are digital, which means they offer greater speed and reliability than earlier mechanical devices.

T-carrier system is a hierarchy of digital transmission capabilities designed to operate at various rates, designated T1 (1.544 megabits per second [mbps]), T2 (6.312 mbps), T3 (44.736 mbps), and T4 (274.176 mbps). T1 circuits have 24 channels, each carrying 64 kilobits per second of information.

tariff is the published rate for a service, piece of equipment, or facility as established by the common carrier and approved by the Federal Communications Commission or the state public utility commission.

telecom is short for telecommunications.

telecommunications is a general term for the electronic transmission of information of any type, including data, television pictures, sound, facsimiles, and so on.

Telecommunications Development Fund is a fund authorized by Section 707 of the Act to promote access to capital for small businesses, stimulate new technology development, and support universal service objectives.

telecommunications relay service (TRS): See dual party relay service.

telephone is an instrument connected to a network that enables the customer to communicate over distance with anyone, regardless of location, who also has access to that network.

telephony, according to *Webster's*, is "the use or operation of an apparatus for transmission of sounds between widely removed points with or without connecting wires."

toll call is a call made beyond a customer's free local calling area. Charges are determined by distance, time of day, and other factors.

transponder is a device in an orbiting satellite that receives a signal from earth, translates and amplifies it, and retransmits it to earth.

trunk is a circuit between central office switches.

TSLRIC (total service, long-run incremental cost) "of a given service is equal to the difference between the total forward-looking, long-run costs of the firm and the total forward-looking, long-run costs of that firm if it offered everything it currently offers except the service in question." As cited by Gabel (1995).

twisted pair is the term used for the pair of insulated metal wires that connect local telephone circuits to the central office.

unbundle is to cease charging one inclusive rate for two or more components of a regulated service, i.e., to charge separately for them. Unbundle means to price individually the specific components and functions of the telephone network.

uncommon laws, from George Gilder's articles in *Forbes* ASAP (1993-96), except for Kahn's Law:

> Joy's Law (Bill Joy of Sun Microsystems): "Let's be truthful. Most of the bright people don't work for you—no matter who you are. You need a strategy that allows for innovation occurring elsewhere."

> Kahn's Law (Bob Kahn): "What we expect tomorrow, never actually occurs. What we expect far in the future, actually creeps up on us before we realize it."

> Metcalfe's Law of the Telecosm: "The power of computers on a network rises with the square of the total power of computers attached to it. Every new computer both uses the Net as a resource and adds resources to the Net in a spiral of increasing value and choice."

> Gilder's Version of the Law of the Telecosm: "While Moore's Law doubles computer power every 18 months, the law of the telecosm, by the most conservative possible measure, doubles total bandwidth every 12 months. This adds up. Over the next decade, computers will improve a hundredfold while bandwidth will expand a thousandfold."

> Moore's Law (Gordon Moore, chairman of Intel Corporation): "The number of transistors on a single chip will double every eighteen months."

> Moore's New Law: "The costs of a chip factory double with each generation of microprocessor."

Moron's Law, according to Roger McNamee, is "the telecom regulations that stifle bandwidth expansion."

Negroponte's Switch: "In 1989 the most weighty wisdom on the future of media was the 'Negroponte switch,' the theory launched by Nicholas Negroponte of MIT's Media Lab that what currently goes by air—chiefly broadcast video—would soon switch to wires (fiber optic and coax), while what currently goes by wires— chiefly voice telephony—would massively move to the air."

Nilaus Wirth's new Parkinson's laws for software: "Software expands to fill available memory. Software is getting slower more rapidly than hardware gets faster." (Or, as Gilder quotes Nicholas Negroponte, "Every time Andy [Grove] makes a faster chip, Bill [Gates] uses all of it.")

universal service has been conventionally defined as the provision of easy access to the telephone network at affordable cost for all who want it. This definition is likely to evolve as the demand for advanced telephone services increases.

universal service fund (USF) is a federal program, financed by interstate telephone service revenues, that provides support to those local telephone companies whose costs of providing basic service are higher than the national average so that they can charge affordable rates. USF assistance is distributed on a sliding scale, with the highest cost study areas receiving the most assistance. To fund USF, long-distance carriers pay a flat monthly per-line fee based on their number of presubscribed lines. The National Exchange Carrier Association bills the long-distance companies for the charges and distributes the funds to qualifying exchange carriers on a monthly basis.

value of service pricing refers to the concept of charging more for a service if it is perceived as being worth more. People once considered phone service "worth more" in large cities than in rural areas because urban consumers could connect to many more phones than rural customers. This concept will lose favor as local competition increases.

video dial tone is the FCC's term for the conduit through which existing telephone networks provide video services.

virus is a computer program that can infect, replicate, and spread among computer systems.

v-chip is a device that television manufacturers will be required to place in television sets sold in 1998 that can decode a rating signal transmitted with a television show. In enacting this provision, Congress determined that there was a compelling government interest in giving parents technology that would allow them to block television programs that contain "sexual, violent or other indecent material" that they do not want their children to see. See the Act's Section 551, Parental Choice in Television Programming.

VSATs are very small-aperture terminals capable of sending and receiving voice, data, and video signals via satellite.

world wide web is a subset of the Internet. The web is a graphically oriented system that facilitates movement from one topic to another related one. A web site includes multiple topics and, by clicking on highlighted symbols, the user can view additional attached files, which display pictures as well as text. The various linkages of web sites and related topics, the graphical design, and the hypertext have made the web the most popular part of the Internet.

wide area network (WAN) is a communications network that connects geographically separated areas. (See LAN, above.)

wide area telecommunications service (WATS) is a fixed-rate service that allows customers to make or receive long-distance calls without being charged for each one.

wireless refers to radio transmissions through the air. Currently cellular and PCS technologies are the most common wireless communications services. Digital wireless may become the on-ramp to the information superhighway.

Sources: General Accounting Office, *Information Superhighway* (1995), Harvard Business School, *Telecommunications in Transition: Managing Business and Regulatory Change* (1986); GTE Telephone Operations, *Everything you always wanted to know about telecommunications—but didn't know who to ask,* (1995); Organization for the Protection and Advancement of Small Telephone Companies, *Keeping Rural America Connected: Costs and Rates in the Competitive Era* (1994); Frederick Williams and John V. Pavlik, *The People's Right to Know* (1994); A Center for Community and Economic Development, Applied Rural Telecommunications Information, "Resource Guide Glossary," [http://www.yampa.com/aerie/resources/section 4/glossary.html]; American Legislative Exchange Council, *Competitive Telecommunications* (November 1995); and Joel Shurkin, *Engines of the Mind,* (1996).

SELECTED BIBLIOGRAPHY

Armstrong, Rodney. *Creating the Climate for the Information Age: The Nebraska Statewide Telecommunications Infrastructure Plan*. Lincoln, Nebraska: Nebraska Information Technology Commission, October 1995.

Auletta, Ken. "Pay Per Views." *The New Yorker*, June 5, 1995, 52-56.

Bauer, Karon, ed. NARUC *Report on the Status of Competition in Intrastate Telecommunications*. Washington, D.C.: National Association of Regulatory Utility Commissioners, October 4, 1995.

Brand, Stuart. *The Media Lab: Inventing the Future at MIT*. New York: Viking, 1987.

Branscomb, Anne Wells. *Who Owns Information? From Privacy to Public Access*. New York: Basic Books, 1994.

Blackman, Colin, and Hans Schoof. "Competition and Convergence: Toward Regulatory Chaos?" *Telecommunications* Policy 18, no. 8 (1994).

Borrows, John D., Phyllis A. Bernt, and Raymond W. Lawton. *Universal Service in the United States: Dimensions of the Debate*. Columbus, Ohio: National Regulatory Research Institute, June 1994.

Brock, Gerald W., ed. *Toward a Competitive Telecommunications Industry: Selected Papers from the 1994 Telecommunications Policy Research Conference*. Mahwah, New Jersey: Lawrence Erlbaum Associates, 1995.

Campbell, Heather E. "The Politics of Requesting: Strategic Behavior and Public Utility Regulation." *Journal of Policy Analysis and Management* 15, no. 3 (summer 1996).

Carney, Dan. "Congress Fires Its First Shot in Information Revolution." *Congressional Quarterly*, February 3, 1996.

Case, Karl E. *State and Local Tax Policy and the Telecommunications Industry*. Washington, D.C.: Council of Governors' Policy Advisors, 1992.

Caudle, Sharon L. *Reengineering For Results: Keys to Success from Government Experience*. Washington, D.C.: National Academy of Public Administration, August 1994.

Cauley, Leslie. "Not Welcome Here: Competition is coming to the local phone market. But thanks to the Baby Bells, it isn't coming quickly." *Wall Street Journal*, March 20, 1995.

Chamberlin, Whitney. *Telecommunications and Community Economic Development in North Carolina*. Conference Report. Washington, D.C.: Center for Policy Alternatives, 1995.

Cohen, Jeffrey E. *The Politics of Telecommunications Regulation: The States and the Divestiture of AT&T*. Armonk, New York: M.E. Sharpe, 1992.

Conte, Christopher R. "Reaching for the Phone." *Governing*, July 1995.

Cooper, Jamie. *Telecommunications in the States-A Progress Report*. Draft. Washington, D.C.: A Joint Project of the Center for Policy Alternatives and the Benton Foundation, December 7, 1995.

Crandall, Robert W. *After the Breakup: U.S. Telecommunications in a More Competitive Era*. Washington, D.C.: Brookings Institution, 1991.

————. "Waves of the Future: Are We Ready to Deregulate Telecommunications." *The Brookings Review*. Washington, D.C.: Brookings Institution, winter 1996.

Crandall, Robert W., and Harold Furchtgott-Roth. *Cable TV: Regulation or Competition?* Washington, D.C.: Brookings Institution, 1996.

Crandall, Robert W., and J. Gregory Sidak. "The Unregulated Infobahn." *Jobs & Capital*. Santa Monica, California: Milken Institute for Job & Capital Formation, summer 1995.

Crandall, Robert W., and Leonard Waverman. *Talk is Cheap: The Promise of Regulatory Reform in North American Telecommunications*. Washington, D.C.: Brookings Institution, 1995.

David, Paul A. "Computer and Dynamo: The Modern Productivity Paradox in a Not-Too-Distant Mirror." Reprint no. 5. Stanford, California: Stanford University Center for Economic Policy Research. Originally published in *Technology and Productivity: The Challenge for Economic Policy*. OECD, 1991.

Drake, William J., ed. *The New Information Infrastructure: Strategies for U.S. Policy*. New York: Twentieth Century Fund Press, 1995.

Entman, Robert M. *Strategic Alliances and Telecommunications Policy*. Washington, D.C.: The Aspen Institute, 1995.

Firestone, Charles M., and Jorge Reina Schement, eds. *Toward an Information Bill of Rights & Responsibilities*. Washington, D.C.: The Aspen Institute, 1985.

Gabel, David. "Pricing voice telephony services: Who is subsidizing whom?" *Telecommunications* Policy 19, no. 6 (1995): 453-464.

Gallt, Jack. "State Telecommunications Activities." Memorandum. Lexington, Kentucky: National Association of State Telecommunications Directors, April 6, 1993.

Gasman, Lawrence. *Telecompetition: The Free Market Road to the Information Highway*. Washington, D.C.: Cato Institute, 1994.

Gates, William H. *Creating the Global Information Society. Looking Ahead*. White paper. Redmond, Washington: Microsoft, 1995.

General Accounting Office. *Information Superhighway: An Overview of Technology Challenges* GAO/AIMD-95-23. Washington, D.C.: GAO, Report to Congress, January 1995.

————. *Telecommunications: Initiatives Taken by Three States to Promote Increased Access and Investment* GAO/RCED-96-68. Washington, D.C.: GAO, Report to Congress, March 1996.

Gilder, George. *Telecosm*. New York: Simon & Schuster, forthcoming 1996. See also his series of articles in *Forbes* ASAP, 1992-96.

Gleick, James. "The Telephone Transformed-Into Almost Everything." *New York Times Magazine*, May 16, 1993.

Governor's Blue Ribbon Telecommunications Infrastructure Task Force. *Convergence, Competition, Cooperation*. Madison, Wisconsin: Department of Administration, November 1993.

Governor's Telecommunications Policy Coordination Task Force. *Building The Road Ahead: Telecommunications Infrastructure in Washington*. Olympia, Washington: Department of Revenue, April 29, 1996.

Gregory, Michelle. "When Cells Multiply: Regulating Cellular-Tower Siting for the Public Good." *PTI Prism*. Washington, D.C.: Public Technology, Inc., winter 1995/96.

Hammer, Michael, and James Champy. *Reengineering the Corporation: A Manifesto for Business Revolution*. New York: HarperBusiness, 1993.

Honabarger, John W., ed. *Everything you always wanted to know about telecommunications—but didn't know who to ask*. Irving, Texas: GTE Telephone Operations, 1995.

Howe, Lloyd, and Dick Gardner. *Telecom '92: Connecting Idaho to the Future*. Boise, Idaho: Idaho Department of Administration, 1992.

Information Highway State and Local Tax Study Group. "Supporting the Information Highway: A Framework for State and Local Taxation of Telecommunications and Information Services." *State Tax Notes*, July 3, 1995.

Institute for Information Studies. *Crossroads on the Information Highway: Convergence and Diversity in Communications Technologies* (1995), *The Emerging World of Wireless Communications* (1996), and *Universal Telephone Service: Ready for the 21st Century?* (1991). Queenstown, Maryland: The Aspen Institute and Nashville, Tennessee: Northern Telecom, Inc.

Kupfer, Andrew. "The Future of the Phone Companies." *Fortune*, October 3, 1994.

Malone, Michael S. "Chips Triumphant." *Forbes ASAP*, February 26, 1996, 53-82.

McHugh, Richard. *The Telecommunications Industry in Utah and Its Implications for General Sales Taxation*. Atlanta, Georgia: Policy Research Center, January 15, 1996.

MCI. *Preserving Long Distance Competition and Promoting Local Competition: 21st Century Telecommunications Policy.* Washington, D.C.: MCI Communications Corporation, 1995.

Mechling, Jerry. "Reengineering Government: Is There a 'There There'?" *Public Productivity and Management Review* 18, no. 2 (winter 1994).

Mueller, Milton. *Universal Service: Competition, Interconnection, and Monopoly in the Making of the American Telephone System.* Cambridge, Massachusetts: MIT Press/American Enterprise Institute for Public Policy Research, 1996.

NARUC Committee on Communications. *Universal Service Project.* Washington, D.C.: National Association of Regulatory Utility Commissioners, July 1994.

National Association of State Telecommunications Directors. 1995 *State Reports.* Lexington, Kentucky: Council of State Governments/NASTD, 1995.

National Governors' Association. *State Technology Inventory.* Washington, D.C.: State Management Task Force, NGA, July 1994.

————. *Telecommunications: The Next American Revolution.* Washington, D.C.: NGA, 1994.

Negroponte, Nicholas. *Being Digital.* New York: Alfred A. Knopf, 1995.

Olson, Robert L., and Clement Bezold. "Back to the Future: Revisiting the Information Millennium." *Insight.* Livingston, New Jersey: Bellcore, winter 1990.

Parker, Edwin P., and Heather E. Hudson, with Don A. Dillman, Sharon Strover, and Frederick Williams. *Electronic Byways: State Policies for Rural Development Through Telecommunications.* Boulder, Colorado: Westview Press/The Aspen Institute, 1992.

Pelton, Joseph N. "The Globalization of Universal Telecommunications Services." *Universal Telephone Service: Ready for the 21st Century.* Queenstown, Maryland: Institute for Information Studies/The Aspen Institute/Northern Telecom, 1991.

Perlman, Ellen. "Ringing in a New Era of Telecom Investment." *Governing,* November 1994.

Pool, Ithiel de Sola, ed. *The Social Impact of the Telephone.* Cambridge, Massachusetts: MIT Press, 1977.

Rabinovitz, Jonathan. "Competition to Begin for Local Phone Calls, Ending a Monopoly." *New York Times,* January 6, 1996.

Rivkin, Steven R., and Jeremy D. Rosner. *Shortcut to the Information Superhighway: A Progressive Plan to Speed the Telecommunications Revolution.* Washington, D.C.: Progressive Policy Institute, 1992.

Schwartz, Gail Garfield. "Telecommunications and Economic Development Policy." *Economic Development Quarterly* 4, no. 2 (May 1990).

Sclove, Richard E. *Democracy and Technology*. New York: Guilford Press, 1995.

Shurkin, Joel. *Engines of the Mind: The Evolution of the Computer from Mainframes to Microprocessors*. New York: W. W. Norton, 1996.

Spulber, Daniel F. "Deregulating Telecommunications." *Yale Journal of Regulation* 12, no. 1 (winter 1995): 25-67.

Stoll, Clifford. *Silicon Snake Oil: Second Thoughts on the Information Highway*. New York: Doubleday, 1995.

Telecommunications Strategic Planning Committee. *Connections to the Future: A Telecommunications Strategic Plan for Kansas*. Topeka, Kansas: Telecommunications Strategic Planning Committee, January 1996.

Teske, Paul Eric. *After Divestiture: The Political Economy of State Telecommunications Regulation*. Albany, New York: State University of New York Press, 1990.

Teske, Paul E., ed. *American Regulatory Federalism & Telecommunications Infrastructure*. Hillsdale, New Jersey: Lawrence Erlbaum Associates, 1995.

Teske, Paul. "Interests and Institutions in State Regulation." *American Journal of Political Science* 35, no. 1 (February 1991).

————. "Rent-seeking in the deregulatory environment: State telecommunications." *Public Choice* 68 (1991): 235-243.

————. "State Telecommunications Policy in the 1980s." *Policy Studies Review* 11:1 (spring 1992).

U.S. Congress, Office of Technology Assessment. *Making Government Work: Electronic Delivery of Federal Services* OTA-TCT-578. Washington, D.C.: U.S. Government Printing Office, September 1993.

————. *Rural America at the Crossroads: Networking for the Future* OTA-TCT-471. Washington, D.C.: U.S. Government Printing Office, April 1991.

Vietor, Richard H.K. *Contrived Competition: Regulation and Deregulation in America*. Cambridge, Massachusetts: Belknap Press of Harvard University Press, 1994.

Vietor, Richard H.K., and Davis Dyer. *Telecommunications in Transitions: Managing Business and Regulatory Change*. Boston: Harvard Business School, 1986.

Williams, Frederick, and John V. Pavlik. *The People's Right to Know: Media, Democracy, and the Information Highway*. Hillsdale, New Jersey: Lawrence Erlbaum Associates, 1994.

Wilson, Robert H., and Paul E. Teske. "Telecommunications and Economic Development: The State and Local Role," *Economic Development Quarterly* 4, no. 2 (May 1990).

Zysman, George I. "Wireless Networks." *Scientific American*, September 1995.

OTHER CGPA PUBLICATIONS

Building Results: New Tools for an Age of Discovery in Government

A Convergence on Crime: Emerging Similarities in How States Should, and Are Reducing the Impact of Crime

Creating Opportunity: Reducing Poverty through Economic Development

Experiments in Systems Change: States Implement Family Policy

The Game Plan: Governance with Foresight

Getting Results: A Guide for Government Accountability

A Guide to Community-based, Collaborative Strategic Planning

Improving Public Policy: States and Grantmakers Working Together

Managing the Policy Agenda: Organizational Options for Governors

New Alliances in Innovation: A Guide to Encouraging Innovative Applications of New Communication Technologies to Address State Problems

New Businesses, Entrepreneurship, and Rural Development: State Policies and Generating Rural Growth from Within

A New Vocabulary for Governing in the 1990s: A Lexicon for Governors' Policy Advisors

The Safety Net as Ladder: Transfer Payments for Economic Development

Scenarios of State Government in the Year 2010: Thinking About the Future

Seven Things States Can Do to Promote Fatherhood

The States Forge Ahead Despite the Federal Impasse: CGPA's January 1996 Survey of States on the 'Devolution Revolution'

State Technology Programs: A Preliminary Analysis of Lessons Learned

State and Local Tax Policy and the Telecommunications Industry

Strategies for Rural Competitiveness: Policy Options for State Governments

Strengthening Families: A Guide for State Policymaking

Thinking Strategically: A Primer for Public Leaders

Trading Water: An Economic and Legal Framework for Water Marketing

Understanding State Economies through Industry Studies

The Value Choices in State and Local Spending: A Workbook for State Policymakers

Voices From the Field: Lessons from the Family Academy

The Wealth of States: Policies for a Dynamic Economy

ABOUT THE AUTHOR

Tom Bonnett is the director of economic development and environment. He came to CGPA with extensive experience in all levels of government and in the nonprofit sector. He was elected to the Vermont House of Representatives in 1974 and reelected in 1976. During the 1980s, he directed the Neighborhood Economic Development Division of the New York City Department of City Planning and served as executive assistant to the deputy administrator of the New York City Human Resources Administration, where he conducted research and developed programs for the city's homeless. He also served as executive director of the Downtown Flushing Development Corporation, a nonprofit community-based organization.

In Washington, D.C., Tom worked for a member of Congress and for the American Federation of State, County, and Municipal Employees. His published work includes articles and reports on the politics of redistricting, school finance reform, tax evasion, scenario development for long-range transportation planning, and rural economic development. Tom has authored the following CGPA publications:

Scenarios of State Government in the Year 2010 (with Robert L. Olson), 1993;

Strategies for Rural Competitiveness: Policy Options for State Governments, 1993;

A New Vocabulary for Governing in the 1990s: A Lexicon for Governors' Policy Advisors, 1994; and

Preparing for Block Grants and State Autonomy on Social Welfare Programs: A Survey of How the States are Planning for the 'Devolution Revolution' (with Eric Brenner, Richard P. Nathan, and William O'Heaney), October 1995.

Tom Bonnett received a BA from Bennington College and an MPP from the University of California. He lives in Park Slope, Brooklyn, New York.